Jerry- My f
MARINERS FAN
you enjoy the stories!

Born Into Baseball

Jim Coughlin

Jim Coughlin SR
#25

About the Author

Jim Campanis, Jr. is the son of former major leaguer Jimmy Campanis, and grandson of long-time Dodgers' General Manager, Al Campanis. Jim Jr. is a third generation professional baseball player, whose on-the-field career included All-American honors at USC, selections to the 1985 USA Junior National Team & Team USA in 1988, plus six seasons as a catcher in the minor leagues with one year on the major league 40-man roster.

From the time he was drafted in the third round in 1988, Jim rose steadily through the minor league ranks, and was destined to reach the majors as his father and grandfather had, until he suffered his toughest break—a broken wrist the very day he was told he was to be a September call-up.

Jim decided to leave baseball in 1995 and explore new opportunities. He found a new career path in advertising and marketing, and then founded his own full-service agency, Campy Media, Inc. Jim divides his time between his work, active participation in the baseball community, writing music, and enjoying his family at his home in Southern California.

Born Into Baseball

Laughter and Heartbreak at the Edge of The Show

Jim Campanis, Jr.

SUMMER
GAME
BOOKS

Published by Summer Game Books

ISBN: 978-1-938545-79-5 (paperback)
ISBN: 978-1-938545-80-1 (ebook)

For information about bulk purchases or additional distribution, write to
Summer Game Books
P. O. Box 818
South Orange, NJ 07079
or contact the publisher at
www.summergamebooks.com

Front cover photo descriptions, clockwise from upper left hand corner: 1. My Grandpa Al, Sandy Koufax and Fresco Thompson at press conference announcing Sandy's first contract with the Brooklyn Dodgers. 2. My Grandpa Al, my dad and I in 1985 at an event at Dodgers Stadium. 3. Oil painting of my dad playing for the Kansas City Royals by artist Matt Blansett. 4. (L to R) Me and the LEGENDARY Dave "Lats" Latter looking HOT on Halloween night, 1987. 5. Me and "Lats" in 2013. 6. Photo from Topps Baseball Card shoot at my first Spring Training in 1989. 7. Going deep at USC. 8. The medallion awarded to me by USC and installed in Heritage Hall for being named All American in 1988. 9. My dad sliding into home plate when he played for the Seattle Angels (AAA) in 1966.

Dedication

To my Mom and Dad for their love and support from the beginning.
To my wife, Lisa, who decided to go on this wild ride with me
over 25 years ago.
To my sons, Alex and Tommy. I love you both, and am proud
of the men you are becoming.
To all the people who encouraged and supported my writing—I can't
thank you enough for motivating me to finish this book.
To Lats, Riles, and Bilski—Fight On Brothers!

Acknowledgments

Mom/Dad
Lisa/Alex/Tommy
Grandpa Al/Grandma Bessie
Grandpa John/Grandma Gladys
Grandma Tulla
Andrea/Joe/Emily
Alexa/Dustin/Dustin Jr.
Nick/Tianna
Uncle George
Matt/Skye/Leilani/Maya
Lenice/Chance
Aunt Linda/JD/Neil/Hannah
Aunt Elizabeth/Roger
Vanessa/Diane/Mary
The LEGENDARY Dave "Lats" Latters
Chris "Bilski" Billig/Martha
John "Riles" Reilley/Debbie
Peggy Ruley
Terrance Morgan
Eric Lenaburg
Jim Henderson

Jason Himelstein
Brian BcA Cramer
Pete/Tracy Felix
Greg/Teresa Meeder
Jimmy Von Eps
Ben Davis
Luis Loucks
Matt Blansett
Jerry Plowman
Barbara Young
Laurie Sanchez
Paul Crabb
Mike Reinberger
Steve/Keri/Maddie/Kennedy Clave
Walter Friedman
Tom Owens
Michelle Balling Smith
Michael Austin
Matt Barsanti
Tom & Debra Barsanti

And finally a HUGE THANK YOU to countless old and new friends for their support and encouragement. Special thanks to friends from Van Buren Elementary, Kraemer Junior High, Valencia High School, The University of Southern California, and my AWESOME network of professional colleagues and online amigos on various Social Media sites.

Contents

Foreword

by Jim Henderson

When I first met Jim Campanis, he had a boner. But I'll get to that.

In the fall of 1987, I arrived as a Freshman at the University of Southern California intent on taking the college baseball world by storm. My first day on campus, I walked over to the baseball office with a few other players, and sitting in one of the chairs was Jim.

I was a catcher, and I knew Campy would be my competition, so I was determined to hate him. That determination, however lasted about five minutes. He was the same gregarious, self-effacing, entertaining guy that you'll discover while you're reading his stories. I don't think anyone could hate him.

Over the next year, and like any teammates playing the same position, I got to know Campy well. We talked about baseball, family, college, and girls—things that everyone talks about—but mostly we talked about life. He introduced me to block parties on fraternity row, the new band Guns N' Roses, and, of course, cheerleaders. For me, however, the coolest thing was that Jim never treated me like a freshmen.

A clue about the kind of guy Campy was came from watching him interact with his best friend, Dave Latter. Dave—Lats—was a pitcher, and the two were literally inseparable. In a way, he was the mirror image of Jim: funny and sarcastic, but without a mean bone in his body. As you'll see, Lats is the subject of more than a few of the stories in this book, and he's worthy of every last one. The two of the them remained best friends until Dave passed away in 2014. Jim never told me as much, but I'm fairly sure this book is a final goodbye and tribute to Lats.

Even though Campy became a friend, I still wanted to be the starting catcher at USC. But a few things got in the way. While I'll go to my grave believing that Jim ended up as the starter that year because I had arm surgery, the reality was that it may have been because he hit 23 home runs and was named an All-American. The year was tough on me, but Campy never treated me with anything but respect. That was our only year together in college, because he left after being drafted by the Seattle Mariners, and I ultimately transferred to Arizona State.

While I bumped into Jim once or twice over the years, we really didn't reconnect until I found him on—you guessed it—Facebook a few years ago. He knew I was a lawyer, and he told me about a little legal issue he had with a former business partner. I told him I'd handle it in exchange for a lunch or two if we could get it resolved without devolving into a lawsuit. Fortunately for Campy (and unfortunately for my income), we got it taken care of without him spending a nickel.

The best part of it, though, was reconnecting with Campy. Many years had passed, and the lunches were filled with countless stories: some happy, some sad, but all told with a smile and a laugh. We talked—and still do— regularly, and Jim even came to my wedding. I'll never be Lats, but that's OK. Campy has enough heart to go around.

We also spent a lot of time discussing the short vignettes about baseball that Jim was writing on Facebook, and the extraordinary reaction they were getting. For me (and hopefully for you), his stories capture that same piece of magic that "Field of Dreams" did by telling a tale that's ostensibly about baseball, but in reality illuminates the hopes, dreams, fears, laughter and heartache that life brings to us all. There's even one in the book about me, and while I'm a little prejudiced, I think Campy managed to weave all those emotions in my story.

Anyway, when we all got up to leave the baseball office when I first met Campy some 29 years ago, he just remained in his chair. Lats, I believe, asked him why he wasn't leaving. Campy, with a book on his lap, responded as only he could:

"I've got a boner. I can't stand up until it goes away."

And that is how I met Jim Campanis.

Introduction: Carrying on the Family Business

On August 27, 1967, my dad stepped into the batter's box to pinch-hit for the Los Angeles Dodgers at Dodgers Stadium. He hit a rocket to left field but directly at the left fielder. As he returned to the dugout, Walt Alston told him he was out of the game. So my dad quickly changed and sped off with my Grandpa Al, listening to the game on the radio, racing to St. Jude's Hospital in Fullerton and arriving just in time to see me being born.

By 1969, we were in Kansas City, because within 15 minutes of the Dodgers hiring my Grandpa Al as their new Vice-President/General Manager, he traded my dad to the Kansas City Royals for two minor leaguers and $100,000 cash!

From my first moments of consciousness, and for as long as I can remember, baseball has been the center of my and my family's lives. I remember playing in the sand box with a bunch of kids when one of them yelled, "The game's on!" and we ran inside to listen on the radio to our dads play baseball. Among my first memories are my dad catching for Kansas City at Overland Park, KS.

So yes, I was literally "born into baseball" – a third generation ballplayer with all its challenges and thrills – an opportunity for which I am extremely grateful.

From the time I was about 4 years old until the age of 8, I was like another player on my dad's teams. I played catch with pro players, shagged fly balls, took batting practice with a sawed off Louisville Slugger, and helped the bat boys while wearing a cut down Pittsburgh Pirates uniform. I was all in at an early age, right down to my vocabulary. I knew a "pickle" from a pickle and a "donut" from a donut!

As you'll see from the stories throughout this book, my parents, and later my wife Lisa, and I sacrificed everything to chase the dream of my becoming a successful major league baseball player. In hindsight, I realize I really had no other career path besides baseball, but that was alright, because there was nothing else I would have rather been doing.

Due to her gender, my younger sister Andrea didn't have a chance to experience the same things that I did being a clubhouse rat and living a baseball life from early childhood. Even so, growing up she was my best friend, even though we still fought like cats and dogs, mostly out of boredom. I used to wish she was my little brother so we could go out on the ball field and play together, not just in the back yard. By the way, Andrea was an outstanding player, and even at a young age could handle the heat I threw at her.

My dad was traded to the Pirates in 1971 and my sister Alexa was born during the baseball season in Charleston, WV, home of the Pirates AAA affiliate Charleston Charlies where my dad was the catcher and cleanup hitter.

As I got older, we would tell stories about growing up on the road to our younger brother Nick, who is 12 years younger than I and came on the scene after my dad had retired. He'd look at us in envy, like, "Man, that sounds like fun…no fair!!!"

Two or three times each month, my mom, Andrea, Alexa, and I would take my dad to the field with the car loaded up with his suitcase and gear as he was about to embark on a 5, 10, or even 15-day road trip. We would all cry as we said good-bye, but my dad would pull me aside and tell me to be strong since I was the man of the house until he returned. I took that responsibility seriously, but of course my mom was the real rock in our family who kept things together and moving forward in our complicated lives.

To me it was just normal, the only way I knew. It would have seemed odd for my dad to go to work in the morning and come home by dinnertime. It would have been odd to go on a road trip where a baseball game wasn't the destination.

My dad retired right when I began playing little league, and he was there at every game, watching and also continuing my baseball education. In fact, he was right there with me, always ready to offer guidance and advice, until my last hack as a pro.

In this collection of stories, I chronicle my experiences inside the game from my early childhood, through high school, USC, pro and winter ball, and ultimately the toll it took on me when I was not able to fulfill my one and only dream in life—to play in the major leagues.

Through it all, the experience of being part of baseball, and baseball being part of me from my first waking moment, has made me rich beyond my wildest dreams. Maybe not financially rich like many of those who do make The Show, but rich with memories, lasting friendships, and an intimate knowledge of baseball that I share with youngsters chasing the same dream I did.

Sometimes it's not the destination that makes the trip memorable…it's the ride getting there. I try to remind myself of that every day, and I hope you do, too: Wherever you are going, enjoy the ride!

Jim Campanis, Jr.
December, 2015

Developing my taste for the game.

1
Growing Up Campanis

The first chapter of life is so important. It often sets the tone for each of us as we choose which path to follow. In my case it was the game of baseball and the awesome people around it.

I grew up in ballparks all over the world and feel a special kinship for those who love the game the way I do.

Some of the stories in the first chapter go back to before I was even born, to the tales I heard around the dinner table. These stories became the soundtrack to my childhood and shaped the way I played ball in Little League and High School.

Then, on April 6, 1987, when I was 19, the Nightline interview aired, and my childhood ended abruptly. Life was never the same after that.

On the Road - AGAIN!

From my earliest memories, I was traveling…planes, trains and automobiles all over the world chasing my dad's team around. Years later I was traveling all over the place to play this wonderful game of baseball as well.

My mom estimates that she moved us 43 times while my dad played.

My wife and I moved about 25 times with our son Alex.

Traveling and living months on end in these random places was a great experience that I treasure…especially the regional food! Tacos al Carbon in Mexico, pinchos in Puerto Rico, boiled peanuts in the South, jambalaya in Louisiana, salmon in Alaska, roasted pig in Hawaii, kobe beef in Japan, fried catfish in Memphis, tri-tip in Santa Maria, and of course…In-N-Out Burger in SoCal!

Some of my baseball buddies have traveled much more than I have. It's part of the deal.

All in all I really enjoyed the "Trip"—and it was just that. All night bus rides, sleeping in the overhead luggage rack or on a blow up mat then later waking up in a strange hotel room was all part of the job. But by far the toughest thing to deal with was simply eating.

I swear some teams either put us up right next to nightclubs and/or strip joints to distract us, while others put us up in the middle of NOWHERE with nothing to eat for miles. How is a guy supposed to eat on $8 a day when you have to take a cab to get lunch and dinner!

We would sometimes walk miles to get to an Applebee's just so we could eat something remotely healthy like a salad.

When I was finishing my career in the California League, the travel was pretty easy. So easy, the wives and girlfriends would follow the bus, meaning we had cars when we arrived. That made the trips more like a party. But cities like Lynchburg, VA and Birmingham, AL made our lives tough. Durham's hotel was so close to a strip joint you could hear the bass through the walls of that Red Roof Inn! Sure I had to check it out, but it was because they had a free buffet…food buffet, that is!

In my opinion, and I still feel this way, the more you travel the world and observe the local customs, the more you grow as a human being. I can't tell you how many times someone has told me where they are from and I immediately have a local story for them. Recently, someone told me they were from North Carolina. I asked which city. He said Winston-Salem. Well, I knew that was the home of Krispy Kreme Donuts, which was a great

My Baseball Travels

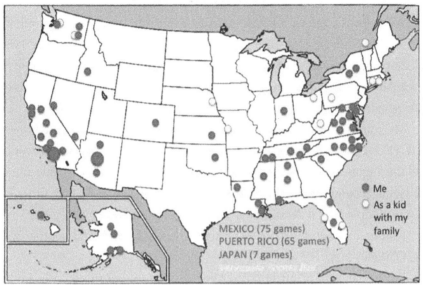

MEXICO (75 games)
PUERTO RICO (65 games)
JAPAN (7 games)

● Me
○ As a kid with my family

ice-breaker and it really impressed him. My extensive traveling has helped me in business countless times.

Get out and take 10-day roadie, anywhere. It's totally worth the expense!

Here is a map showing where I played—over 100 different cities—sometimes for one night, sometimes for six months.

The Box

Growing up, my dad was a player and grandpa was an ex-player. I had a unique childhood, but similar to other kids of pro players.

I've discussed this odd childhood with guys like Pete Rose Jr., Bret Boone, and Ken Griffey Jr.

The one thing that was different for me was that my grandpa was an executive for the Dodgers which brought its own set of benefits.

When I was a kid, we NEVER sat in a regular seat. We sat in my grandpa's box on the Club Level behind home plate. In fact, it wasn't until the 1980 All Star game at Dodgers Stadium, when I was 12, that I watched a game in a regular seat for the first time. By then I had watched literally hundreds of games in that box.

My grandpa's box was set up with two rows, an upper row and a lower row. He sat in the far left seat on the lower row next to a phone. He would call the dugout several times a game. He would yell, he would ask questions, he would recommend an outfielder move right or left, and other times he would complement a decision made by the coaching staff.

Believe it or not, it was one of only two boxes back then; the other was the O'Malley box.

Just to the right of my grandpa's box was the coolest thing—Vin Scully broadcasting live. I could hear his natural voice around the corner of the box and then hear the echo of transistor radios in the crowd. I would get in trouble with the broadcast producer for constantly looking around the front corner of the box to watch Vin.

My grandpa was always teaching me about baseball and would call me over for lessons. He would ask why we should bunt here or he had me watch how the batter was trying to score a runner from third. That was my favorite part.

Over the years, we had so many memories from that box—celebrity visitors, a former President, throwing paper airplanes onto the field, streakers, Strawberry Haagen Daz, Easter, July 4th, the playoffs, the World Series, and numerous great games. We even watched a Jacksons concert from that box.

After my grandpa was fired in 1987, all of this ended.

Today, my grandpa's box is gone. The new stadium design has replaced the old boxes with luxury suites sold to businesses for schmoozing. But Vin is still there doing play-by-play from that same spot.

I ran into Vin a couple of years ago. Remarkably, he remembered me, knew about my playing career, and remembers my grandpa and that box very fondly. He told me that he used to room with my grandpa on road trips in the late 50's and 60's. I didn't know that! We reminisced about the good old days and he wished me luck in my business endeavors. What a class act.

All things must come to an end; I've accepted the end of my grandpa's run. But when Vin hangs up his mic, it will be a sad day for baseball fans all over the world.

Jackie at Show and Tell

Many of you know that my grandpa made comments on *Nightline* that were construed as racist, but here's the real deal:

In 1946 my grandpa was offered a once-in-a-lifetime opportunity by the President of the Dodgers, Branch Rickey. He was offered a job in the front office after the 1946 season under one condition. He had to play in Montreal and teach Jackie Robinson how to play second base.

My grandpa and Jackie had already played together on Jackie's barnstorming team prior to the 1946 season, and they knew each other very well. That barnstorming team was one of the very first interracially mixed pro teams ever! It was also deliberately set up by Branch Rickey to let fans see players of mixed races on the same team. As crazy as it sounds now, this was something fans had never seen before! The barnstorming team was a success for Jackie and it helped my grandpa lay the foundation for teaching Jackie how to play second base.

When the 1946 season started in Montreal, my grandpa and Jackie were working intensely on the proper footwork for double plays, angles for relays, covering first on a bunt, and how to get a good jump on ground balls. Of course, Jackie was an excellent student. My grandpa and Jackie were also roommates on the road, something unheard of in the 1940's.

My dad (far left) at about age 5, with my Uncle George (middle), and Grandpa Al, around 1948.

Mr. Rickey kept his promise to my grandpa who in 1947 became an executive working in the front office, while Jackie went on to Rookie of the Year honors.

A few years later, my dad, who was in third grade at the time, needed something for his Show and Tell that week. He asked my grandpa if he could get a ball or bat signed by Jackie to use. My grandpa said he would try…

As my dad was delivering the "Tell" part of Show and Tell, there was a knock on the classroom door. It was my grandpa. My dad said, "Oh, did you bring a Jackie Robinson ball or bat for me, dad?" My grandpa replied, "Why don't you ask for one yourself?" And into that Brooklyn classroom walked Jackie Robinson.

My dad remembers the teacher was in complete shock and could barely speak. Of course, my dad received an "A" for his show and tell. Soon, the rest of the school had heard, and they set up a table for Jackie who signed autographs for hours before he had to leave for the game.

Jackie and my grandpa remained friends for the rest of their lives. I know that if Jackie had been alive after the *Nightline* show, he would have completely defended my grandpa and his character. Who knows how different things would have been for him…and for me.

Hiding Clemente

Before there was an amateur draft for major league baseball, scouts would have to scour the world for talent, then bid for that talent against other teams.

Back in the 50's, there was a rule to protect the smaller market teams from losing quality talent to the big market teams. This rule stated that if a player received a signing bonus of more than $4,000, that player had to be on the Major League team for at least two years or other teams could pick them up in the "Rule 5 Draft." There is still a similar rule.

In 1954, my grandpa held a tryout camp in Mayaguez, Puerto Rico and saw this player who was like a man compared to the other boys trying out. His name was Roberto Clemente.

Roberto was so talented, my grandpa felt like he struck gold but knew every other team in MLB would want him, too.

He called his boss, Buzzie Bavasi, and recommended that he sign Clemente for $10,000 and have him report directly to Brooklyn for the season. But Mr. Bavasi threw my grandpa a curve and said OK to the $10,000, but he had him sign a AAA contract with the Montreal Royals. My grandpa knew this was a BIG gamble, but Bavasi didn't want to lose a roster spot for an untested rookie.

That Spring Training, Clemente reported to Dodgertown in Vero Beach and completely dazzled everyone, especially Bavasi. But the decision to start him in AAA was final and Clemente was sent to Montreal to start the season.

If you know baseball, you know the scouts get to the games early to watch batting practice plus watch the player's defensive work and arm strength. The Dodgers management knew scouts would drool over Clemente so they would not allow Clemente to even be on the field when the scouts were in the stands.

They also had Clemente batting 9th in the lineup on a rare start! That's right, even the PITCHER batted ahead of Clemente so the scouts wouldn't be able to see his talent.

One game, the Montreal team rallied in the first inning and Clemente was on deck to hit. That's when the manager called Clemente into the dugout and ordered someone to pinch hit for the future Hall of Famer IN THE FIRST INNING! That's how bad the Dodgers were trying to "hide" Clemente from the other teams.

When that happened, Clemente went into the locker room, packed his bag, and quit baseball. He didn't care about the so-called Rule 5 Draft, he just wanted to play, but not like this. It took several meetings to convince him to come back and play again.

The former President of the Dodgers and the man responsible for bringing Jackie Robinson in to break the color barrier was Branch Rickey, who was now the President of the Pittsburgh Pirates.

One of his scouts happened to see Clemente and wrote a glorious report about him. When Mr. Rickey read the report, he decided to pick Clemente in the first round of the Rule 5 Draft in 1955. The Dodger's efforts to hide Clemente had failed; my grandpa was devastated.

The next year, in 1955, my grandpa signed a lefty by the name of Sandy Koufax and gave him $14,000 to sign, and because the Dodgers signed him for over $4,000 they were faced with the same dilemma. After losing Clemente, they decided to send Koufax directly to the Dodgers. Koufax never played one minor league game. In 1955, both Clemente and Koufax made their MLB debuts.

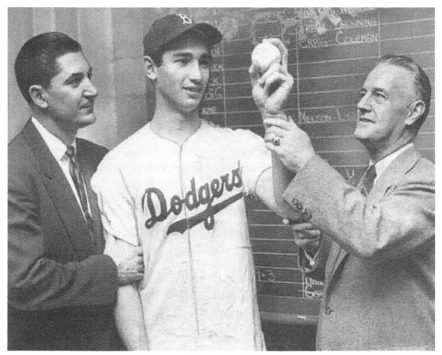

At a press conference for Sandy Koufax, with my Grandpa Al on the left and
Fresco Thompson on the right.

Fifteen years later, in 1970, my dad was traded to the Pirates. Clemente
was still very fond of my grandpa for signing him and befriended my dad.
He called him "Campan-ee."

My dad tells this story of Clemente's talent all the time.

They were both inside an enclosed rectangular batting cage at Spring
Training. Clemente bet my dad a Coke that he could hit ten line drives
(or as he called them, "lineas") IN A ROW off the back square of the cage
without hitting the side or top nets. That's nearly impossible for anyone,
but Clemente did it all of the time. Good thing a Coke was only 5 cents
then!

Unfortunately, we lost a legend on New Year's Eve 1972 in a plane crash
as he was going to help victims of an earthquake in Nicaragua. But the legend of Roberto Clemente lives on and will as long baseball is played.

The Amazing Return of Bobby Darwin

My grandpa Al told me this amazing story back when I was just a kid, about a former major league player, Bobby Darwin.

Bobby was originally signed by the California Angels as a pitcher. He had a cannon for an arm and was sent to San Jose in the Cal League to be one of the starters in their rotation. He started 26 times and had 9 complete games striking out 202 batters. But he also walked 149 in 153 innings. That's A LOT of walks!

The next year the Baltimore Orioles picked up Bobby off waivers and sent him back to the Cal League, this time Stockton. But he continued with his control problems—lots of strikeouts but also a lot of walks.

This was Bobby Darwin's story for the next SIX seasons. But his great arm was keeping him in the game as the scouts felt if he matured and found control, he could be a 20-game winner in the big leagues.

After the 1968 season, Bobby was released by the Orioles. He figured he's better get a job so he started working as a tow truck driver for AAA.

It was at that same time that my grandpa was driving through the LA area and blew out a tire. He called AAA and guess who came to tow the car? BOBBY DARWIN!

Bobby recognized my grandpa and started to tell him about his recent career as a pitcher and his desire to play again. My grandpa really liked his great attitude and took his phone number with him.

A few days later, he read some old scouting reports on Bobby and decided it would be a chance worth taking to sign him. So he called him up and Bobby Darwin signed a minor league contract.

When he showed up to Spring Training, he impressed many of the coaches and scouts with his arm strength, but also became somewhat of a legend taking batting practice.

It turns out Bobby Darwin could flat out HIT! The sound of the ball off of his bat was louder than even the star players on the Dodgers major league team. He used to put on a show in batting practice that none of the other players couldn't equal.

Bobby started that first season with the Dodgers in AAA as a reliever, only throwing in 61 innings, and compiling a 6.49 ERA. However, he continued to put on a show in batting practice, which got my grandpa thinking. He decided that even though Bobby had an amazing arm, he would never make it as a major league pitcher, so he offered him a challenge—move to the outfield.

Bobby was very open to the idea of playing the outfield. After the Spring Training 1970, Bobby was starting in the outfield for the Bakersfield Dodgers in the Cal League—his third season in the league, but this time as a position player.

He crushed the ball that season hitting just under .300 with 23 home runs. He followed that up with an even better season in Triple A the next year, and by the end of 1971, he was called up to the Dodgers! What a turnaround!

Bobby went on to play nine years as an outfielder in the major leagues, hitting as many as 25 home runs for the Twins in '74. For many years since his retirement as a player, Bobby has been a scout for the Dodgers and has been honored by the Dodgers for his lifelong service.

The Charleston Charlies

My earliest memories in life involve my dad playing pro baseball, especially for the Pittsburgh Pirates Triple A team, the Charleston Charlies, at Watt Powell Park.

I was in kindergarten at that point and remember my mom had me go to a meeting with our elementary school principal to make a special request.

My mom asked if she could home school me for the remainder of the school year so we could go to West Virginia to be with my dad. Mr. Graham said YES and we started our drive from Southern California to Charleston—just my pregnant mom, sister Andrea, and me driving alone across the USA.

Working out with the Charlies in 1973. I was 5.

When we arrived, my dad had rented a mobile home. My mom was not very excited about living in this box all summer, but it had A/C and wasn't too far from the baseball field or the hospital where my sister, Alexa, would be born.

The first day we arrived in Charleston, my dad took me with him to the stadium. I remember this like it was yesterday. The stadium was a classic old park near the river, with a metal roof. There was a railroad track above the right field wall that was so loud when the trains rolled by you could barely hear the announcer.

My dad grabbed an old uniform after the first game and took it home. Then my mom took out all of the seams, cut down the uniform and re-sewed the seams to make a perfect little uniform for me. Now I was ready to hit the field!

My dad would always include me in his pre-game routine. He would play catch with me, hit me ground balls, fly balls and I even hit on the field with a sawed off bat.

When people ask why I was so good in little league, it was because I was taught the basics by pro players and practiced with them at age 5! What an advantage for me! I was literally catching major league fly balls in right field and throwing the ball all the way to 2nd base. I was like a little baseball toy for the players and they enjoyed testing my skills.

One time, my dad's group was hitting and I was in right field. They had a contest to see who could hit the most pitches at me, and then, how many I could catch. I remember my dad celebrating when I caught one of his monster fly balls.

My dad played in the Pirates' system for the next three seasons and so did I. Occasionally he would get a two- or three-week call up to Pittsburgh, but we just stayed in Charleston until he was sent back down.

Through those years, I learned how to behave in the dugout during a game, how to behave in the clubhouse before and after a game, especially after a loss. I was trained to say NOTHING and did just that.

As time went on, my dad became a town favorite. He would appear often on Charleston TV with his massive collared polyester shirts accompanied by the platform dress shoes and skin-tight bell bottoms...quite stylish for the early 70's.

As a publicity stunt, the team had my dad take on Mickey Mantle in a home run hitting contest. The Mick was retired and in his early 40's at that time but could still hit bombs. It was close but my dad beat the Yankee legend and the fans went crazy.

When I looked back at my dad's stats, he was CRUSHING the ball those years, but the Pirates were stacked with players.

Over the four seasons my dad was in the Pirates' organization he played with guys like Tony LaRussa, Dave Parker, Kent Tekulve, Richie Zisk, Ed Ott, Bruce Kison, Gene Garber, Doug Bair, Rennie Stennett, Art Howe, John Candelaria, Mario Mendoza (Known for his "Line"), Omar Moreno, and more. Maybe worst of all, ahead of him on the Pirates' catching totem pole, was the great Manny Sanguillen.

After leading the team in 1974 once again in HR's and RBI's my dad decided enough was enough. At 30 years old he felt like he wasn't going to get another chance to be anything more than a Triple A player and felt like he could do more with his life. That's EXACTLY how I felt when it was time for me to make a choice.

When he retired, he was home all the time and began to coach my little league teams. He was always there helping me through good times and bad my whole career.

Growing up on the field with my dad was the greatest baseball experience a young kid could ever have. It deeply infused in me the love of the game and I've tried to pass along that passion to my boys also.

Being "Roger the Dodger"

From my earliest memories, there was always this book in our home, "The Dodgers Way to Play Baseball," written by my grandpa Al.

Most people are surprised to learn that my grandpa was an author. He wrote this book in 1954 and it was reprinted 20 years later in paperback with a catchy cartoon cover of a batter stepping in the bucket while his coach is reading how to correct it.

This book was a detailed instructional look into how to do all things baseball—pitching, hitting, fielding, bunting, stealing bases, catching, even bunt defenses and double relay assignments. This book was revolutionary in 1954.

In the late 70's, the re-release of the paperback version was selling well. It could be found at select bookstores and also at Dodger Stadium where dozens were sold daily. The sales helped my grandpa earn more money as an author than the GM of the Dodgers in those years!

My grandpa's publisher was pleased with the sales of the paperback, but felt the book was way too technical for mass appeal. If you read it, there is a whole chapter dedicated to the proper way to cross over your feet when starting to steal a base. It was very detailed and targeting elite players and coaches, a very small universe.

The publisher suggested that he dummy down the instructional parts so kids could understand them. Plus he suggested that the book be presented in the same format as famous children's books from that era like Dr. Suess and a book that the publisher liked called, "Danny and the Dinosaur," written and illustrated by Syd Hoff.

The children's book format uses brightly illustrated images with cartoon characters that were very appealing to younger readers. My grandpa liked the idea and he came up with the title "Play Ball with Roger the Dodger." I remember he came over to our house for a family get-together. During dinner he mentioned the "Roger the Dodger" book but he had some issues to overcome. He mentioned that he was able to strike a deal with the illustrator Syd Hoff to draw the pictures for the entire book. This was a BIG deal since Syd Hoff was one of the elite children's book authors of the day and it would widen the appeal of the book.

The challenge was how my grandpa was going to direct what Syd would draw. How would my grandpa insure the drawings were technically correct? For example, when showing the proper way to field a ground ball, the drawing needed to show the player with his glove low to the ground, arms extended, knees bent, eyes on the ball, etc. This was proving to be a real challenge and making it difficult for both my grandpa and Syd to get on the same page.

That night at dinner my dad gave my grandpa a suggestion. He said, "Why don't we go out to the little league field and take pictures of Jimmy in the proper poses?" A light went off in my grandpa's head and he agreed that that would be the best way to direct Syd Hoff on how to draw the images for the book.

So a few days later I strapped on a miniature Dodgers uniform and we rolled out to the Yorba Linda Little League field armed with a Polaroid camera and loads of film.

Since my grandpa had already written the text for the "Roger the Dodger" book, he brought it along so we could set up each shot.

The photos started with the proper grip on the ball, the proper arm angle when throwing, etc. I would do what was directed to get the right shot for Syd to draw. The Polaroid camera was perfect for this job. My grandpa could see the shots and approve them on the spot.

They must have taken 150 pictures of me posing as a batter, base runner, catcher, pitcher, infielder, and outfielder making all of the technically correct moves. They also had me do all of the WRONG moves like fielding a ball with straight legs bending too much at the waist, swinging with a poor bat angle, throwing sidearm, etc.

We had some fun with the photos also. One was shot showing me jumping over the outfield fence, stealing a home run. That was not used, however.

My grandpa selected the photos and wrote notes on each photo to help Syd draw the image. Sometimes he wrote, "Draw exactly like this" or "Make sure to show eyes off the ball." Now it was Syd's turn to take this direction and execute it.

A couple months later, a large envelope arrived at my grandpa's house from Syd Hoff. It contained the basic drawings for the book taken from the photos of me at the little league field. They were PERFECT! Syd really nailed the drawings especially those showing proper or improper technique. My grandpa was very happy with the results and felt that young kids just learning to read could benefit from the book by simply following the illustrations.

When the publisher read the text and saw the pictures he was thrilled with the book and off to the presses it went.

I remember a few cases of books arriving at my grandpa's house. I couldn't wait to read it and see how I looked as a cartoon. It was so cool. The kid Syd drew bore a striking resemblance to me at 9 years old, especially the cover image.

The book was a hit right away and sold thousands of copies at Dodgers Stadium and in limited release at book stores.

As the years rolled on and my grandpa passed away the book went out of print.

A couple of years ago I decided to find out who owned the rights to the two books and I contacted the former publisher. They replied that I could petition for the rights to the text of the Roger the Dodger book and the entire 'Dodgers Way to Play Baseball" book also but the estate for Syd Hoff owned the drawings.

I sent in my request for the rights and within a few weeks was sent the legal paperwork transferring the rights to the Campanis family.

One of these days I will update the "Dodgers Way to Play Baseball" by adding more modern hitting and catching techniques, new concepts like sabrmetrics and shifts, new pitches like split finger fastballs, and updated images of equipment like the hockey-style catchers masks and modern catcher's gear to the book.

Stay tuned as the "The Dodgers Way to Play Baseball" will be available once again for younger generations to learn how the game should be played…even in today's Moneyball era.

Three generations of Campanis, though only two ties.

Grand Canyon Slam

Like many families, we took a trip to the Grand Canyon. I was about 10 years old when we went.

As we were packing up, my dad told me to bring my baseball bag in case we found a batting cage on our trip. But actually, he had another plan in mind.

When we arrived at the South Rim he kept driving further and further away from the tourist spots and found a beautiful area where we stopped and set up a picnic.

My dad grew up in Brooklyn where my Grandpa was working in the front office for the Dodgers. Then in the winter, my grandpa would go to Cuba or the Dominican to manage and scout Latin players. As I was growing up, my dad used to tell me how much he would miss his dad when he was my age. So when he was still hitting 25 HR's in AAA for the Pirates he had to make a choice, keep sacrificing to prolong his career, or retire and raise a family. He chose us, which was very lucky for me, being the oldest and also a pretty good ballplayer. He never went on family trips with his dad unless it involved baseball, so this Grand Canyon trip was special to him.

It was at that point he told me to get my baseball bag.

We played catch for a while, and then to my amazement he said, "OK, now throw the ball over the edge." So I did. Then he said "Well, now you can tell everyone, you can throw the ball a mile!"

He then had me pull out a bat. He tossed me a pitch and I whacked it—A MILE!

I learned later that when my dad was playing for the Salem Dodgers managed by Stan Wasiak, the team was driving home after a series of tough losses. In an effort to boost morale, Stan ordered the bus driver to pull off the highway and head to the Grand Canyon. This team had future big leaguers Bill Kelso, Roy Gleason, and future Rookie of the Year, Jim Lefebvre yet they were slumping.

After a while, Stan jumped up and told the bus driver to park. Then he ordered the players to get their gloves and bats and he threw the team batting practice on the edge of the rim until EVERY ball was gone. This little trick helped the team get back on track. Even though they had no baseballs when they arrived at their next game to take batting practice, they scored 10 runs and won five straight games on their way to the Northwest League championship in 1963.

Baseball on the Family TV

For those lucky enough to grow up in a baseball family like I did, we were taught the fundamentals of baseball at a very young age, often by watching games on TV.

I had a nice chat with Bret Boone the other day and we both agreed that our family's "business" really helped us have an edge over other players. We both talked about having access to advanced concepts, gear (gloves, batting gloves, spikes) and the knowledge of hitting, fielding and throwing drills taught to us by our families.

From my earliest memories, watching baseball on TV with my grandpa and dad was exhausting.

Most Sunday's growing up, we'd go to church and then over to my grandpa Al's house for a day of swimming followed by a big family dinner.

As my grandpa got older, he went to fewer and fewer road games. Of course, he couldn't miss watching the games, so he had a massive satellite dish installed in his backyard. He could pick up the Dodgers now wherever and whenever they were playing.

I remember my grandpa used to literally scream at the TV. He would blurt out, "Ahhh, for God's sake (insert player's name), hit the cut-off man!" Or "Come on (insert coach's name), that guy is a dead fastball hitter!"

If he saw the same thing happen over and over, he would CALL THE DUGOUT from his house! I recall a time when the Dodgers were playing the Expos in Montreal when he felt so compelled by what he saw he called the dugout phone and pitching coach Ron Perranoski answered. Immediately the shot on TV was Perry answering my grandpa's call and then Vin Scully said on TV, "Looks like Perranoski is calling the bullpen to get someone loose." But it was just my grandpa telling him from 3,000 miles away to shift over an outfielder 20 feet!

Watching a game with my dad and grandpa, it was like they were actually playing. Both of them would literally twitch when the ball crossed the plate like they were batting. They were so into the game that they tracked the ball out of the pitcher's hand and with perfect game-speed timing would mentally swing at pitches. At first I thought this was crazy but as I learned why they did this, it made sense. It helped develop their "Game clock."

All players are familiar with the speed of the game—what we called the game clock. It's the time you know you have (or don't have) when a ball is hit to you. As a shortstop you learn that you can lay back on hard hit balls and make the play, or that you have to charge slow hit balls and throw on the run. If not, the clock will run out and runner will be safe.

Watching baseball on TV with my family helped introduce me to the feeling of the game clock and also helped to define the critical rhythms of the game, especially the rhythm of the pitcher.

Occasionally, my grandpa would also use his satellite dish to pull up games of teams the Dodgers were set to play in upcoming weeks. He would pull out his scouting sheets and set up a TV tray to write on, and then watch the game intensely. I remember when I was around nine years old we watched the Cubs play the Braves one afternoon. He was particularly interested in some of the players on these two teams. I remember he said, "Watch this player's swing—it's perfect!" He was talking about Rick Monday whom he later traded for. He also told me the Dodgers needed an outfielder so he had me watch the Braves left fielder, a guy named Dusty Baker.

I was one lucky kid learning about such fine details of baseball before I had even turned 10 years old. I had an average body with an average arm and average power, but the knowledge of the game really helped me develop into a good player despite my physical limitations. By high school, I had adopted the "Campanis TV Twitch" as well.

After my playing career ended, I coached my son's Pony league and travel ball teams for 13 years and preached the "Game Clock" concept. I begged the kids to watch as much baseball on TV as possible to develop a better game clock. The kids understood this concept just like I did when I was their age.

As I began working jobs, the guys in my office have noticed this little oddity as we watch ballgames on TV and laugh at me. But I can't help it, my game clock is STILL ticking!

Nailing Guerrero

It was spring of 1984, I was 16 and a junior in high school when my grandpa asked me if I wanted to take batting practice and field grounders at Anaheim Stadium before a Freeway Series game between the Dodgers and Angels. Of course I said YES!

The game was on Saturday but on Friday night I pitched about 5 innings for my high school team and my arm was DRAGGING. I wasn't a pitcher but in desperation the coach would throw me in there.

The next morning I was on the field at the Big A. They even wrote my name into one of the groups on the batting practice schedule!

My group hit first and I used a wood bat. All in all, the players complimented me for hitting that well at 16 so I guess I held my own.

Then it was time to take ground balls, but my arm was BARKING!

I remember playing catch with Bill Russell before we went on the field. I told him my arm was killing me, so he said to just take it easy. No reason to get hurt in BP.

When we went out to shortstop to take grounders, Coach Mark Cresse was ready with his fungo. Russell took the first grounder and flipped a strike across the diamond to the first baseman. Then it was my turn. I fielded the groundball and just lobbed it over. Then the next one I did the same thing.

Out of nowhere, infield coach Joe Amalfitano runs out to shortstop and starts ripping me a new one. Even Bill Russell tried to explain why I wasn't throwing the ball hard. I was sore as hell!

He didn't care and kept yelling at me. So I caught the next grounder and threw it to first base as hard as I could.

The first baseman was following the track of the ball and began to prepare to jump but it was WAAAY over his head. In fact it was so far over his head it was going to make it in the air to the Dodgers' dugout.

In the dugout the star of the team, Pedro Guerrero, was recording a radio interview with Jerry Doggett when my errant throw nailed Pedro directly on his right collarbone…and he dropped to the ground in pain.

I was scared out of my mind. Two days before opening day and I just drilled the best player on the Dodgers! After about 10 minutes of medical attention, Pedro said he was OK to play. I was so relieved. Before the game he showed me his swollen collarbone. I hit him so hard it left a lace mark!

Pedro also told me a story. He said that when he just finished his first Rookie Ball season and returned to his home in the Dominican, he saw my grandpa walking on the beach. He said my grandpa asked how he doing and he told my grandpa he was very hungry and had no money. My grandpa gave him $200 and that fed him and his family for weeks.

But Pedro still made sure to give me crap the rest of the day. Thankfully he hit over .300 again that year!

Batboy for the Angels

I grew up at Dodgers Stadium but around the time I was 15, I spent dozens of nights working out and being batboy with the Angels.

Baseball is a VERY small world. My grandpa Al had worked in the Dodgers front office for years. He had become good friends with Preston Gomez who had previously coached for the Dodgers but also had managed both the Padres and Astros. Preston then took a job as the Dodgers third base coach in the mid 70's.

In 1981, he started a long run with the Angels as a coach and consultant. The team was managed by John McNamara back then.

Preston moved to nearby Anaheim Hills and came to my parents' house for a party after the 1983 Spring Training. While he was there, he saw me playing wiffle ball and invited me to come out to Anaheim Stadium to work out with the team.

He picked me up the next game at 2 PM and off we went. I was so excited.

At the time, the Angels had some GREAT players: Bobby Grich, Doug DeCinces, Brian Downing, Mike Witt, Reggie Jackson, Rod Carew, Tommy John, Fred Lynn, Rick Burleson, Bob Boone, Ellis Valentine and more.

When I first arrived, I couldn't believe how small the Angels clubhouse was compared to the Dodgers. The batboy locker was way over in a corner and shared by all of the other batboys. Our locker was closest to Reggie's locker.

I learned from my dad to keep to myself unless spoken to in the clubhouse and not say ANYTHING after a loss. So that's what I did.

I met the other batboys and also some of the player's sons, like Bret Boone, who was later a teammate of mine at USC and with the Mariners.

One day, I was in right field when Ellis Valentine asked if I would warm him up. He was on the DL at the time but wanted to keep his arm in shape. In fact, he was experimenting as a pitcher since he had one of the best throwing arms in the game. As he began to get warm, he was throwing 90 MPH with very little effort. Then we would play long toss and he could throw a bullet, on a line, from 200+ feet…amazing.

Once he went into the right field bullpen and began to pitch. I remember seeing the pitching coach and other scouts huddled around watching this spectacle. He was throwing damn near 100 MPH. The catcher's glove was popping so loud it made an echo throughout the stadium.

The Angels players were very cool to me, but none of them knew my grandpa was with the Dodgers until he came to an Angel game.

The Dodgers had a day off and to my surprise my grandpa walked into the Angels clubhouse.

He was met by John McNamara and went into his office for a chat. A little bit later he stopped by my locker and asked me how things were going. That's when the #1 superstar in baseball, Reggie Jackson, walked over.

Reggie said, "Al, how do you know this young man?" My grandpa explained that I was his grandson. Reggie then said, "I've been watching him over the last few months. He is respectful to the players, minds his own business, has not asked for any autographs, and WOW, can this kid play ball!" I could tell my grandpa was proud of me at that moment.

Within a few years I was moving on to start playing college baseball and couldn't find the time to batboy anymore.

When I think back on my childhood, I firmly believe that my collective baseball experiences helped me to develop the confidence in my abilities and the belief that I had a legit chance to play pro someday. From catching fly balls in the outfield at 5 years old, to hitting with a sawed off big league bat, to learning clubhouse etiquette, to watching how hard pro players worked. Together it shaped my future.

Unfortunately, Preston was in an accident and passed away in '09 at the age of 85. To honor this extraordinary man, the Angels wore a black diamond patch on their uniforms with the name "Preston" for the 2009 season.

The years working out with the Angels were near the top of my list of awesome baseball experiences. I'm still a fan of the team, the new players like Mike Trout, Manager Mike Scioscia and those Angels LEGENDS from the 80's…especially Reggie Jackson!

Dodgers Old Timers Games

When I was a kid, my dad played in the Dodgers Old Timers game every year.

These games were always a lot of fun for my dad as he loved to reminisce with his old buddies from his playing days. They told war stories about old players and games long gone. They'd say, "Can you believe that was 20 years ago?"

My dad took this one game very seriously every year and we used to go to the batting cages for weeks to get him in shape. He was in his late 30's and early 40's and still had some pop in that old swing of his…one year he missed hitting a home run by one foot! The crowd went crazy that day when he unloaded on that pitch from Pete Richert.

I remember a special year. The Dodgers Old Timers were matched up against the Major League All Stars including some of the greatest legends to ever play the game. I was dressed up in a Dodgers uniform and was the batboy for the game.

Before batting practice started, my dad introduced me to a bunch of the old time players. One was Hank Greenberg and my dad said, "Hank hit 58 home runs one year, and played against a pretty good hitter on the Yankees…a guy named Babe Ruth!" I couldn't believe it!

He introduced me to Mickey Mantle who my dad beat in a HR contest in the early 70's when my dad was in Triple A. Mickey remembered that contest at Watt Powell Park in good ole Charleston, WV. Then I was introduced to Sandy Koufax, Don Drysdale, Johnny Roseboro, Maury Wills, Lou Brock, Del Crandall, Willie Mays, Juan Marichal, Jim Lefebvre, Bob Gibson, Wes Parker (who made an appearance on The Brady Bunch), and the list went on and on. I must say, I only knew their names from books and never saw them play. I knew they were legends, but to me, so were the current Dodgers like Ron Cey and Dusty Baker…even more so. Except for one player…

Growing up with my dad playing baseball, I was taught one BIG thing: I NEVER, EVER asked a player for an autograph. It was considered tacky and inappropriate and my dad didn't want some player on his team getting irritated by me. But then my dad introduced me to Hank Aaron.

I was so nervous when I shook his hand that I could barely speak. Then I decided, if I was going to get a first autograph, it would be from the Home Run Champion of all time! But I had to have patience and ask him the appropriate way. So I waited until after the game when he was done showering. Then I waited until he was fully dressed when I decided it was the right time to approach him for my first autograph request ever.

It seemed like every time I got closer, someone else would jump in to talk to him. Finally I got up the nerve, walked up to him and said, "Excuse me Mr. Aaron, would you please sign my ball?" He said "Aren't you a Campanis?" I nodded. He said "OK, but first go into Dusty Baker's locker and get me a pick then I'll be happy to sign your ball."

So I said, "Sure Mr. Aaron, I'll be right back!" I ran into the Dodgers clubhouse that was about 30 yards from the Old Timer's clubhouse but Dusty was already on the field warming up and there was no one else around.

I ran back to my dad's locker and right away he asked me if I got Hank Aaron's autograph. Flustered, I explained I needed to get Dusty's pick first. Then I asked, "Dad, what's a pick?"

My dad completely cracked up laughing. "A pick is slang for an afro-comb."

Then I knew EXACTLY what Hank Aaron wanted so I ran back to Dusty's locker, found the pick, and delivered it to Hank. He didn't have a ton of hair, but it took him like 10 minutes to pick that 'fro and make it look perfect before he would sign my ball. Finally he said, "Alright, give me that ball. There you go, son. Now take the pick back to Dusty's locker."

My first autograph was from Hank Aaron!!! I ran back to Dusty's locker and returned the pick. Then I met my dad at his locker where I showed off my prized Hank Aaron autographed baseball.

A few weeks later we were playing "Over the Line" on the street in front of my house and lost a ball down the sewer. As hard as we tried to retrieve it, it was too far down there. So I told my friends to hang on a minute while I searched my room for another ball. Finally I grabbed one and we played Over the Line on the street all day until the lights came on…with that Hank Aaron autographed ball.

The Campanis Target Mitt

When I was a kid, my grandpa was the GM of the Dodgers. He was an innovative thinker and is credited for many of the systems still used in baseball scouting to this day including the Dodgers' scouts rating system, batting and fielding practice tools and specialized drills to increase performance.

After a tough loss in the early 70's, he went to the clubhouse to discuss the game with Walt Alston and the pitching coach. His concern was the lack of control the bullpen seemed to have. They either couldn't throw strikes or they couldn't hit their spots and were getting crushed by opposing hitters.

He thought there had to be a reason why, so he asked a few pitchers what their excuse was. To his amazement, a couple of guys said they couldn't focus on the glove and were erratic as a result. This stuck in my grandpa's brain for a couple of years and then a revelation!

When he was driving home after a night game, Cal Trans closed a couple of lanes on the 5 freeway. As he was slowing down, he couldn't help but notice the workers were wearing BRIGHT orange vests that were impossible to ignore, and it got his wheels turning.

The Campanis Target Mitt.

As soon as he got home he drew a catcher's mitt with a bright orange strip around the pocket. He knew this would help pitchers focus on the catcher's glove.

Later that week he had my great grandma Tulla sew two bright orange patches onto a catcher's glove, and he started making some calls to glove makers. My grandpa needed some assistance from my dad and uncle so they were added as partners.

The "Campanis Target Mitt" was patented and my family was offered deals by ALL of the major glove companies. They finally accepted a contract with Rawlings.

Right away the best catchers in the game were using the glove, including Steve Yeager, Johnny Bench, Lance Parrish, and more.

The glove sold pretty well, but remember how niche catcher's gloves are to begin with, and then consider the sub-niche of a glove with a target, so we're not talking huge money. But I recall my parents getting royalty checks every quarter. It wasn't a lot but it really helped.

I was converted to a catcher in 1985 and immediately started using the Campanis Target Mitt.

I caught well over a thousand games with those gloves and can't remember a pitcher EVER saying he didn't like it. In fact, some pitchers preferred when I caught, thanks to the glove.

Ironically, my grandpa tried to patent a first baseman's glove with the same target area but was denied since he was infringing on HIS OWN patent.

Today, the patent is up so ANY company can make a "Target" glove, but you just don't see them anymore. Based on the way many of relievers are pitching, maybe it's time to bring back the Campanis Target Mitt!

High School Hazing

My freshman year of High School, a new baseball coach, Kevin McConnell, arrived at Valencia. The varsity team wasn't doing well, so after a few games, he decided to call me up to varsity. I was immediately batting second and starting at 3rd base. The upperclassmen were not exactly crazy about the development. When I got called up, I was given a locker in the Varsity Locker Room. I was so stoked—I was on VARSITY and had my own locker!

The upperclassmen, on the other hand, decided it would be fun to make me pay a price for my fast promotion and set out to haze me a little... Prior to practice one day, I was jumped by several juniors and seniors in the locker room. I was a 14-year-old kid and they were 18-year-old MEN!

It started with them taping me to the bench...NAKED! Then they applied eye black all over me. To make matters worse – much worse – they squirted a whole tube of Ben Gay on my junk.

Laughing like crazy, they left me there and went out to practice, while I squirmed to get free, more than a little bit uncomfortable.

Meanwhile, out on the field, the coach was yelling "Where the hell is Campanis?" They all played dumb and said I must be blowing off practice. I was eventually freed by someone and scrambled out to the field where Coach was PISSED at me.

Now it was my turn to act. Instead of fighting back, I decided to change tactics. I invited the two ring leaders to go to a Dodgers' game, to hang out in the clubhouse, and watch the game from my grandpa's box. They got the royal treatment under one condition—that they become my bodyguards.

When some of the other guys tried to haze me again, the two guys stepped up and said, "No, leave him alone, he's part of our team now." I went on that season to bat just under .300 and made All-Orange League Honorable Mention.

It was a good life lesson...but Ben Gay on my junk?

Funding My Night at the Prom

After high school one day I was driving home and noticed a new baseball card shop had opened up in Yorba Linda so I went in to see what they had.

Besides a ton of old cards, I saw jerseys on the walls and a bunch of Pittsburgh Pirates memorabilia.

I asked the guy how much would he pay for a Pirates jersey that I had back home. He said it could be worth about $100 but he would have to see it first.

I jumped in my truck, drove home, and brought it back to the store.

My dad played pro baseball from '61 to '75 and had maybe 15 to 20 old jerseys so I figured he wouldn't miss just one...right?

At the time, I was trying to save up for Prom and figured this jersey could fund the tickets, my tux, and dinner, so it was worth it—simple logic for a 16-year-old.

When I brought the jersey into the card shop the guy was drooling. I could tell he really wanted it. When I started negotiating with the guy, he started low balling me. But I stuck to my guns and ended up getting $150 for the jersey. I bought the tickets, rented my tux, had dinner at Bobby McGee's and a lot of fun at prom.

Some years later, in 1988, I was at USC and my dad called me to ask where this particular jersey was. I finally admitted that I had sold it for $150 to fund my prom expenses. I continued to say that I saved him money that I would have otherwise had to beg him for. He said, "Jimmy! Do you know whose jersey that was?" I had assumed it was his.

No such luck. Turns out it was Willie Stargell's sleeveless grey road jersey from the early 1960's. To make matters worse, Stargell had just been inducted into the Baseball Hall of Fame, making that jersey worth 5 times what I sold it for!

My dad still reminds me of that brilliant move. Another live and learn moment.

April 6, 1987

On April 6, 1987 my life changed forever when my grandpa Al went on *Nightline* and made comments that were construed as racist. The frustrating part was that he wasn't even close to being a racist, but for whatever reason, he was defending baseball's lack of African Americans in management positions.

I was a sophomore at USC and on the baseball team. That particular night, I had a day off from baseball and school, so I took a friend up to our family cabin in Lake Arrowhead. Oddly enough, the phone rang at about 9 PM and it was my grandpa. He asked for my mom. It was her birthday and he wanted to wish her a Happy Birthday, but she wasn't there. Then he told me to watch *Nightline* that night. He said there may be some people who think he said some controversial things. So we flipped to ABC to watch the interview.

Since I knew my grandpa well, the first thing I thought of when I heard his "lack the necessities" line was that it was a reference to experience and not cognitive capability. But my friend, who was a journalism major, was cringing after each comment. I kept saying, "He makes me work my ass off doing gardening just to earn $20, that's how he is, you have to earn what you get." But my friend told me flat out that his comments meant something totally different to her.

I didn't think much of it until we were back in LA and I saw that his comments were now making national headlines and people were picketing Dodgers Stadium demanding his dismissal as General Manager.

My dad called me to tell me the latest developments and things were not looking good. Then finally some good news, Mr. O'Malley said he would not fire my grandpa for this incident and simply asked him to make a public apology. I thought the whole thing would blow over quickly and everything would get back to normal. But the protests continued and the pressure on the Dodgers to do something kept building.

My dad called again to tell me that my grandpa was resigning to take the heat off the team he loved for over 55 years. It meant more to him to walk away from this fight than to cause any more grief for the players and front office. So to set the record straight, he was not fired by the Dodgers, despite what was written and reported.

Ironically, he was offered the job of GM for the Seattle Mariners as soon as he resigned, the team I would be drafted by a year from then. But protestors heard of my grandpa's offer in Seattle and began picketing that stadium as well. So my grandpa called the Mariners owner, thanked him for the offer, and officially said no thank you to the job.

It was a no win situation, so he decided to try to repair the damage he had done, but not publicly. Instead, he went right to some leading African American figures like Dr. Harry Edwards, a professor at Cal., to open a dialogue about helping African American players make the transition to management both on the field and in the front office. I'm very proud to hear great managers like Dusty Baker say that although what happened to my grandpa was unfair to a man who was not racist, my grandpa's efforts afterwards did help Baker get interviews and eventually a job as a major league manager.

My entire family had to deal with being a Campanis in 1987; it was a very difficult time for all of us. So, as the USC team entered the PAC-10 season, I was under a bit of a microscope to say the least.

The next day at practice everyone was joking on me about it, everyone except for Rodney Peete, John Jackson, and the other African American players. They were giving me some seriously hard looks and then whispering things amongst themselves. Finally Rodney called me over to their group and they jumped me—with HUGS! They reminded me that we were all friends and teammates. They said they had my back and would support me through the nightmare. That moment meant so much to me. I will never forget it.

A couple of days later we were playing a three-game series at Arizona State, where the most obnoxious and stupid fans in the PAC-10 reside. When I was announced as the batter the heckling started." Hey Campanis, your family is racist." "Hey Campanis, is your grandpa mad you play with black guys?" "Hey Rodney, how can you play with a bigot?"

As I stepped up to the plate, Rodney was on first. I hit a double scoring Rodney from first. That shut them up, but only temporarily. They continued their heckling through the weekend, but despite their efforts to knock me off my game, I had a great series. I think my play earned some respect from them. I know my coaches were proud of the way I handled the situation.

By the time we flew back to LA this whole situation was out of control... and everyone knew the Campanis name...but NOT in a good way. I happened to be taking a Sports Writing class as part of my major. The professor told us on the first day of class that if any of our class assignments were published we would get an automatic "A" in the class.

I met the professor and told him the story of my recent experiences. He said to immediately go home and type it out. So I did, and turned it in the next day. A week later he called me to his office to tell me my story was getting published in the OC Register and that I didn't even need to show up to the final!!!

The article was well received and I like to believe it began the process of educating the average fan that my grandpa was actually the opposite of how he was being portrayed on the news.

My grandpa roomed with Jackie Robinson in the 1940's. He was on one of the first-ever racially integrated professional baseball teams with Jackie Robinson. He signed top Latin players like Roberto Clemente and Pedro Guerrero. His only prejudice was against lousy baseball players...of all races!

His life was never the same after April 6, 1987. I think it accelerated his health problems and caused him to become depressed, forced to becoming a baseball outsider. The feeling of being part of a team was gone and he struggled with it.

Prior to the 25th Anniversary of the *Nightline* interview we were contacted by ESPN who wanted to do a special show about how that interview changed the game. At first, my dad and I were against it. But it was to be on Outside the Lines with Jeremy Schaap. His producer assured us that the story would be positive, and for the most part it was. There were three versions of the show produced. I was in one of them and my dad was in two of them.

Please check out one of the versions of the show on the link below.

http://espn.go.com/espn/otl/story/_/id/7751398/how-al-campanis-controversial-racial-remarks-cost-career-highlighted-mlb-hiring-practices

2

Big Dreams at USC

It was a BIG decision to attend USC over several other great schools. In this chapter, you will be introduced to the LEGENDARY Dave "Lats" Latter, my former USC roommate, winter ball teammate, and best man in my wedding. There will never be another Lats!

These years were important to not only my development as a baseball player, but I was introduced to so many great people that I still keep in contact with.

The Nightline *interview continued to be what most people in the media focused on whenever I did something newsworthy. I was often mentioned in the paper with the line, "USC catcher, Jim Campanis, Jr., grandson of former Dodgers GM who was fired for his racist comments…"*

All I could try to do was…Fight On!

Big Mouth in a Big Pond

This experience was a major "Live and Learn" moment in my life…

My sophomore year in high school, I received my first recruitment letter from a college to play baseball. It was from Long Beach State and I was so excited.

By my senior year, I was getting letters from numerous schools and had to decide which campuses to visit. You are only allowed a certain amount of local visits and travel visits so I set them up.

I decided to visit Cal State Fullerton, Fresno State, Cal State LA, USC and Cal Poly.

Each school had its perks. So I had to figure out where was the best fit for me.

When I visited Fresno, they gave me the red carpet treatment. They flew me up from John Wayne airport and had some hot girls pick me up in Fresno. They took me straight to the game at a beautiful stadium on campus. I couldn't believe how nice this place was.

The coach talked to me for a while and invited me to sit in the dugout for the game.

When the game started, I was sitting in the far corner of the dugout. The batter was late on a fastball and shot a missile into our dugout. The ball started ricocheting all around the cement dugout until it smoked me in the back of the head.

I knew it was a sign from God.

The next morning they offered me a half scholarship and were HARD selling me to commit or they were going to give my scholarship to someone else. I was very disappointed in the way they pressured me and I flew home bummed out.

I went to USC a few times for visits and loved the school but they only offered me a half scholarship and I didn't want my parents to have to pay anything if I could get a full ride elsewhere. I did see Randy Johnson pitching for USC and I thought, "Look at the size of this guy!"

When I visited Fullerton, Jose Mota was assigned to show me around. We knew each other from many years of practicing on the field with the Dodgers. He was telling me all about the school, the nice ballpark, the travel to fun places, and that I had a good shot of playing since so many players were graduating.

The coach offered me a full scholarship to Fullerton and said to stop by the next day to sign my "Letter of Intent." I could barely sleep that night thinking about committing to CSUF. This was going to be AWESOME!

We happened to have a high school game the next day so I stopped by the CSUF baseball field afterwards, still dressed in my uniform, to sign the letter. But the coach told me that his assistant was sick that day and didn't type it up. He said to just come back the next day.

I was disappointed but figured I could wait another day.

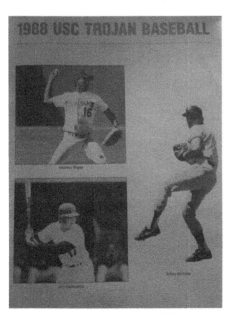

Cover of the 1988 USC Baseball Program.

Within a few minutes of returning home that night, the phone rang. It was the legendary USC coach, Rod Dedeaux who said, "Tiger, you were born to be a Trojan and we are prepared to offer you a full scholarship if you play both football and baseball at USC." I almost fell out of my chair!

That Saturday, Coach Don Buford met my dad and I at Julie's and I signed my letter of intent to USC on the trunk of Buf's Benz.

When word got out that I signed with USC, the OC Register called me for comments.

They asked why I chose USC over CSUF, and here was where my live and learn moment started. My grandpa liked to use the term "Big Fish in a Big Pond" so I said "I want to be a big fish in a big pond and not a big fish in a small pond."

Seemed innocent enough at the time…until my first game against CSUF.

As I prepared for the first pitch, I saw that it was coming straight at me and BOOM! I wore a 90 MPH fastball on my shoulder blade.

When I got to first, I knew the first baseman. He said, "OK Campy, payback is complete." I said, "Payback? Payback for what?"

He then told me that the OC Register article had been pinned up on the CSUF baseball bulletin board for the last several months to inspire the players. My "small pond" comment had lit a fire under these guys' asses.

Later on, during my junior year at USC, I hit three home runs off Fresno State. Afterward, the Fresno coach pulled me aside and said, "Well son, what can I say? We should've offered you a full ride." That really felt good.

Everything happens for a reason. One of the best things ever for me was to play USC baseball with such a great group of players and coaches. I'm proud to belong to the USC Baseball Alumni group and be part of the heritage.

But I did learn my lesson: Watch what you say to the newspaper guys!!!

Football Daze

Today, I've noticed that most kids play only one sport in high school. It seems the coaches want them to focus on one sport and play it all year long.

Back in the day…we played multiple sports.

When I started high school, I intended to play football, basketball, and baseball, but dropped basketball when I learned it interfered with baseball season.

I ended up as a place kicker, punter, and quarterback and really liked playing football. My throwing style was naturally short like a QB is supposed to throw, plus I had pretty good accuracy.

But what no one told me was what it was like to pass when the rush was on. It's like being in the tube of a giant wave and trying to not get wet. Everyone is grunting with the sounds of helmets and pads colliding. It was SUPER intense.

I remember my first TD pass when I was on JV.

It was one of our standard play action fakes to a running back then look for one of two receivers down field. But this play, the linebackers blitzed and were on me too quick. I scrambled for a few seconds, saw Ron Terrill in the end zone covered

Throwing a bomb down the sidelines.

by two defensive backs, and I decided to throw it over everyone's head and out of the back of the end zone.

As soon as I threw it, I was crushed by the defense and was laying on the ground when I heard our fans go crazy.

Turns out, the ball I was trying to throw out of the end zone hit the goal post! Then the ball ricocheted to Terrill who caught it. To everyone's surprise, the ref threw his arms up indicating TOUCHDOWN! Who knew that in High School football, the goal posts are LIVE?

My job as a high school QB was awesome: Fake to running backs Ray Pallares or Bill Buck and hit receiver Richard Savoie down the sidelines for big yardage.

I was a decent kicker and made a 43 yarder with :02 to go for an upset win over El Toro who had won CIF the year before. I missed some too, as some old friends like to remind me when they see me!

There was some interest for me to play college football, and at that time I wanted to play both sports. So I was looking for colleges willing to allow me to do that.

Luckily for me, USC stepped up and offered me the opportunity to play both sports.

When I reported to USC Summer training camp I knew I had bitten off more than I could chew. These guys were HUGE! We actually had a mandatory eating sessions called "Training Table" where the strength coaches would dictate our diets to insure we were getting over 6,000 calories a DAY!

I was sent to work out with the quarterbacks, who included Sean Salsbury and the legendary Rodney Peete. After QB work, those guys went with the starting offensive unit but they sent me to the starting defensive unit. I wondered why?

Then I realized. I was the official first string tackling dummy!

They had me drop back, fake left, and throw to a ball boy on the right— just as the defensive linemen rushed in to block my pass. But they didn't just block the passes, they CRUSHED me, over and over and over again.

When we had kicking practice, I did OK and was optimistic they would have me kick more and play tackling dummy less. But every practice it was more pounding by the lineman.

On the fifth day of workouts, the coaches broke us out by our last names to run the forty-yard dash. They teamed me up with one of the starting offensive tackles, Jeff Bregel. Jeff was 6'4, 290 at the time and picked in the first round by the 49ers later that year.

When the gun went off, we both started chugging as fast as we could, and I lost the race to a guy outweighing me by nearly 100 pounds! These guys were insanely athletic and I knew I was overmatched.

I prayed that my kicking would improve to the point they gave me a red jersey so the lineman couldn't hammer me anymore. But instead, they called me into the head coach's office after week #3.

Ted Tollner was the USC football coach at the time and he asked me to sit down.

He went on to tell me that when I signed my letter of intent, USC was allowed to offer split-sport scholarships, but since then they had been hit with NCAA sanctions. I had to make a decision.

So Coach Tollner said to me, "Son, you have a chance to kick for USC someday, but today you are going to have to choose between football and ba"…and before he could even finish the word, I spouted out "BASEBALL!"

I was so relieved I limped back to my room, packed up, and left within an hour!

The speed of college baseball compared to high school was about 20% greater. But football was so much faster and the guys were so much bigger and stronger than high school, it was truly scary.

Over my three weeks of playing USC football I developed enormous respect for what it takes to play at that level, and I thanked the Lord that I lived through it without breaking or tearing something important!

Hazed But Then Praised

As a baseball player, you have to fit within the social environment of a team, but sometimes that environment is hostile to newcomers.

As a freshman in high school, I was hazed BIG TIME when I was called up to Varsity. When I arrived at USC, I expected no less from the upperclassmen.

Back in the late 80's we had a fall and spring baseball season. We started fall ball right when school started and played 60 games, mostly against junior colleges and pro scout teams.

I played very well in the fall and was hoping to get some playing time when the "real" season started in January.

When the lineup was posted for my first game at USC, I wasn't even listed. That meant I couldn't go into the game, even in an emergency. That really frustrated me, but then I learned I was hazed BY THE COACH! Coach Dedeaux intentionally left me off to make sure I knew my place as a freshman.

I kept a positive attitude and continued to improve but was only getting limited playing time. Then it was time to make our first road trip and I really wanted to have a spot on the traveling team.

Back then we could only travel with 20 players. The 21st guy on the depth chart had to stay home.

We had an older team that season led by Senior Captain, Dan Henley.

When the travel squad was posted on the clubhouse wall, I saw a bunch of guys look for their name and then scream, "F**K THIS!" when they realized they didn't make it. Most of these guys were the older players.

I walked up when no one was around so I, too, could yell an obscenity, but instead I was listed to travel! I was so excited, though I did feel bad for all the other freshmen who didn't make it except one, pitcher Jim Wayne.

Wayne and I were buddies and lived in the dorms near each other. He went to Fountain Valley HS and I had played against him in American Legion so we were already friends by the time we entered USC.

We were given the travel itinerary and told to wear a suit and tie and to be at the field at 8 AM for the bus to the airport.

Wayne and I rode our bikes over to the field together wearing our suits with all our other clothes in our backpacks. Plus, we both played guitar, so we brought along acoustics to jam with at night. This was going to be a BLAST! We were going to Berkeley to play the Cal Bears!

As we were riding over to LAX on the bus, Wayne and I decided to room together since we were the only freshmen on the trip. That's when Dan Henley walked up to us, flanked by a bunch of other juniors and seniors, and the hazing began.

The first thing they made us do was turn our sports coats inside out. Then we had to roll up our pants to our knees. Then we had to pull our shirts through our flies and zip it up for a nice phallic effect. Then the bat girls who traveled with us came over and applied an enormous amount of makeup on us, complete with bright blue eye shadow. Jim Wayne's eyeliner was especially HOT!

As we pulled up to the terminal at LAX, we were forced to exit the bus first and stand where everyone could see us. Then the upperclassmen started throwing coins on the ground and screaming for us to grovel and pick them up. They did this all the way to the security gate where Wayne was detained by the airport police! He explained what was going on so security told the coaches to stop this behavior or people would be getting arrested.

Wayne and I thought it was all over, but the weekend had just begun.

After we landed, the bat girls found us and re-applied the makeup. We had to go and turn our coats inside out again and go through the same treatment as we did at LAX in Oakland. But this time they had an extra surprise for us.

When we went to baggage claim, they made us both stand on the carousel while the bags were coming down the ramp and sing the Star Spangled Banner at the top of our lungs while they hurled coins at us.

Again, security broke up the hazing.

Finally we thought we were out of the woods. What else could they make us do? Hadn't we been abused enough already? Not even close.

USC is known for its awesome Alumni network. There is a HUGE alumni base in the Bay Area and they had set up a banquet for us after our Saturday game. Little did Wayne and I know, but we were going to be the entertainment.

About 45 minutes prior to leaving for the banquet, Dan Henley casually mentioned that we were going to play our guitars for the 500+ alumni, so we might want to think about learning a song. I was panicking!

Wayne and I sat down and started playing all the songs we knew, but neither of us wanted to (or could) sing. What the hell were we going to play?

Then Wayne started playing an old instrumental song from the Ventures called "Pipeline," and we knew that was it.

When we were introduced at the banquet, I was sweating bullets. I had not played guitar in front of that many people before and I had learned this song less than an hour earlier.

As we started playing I could tell the upperclassmen's faces went from happy to downright irritated. Why? Because we were NAILING the song and the Alumni were CHEERING not booing like they expected!

After we finished the song, they gave us a standing ovation and started yelling, "Encore! Encore!" so I started to play a fast Chuck Berry blues song and Wayne ripped through a killer lead. Once again the Alumni went nuts! We looked at each other and literally ran off the stage once we felt like we did a good job entertaining this crowd and fulfilling our hazing commitment.

That was the last time I was hazed.

By the way, Dan Henley is a GREAT guy and told us confidentially that he had to be the leader of the hazing because he was team captain.

As we transitioned from the Dedeaux era and into the Gillespie era, hazing died off. Gillespie didn't like it, and quite frankly, I didn't either. We shifted our form of hazing to inviting the freshmen to hang out with us upperclassmen, and then we stole their meal cards and bought beer all night in a bar they couldn't get into.

By the old USC freshmen hazing standards, Jeff Cirillo, Jackie Nickell, Jim Henderson, and Bret Boone got off easy!

Infectatory Mites

When I was student-athlete at USC, all of the athletes had to provide their own personal equipment like underwear, jocks, cleats, under shirts...etc. Quite a contrast to today's players.

My roommate, The LEGENDARY Dave Latter had an obsessive need to wear these stanky, nylon Bike boxer-brief-type underwear that trapped in all of his sweaty funk. He would wear these to class, then to practice or a game, then home. And believe it or not, he got a NASTY rash all over the whole area those Bike underwear touched.

This rash happened to coincide with our annual physicals at the USC Student Health Center so he figured he'd tell the doctor and get it handled.

That year, the physicals were like a cattle call of all minor sports teams. During our designated time, the Women's Volleyball and Swim teams were waiting to get their physicals also. Lats and I got separated during the physicals. When I was done, I found him in the pharmacy waiting room which is where the Women's teams were lined up to start their exams.

I asked if the doctor was able to diagnose his crotch rot. He said he was waiting for the pharmacy to fill his prescription. As we were waiting, we started chatting it up with the lovely Ladies of Troy. Dave was quite the ladies' man and was deep in conversation with a few of them.

Suddenly, a super LOUD voice came over the intercom saying "YOUR ATTENTION PLEASE, YOUR ATTENTION PLEASE. DAVE LATTER, YOUR PRESCRIPTION FOR INFECTATORY MITES IS READY AT WINDOW B. DAVE LATTER YOUR PRESCRIPTION FOR INFECTATORY MITES IS READY AT WINDOW B.

The girls looked at him with that "Ewwww GROSS" face and quickly said, "Hey, yeah, we'll see you around," and I was like, "Infectatory WHAT?" Needless to say, Dave had a tough year with the ladies and we had to bomb our apartment...TWICE!

Turkeys for Trojans

Junior year at USC my dad was managing a local car dealership and was always coming up with gimmicks to bring in the customers.

That year he decided to buy hundreds of frozen turkeys for his "Thanksgiving Sale Extravaganza." They advertised it in the newspaper as a "FREE Turkey for a Test Drive" and gave away hundreds of turkeys. But there were still dozens left over, so he had me pick up as many as I could and bring them to my USC apartment.

I filled up my truck with like 25 of them. We gave away a bunch to our friends but still had about 8 in our freezer and fridge. I knew just enough about cooking a turkey to be dangerous, but we went for it anyway.

We thawed out one of the turkeys, prepped it like my mom told me to, stuffed it, threw it in the oven, and left for school. We checked on it at about 1 PM and it was looking good. We had to go to baseball practice so our neighbors came over and basted it periodically.

By the time we got home, the apartment smelled AMAZING! We invited everyone over and had an EPIC feast.

Later that week I realized another turkey had thawed in the fridge, so we cooked it the next day. Then another thawed so we cooked it also. This continued for about two weeks. Soon we only had two turkeys left, one completely frozen and one that was rotten from sitting in the fridge too long.

My roommate, Dave Latter, loved to surprise me and make me laugh. So while I was at class, he unwrapped the rotting turkey, took it out to the parking lot and slid it ass-first and waving its wing onto a 4-foot parking barrier pole right in front of where he knew I would lock my bike.

When I got home, it was dark and I didn't see it until I nearly touched that stanky thing sitting on the pole waving at me. I cracked up because I knew Dave had done it. We left that carcass on the pole to see what would happen. It was unbelievable how foul that fowl smelled after a few days!

Flip it...Flip it Good!

As a baseball player, we were constantly looking for ways to entertain ourselves while waiting for practice or games to start. When I went to USC I was introduced to a game called "Flip."

Flip is a game to the death. A group of players form a circle and flip a ball with their gloves between one another until someone makes an errant flip or misses a ball flipped to them. Players flip the ball like a rally in tennis but with gloves instead of rackets. The action gets INTENSE.

When a player misses a flip or makes a bad flip, that player must turn his hat sideways to indicate one miss, then backwards for the second miss, then elimination on the third miss.

At USC, Flip rules were:

1. If you flip a ball above the shoulders you are out.
2. You could not "Screw your neighbor" by flipping to the guy on either side of you.
3. There was a speed limit on flips which was enforced by the group by yelling, "TOO HOT." You could not use your bare hand to assist a flip.
4. However, you were allowed to bounce the flip off any part of your body (except your throwing hand) before flipping to the next player in an effort to deliver a firmer flip....but you had to use your body FIRST and then your glove for the flip.
5. You were suspended from all games that day if you flipped a ball that nailed a player in the lips.

The cool part about Flip is that is forces you to move your feet, focus on the ball, and to be prepared for trickery. Some guys were so good, they looked left and flipped it to the right. Other guys were masters at flipping low. Some guys had tricky Globetrotter between-the-legs moves that were quite difficult to anticipate.

We would have epic games at USC with about 10 guys battling to the end. The finals would be two guys squaring off in a best out of three competition.

A few years later I was playing winter ball in Puerto Rico when a flip game started. The first thing I noticed about the Puerto Rican version of Flip was that these guys were WAAAY better than we were at USC. They also had different rules. For example, you could use your throwing hand to assist you BUT it had to be closed. Plus you COULD screw your neighbor!

I played as often as I could. It really did help my footwork, my concentration, and hand eye coordination. Before I knew it, I was competitive in every game, and as a result my catching was never better than when I was playing Flip on a regular basis.

I recommend this game for those of you coaching kids and struggling to get them to practice defense. Introduce them to Flip. They will improve while having a blast, though maybe you should start with a tennis ball so no one chips a tooth!

From the Gulf Coast to His First Roast

My sophomore year at USC we went to New Orleans and Mobile, Alabama during Spring Break for a tournament against Southern Mississippi, Tulane, University of New Orleans and University of South Alabama. When we first arrived in New Orleans, it rained so hard we had a rare day off. So we decided to hit the French Quarter. What a spectacle! This was right after Fat Tuesday but people were NOT slowing down. It was packed and crazy!

We went bar hopping, ate a boatload of crawfish, and started walking up and down Bourbon Street taking in the sights and sounds of this legendary area.

A few minutes later, one of our teammates started making out with a "girl" right on Bourbon Street in front of a strip club. Then we realized "she" worked there as a TRANSVESTITE stripper. Of course, he never lived that one down! But at least the guy he made out with was pretty hot.

We were also introduced to Jell-O shots with Everclear...and I haven't had one since. No one told us it takes about 20 minutes to feel the effect, so I made the mistake of slamming 2 or 3 or 4 and threw up crawfish the rest of the night!

The next night we played New Orleans and lost when Dave "Lats" Latter fielded a bunt on a very damp field in the bottom of the ninth and threw it nearly out of the stadium. A walk-off loss. Coach Gillespie was pissed!

The next day we rolled into Mobile to finish the tournament against Tulane, Southern Miss, and South Alabama, but once again we were hit with rain. So we decided to throw a party in our hotel room that night.

As we were picking up the party supplies at the nearby Piggly Wiggly Grocery Store, My boy Lats started hitting on the checkout girl.

I could tell he was getting in good with her when she gathered her friends and told them about our little soiree. They all agreed to meet us at the hotel that night about 10 PM when they got off work. These ladies had that killer Southern accent and were awful purdy.

When they arrived, the party was ON! We opened the adjoining doors between the rooms and were bumping Guns 'N Roses while head banging the mullets to "Welcome to the Jungle." It was an EPIC scene.

About an hour into the party my hotel room phone rang. Like an idiot, I answered it, and it was Coach Gillespie! So I put my hand over the phone and yelled, "Hey everyone, SHUT UP it's the f**king Coach, shhhhhhh, be quiet for a second!" I tried to reason with Coach Gillespie but he wasn't having any part of it.

Within a minute he had Coach Sanchez with him pounding on my door.

As I opened the door, the other players started slipping out of my window and the adjoining room window so they wouldn't get busted also. The girls hid in the showers.

Gillespie was no rookie. He walked right into the bathroom, opened the shower curtain, and kicked the Piggly Wiggly girls out. Then he went to the adjoining room and did the same. That's when I knew I was busted and facing serious consequences.

Gillespie said, "Be sure to bring your running shoes tomorrow—and be on the EARLY bus." I knew what that meant and it was going to SUCK!

We arrived very early and ran for about an hour and a half straight when he yelled for me to get ready for batting practice. That's when I saw the line-up for the game. I was not playing—for the first time all season.

I was so pissed off at myself and the situation I was in, I took it out on the baseballs and hit about 15 home runs during batting practice. Gillespie started to egg me on as he KNEW he had lit a fire under my ass. So I started hitting rockets right back at him hoping one would rip through the net and catch his shin or something.

After I was done hitting, I was sent back to the warning track to keep running. Right up until about 10 minutes before game time, when Gillespie changed the line-up and added me at first base.

That game we absolutely crushed (and shut out) a very good Tulane team, then later that day we shut out Southern Miss. The next day we beat ranked Southern Alabama 10-7 to win the tournament!

By then, Gillespie was done being mad at me and now more interested in telling the "Hey shut up, it's the F**king Coach" story to whomever would listen.

Over 20 years later, dozens of former players and coaches met up at a restaurant in Irvine where we had a roast to honor Coach Gillespie. The very first story he told was "The F**king COACH" story.

Coach Gillespie ended up being a huge influence and mentor in my career. I consider myself very lucky to have had Coach Gillespie in my life at that time. Without him, I don't think I would have been able to go as far as I did.

My Furry Little Good Luck Charm

The fall of my junior year in baseball at USC, things were going pretty well, but then I found a good luck charm and had the best season of my life!

One weekend, I went back home to do some laundry. My mom told me she had to adopt a guinea pig from Wagner Elementary where my mom was a teacher's aid, or it would be put down. She also mentioned that she was afraid the cat might get some ideas, like snacking on it, so I volunteered to take it to USC.

Right away, I was attached to this little guy. But he looked so sad in that tiny cage we decided to make him a "free range" guinea pig in our USC apartment.

The guinea pig, who we never named, LOVED running all around the apartment. As time went on, he started picking up on our habits. He would sit under us when we ate burgers and munch on the dropped lettuce or tomatoes. Or he would hear the fridge opening and run over for some celery. Or he would slurp up some water after one of us showered. We never bought him any food; he just sort of lived off our leftovers, and seemed to love it!

About that time and out of nowhere, I really started to play well. The increase in my offensive production was like nothing I'd ever experienced. I had to figure out the reason. Finally it came down to either my hard work over the summer in Alaska or the lucky guinea pig. I gave the benefit of the doubt to the guinea pig!

Coming to the end of the season, I was leading the Pac-10 in HRs, RBI, and players who had a free range guinea pig in their apartment.

When the school year ended, we had to move out of our USC apartment, even though we were still playing and preparing for our regional playoff series in Fresno.

As we moved the desk in our bedroom away from the corner, we discovered quite a surprise. The guinea pig had claimed that hidden corner for all his #2's. Those little pellet craps were piled 3 feet high wedged up against the corner of the walls. We laughed because we just thought he didn't go that often. But he left behind several times his body weight! I bet the cleaning crew had no idea what it was!

We moved into another place on campus for the next couple of weeks and took along my good luck charm.

By now, he was getting fat. When we left for the Regionals that week, we left behind some of his favorite grub—a veggie tray, old burger wrappers, phone books, and a bunch of water.

That week, I had the best tournament of my career, was named MVP, and upped my stock in the upcoming draft considerably...all thanks to the guinea pig!

When we got back to our temporary apartment, we were greeted by an enthusiastic yet considerably skinnier guinea pig. The season was now over and I was off to play for Team USA. I knew I couldn't travel with him.

My mom was volunteering at the Valencia HS preschool so I donated my little buddy. He had a nice big cage and lots of love from the kids.

Come to think of it, I should've taken him with me to the Mariners, because my luck ran out pretty quickly in pro ball!

My Best Bolt Ever!

One of the most critical pieces of a batter's evolution is learning how to wait on breaking pitches.

Watch a major league game and you will see good right-handed hitters name and number on the back of his jersey when hitting. Good hitters keep their front shoulder tucked in and hands ready to fire as they see the ball being released, while recognizing the spin and the speed of the ball. It takes years and years to master this skill. Some never do.

In the summer of 1987, I was sent to play ball in Alaska for Jim Gattis who was the Pepperdine coach and a former minor league player. I can't overstate how important working with Coach Gattis was for my development as a hitter. He proved to me that I could shorten my swing, thereby providing more time to recognize pitches before committing to them. This was a game changer for me.

As we began to play our fall season, I was swinging the bat well and was moved into the cleanup spot. We had a great offense that season, with football star John Jackson (JJ) leading off, Bret Barbarie batting 2nd, USC's QB Rodney Peete batting third, me batting fourth, and Bret Boone batting fifth! Damon Buford batted 9th, which was like a second leadoff man.

Our offensive output was amazing, and we all fed off the guy who was hot that particular day. One day it was Boonie, the next it was Barbs, the next it was Rodney. We had a potent offensive attack but our pitchers were young and a bit inconsistent.

Toward the end of fall ball we would start playing other Division 1 schools in the SoCal area. This was great because it was a preview of who we would face during the regular season when it really mattered. The games were intense and we tried to win each game we played just for bragging rights.

I remember one game like it was yesterday. We were at USC and playing Loyola Marymount in a tight game going into the bottom of the 9th. We were down by a run but had runners at 2nd and 3rd with two outs as I stepped up to the plate.

The crowd of 14 people (scouts, girlfriends, and parents) were on the edge of their seats for the final battle—me against the LMU closer and future major leaguer, Darryl Scott.

Darryl was NASTY. He threw 93-95 MPH, had a decent slider, but lived on his split finger. The bottom would completely drop out of the pitch causing batters to chase pitches out of the zone, and that's exactly how he got me to strike out to end our rally and get the save for Loyola Marymount.

Gillespie saw how down I was. He knew I really wanted to win that game for us and failed. He told me that next time I faced Darryl I would be ready but I should not forget how he pitched to me. And I didn't. I remembered every pitch, and the spin on his split finger was branded in my brain.

The 1988 spring season started out with a bang as we broke the USC record for most wins to start the season going 15-0. We won the 15th game with bottom of the ninth heroics from Bret Boone. He hit a walk off home run to left center that set a bunch of car alarms off when it landed! We jumped around like we had won the World Series. Could you blame us? We had just set the USC record and it still stands!

Toward the tail end of the season we were in a tight race in the PAC-10 South or what we called ourselves, the 6-Pac, and every game was critical to win, even the non-conference games.

As you may know, the NCAA is NOT a perfect entity, and where baseball is concerned it's the same thing. They pick the last few teams that go to the playoffs. If you win the conference, you are a lock, but if you don't, you have to get an NCAA invite, and we knew that was our only hope. Therefore, we HAD to win against other tough teams outside of the 6-Pac…like our non-conference rival, Loyola Marymount.

This time the game against LMU was at the stadium on campus in Westchester. It's a nice little park with a short left field. But the fence is over 40 feet high and then 50 feet above that stretches a net to protect the homes behind the left field fence from getting pounded with home runs. The net is so high, only one person had ever hit one over it, or so the legend went.

I remember the game being tight. LMU had a one-run lead going into the 8th inning, but we had runners on base as I strolled to the plate. That's when LMU's coach decided it was time to bring in their closer, Darryl Scott.

The night before I had done EXTRA visualization techniques, focusing on hitting Darryl. Mentally, I envisioned him in his home uniform, on his LMU mound, and pitching out of the stretch. I slowed down his motion in my mind to see him release that nasty split-finger pitch. And while I was visualizing I kept reminding myself to ONLY swing at that pitch if it was up a little bit. When the split came out of his hand downward, it was going to look good, but fall out of the zone.

Now it was time to face Darryl with the game on the line once again. The go ahead run was on first base so we had a chance to take the lead on an extra base hit.

I watched Darryl warm up and continued to focus on his release point. It was just like I had remembered it.

As I stepped up to bat, I stared down at Gillespie for the sign. He just gave a little fist pump like, "Come on Campy, you can do it!"

Darryl started me off with a fastball that I fouled straight back. Just missed crushing that pitch! 0-1

Then he threw his out pitch, the splitter. I saw it out of his hand and immediately recognized that it was going to be low and I laid off it for a called ball. Now the count was 1-1, but I had seen both of his best pitches.

The next pitch I felt completely relaxed and ready. Darryl checked the runners and began his delivery to the plate.

I'll never forget how big that ball looked as he threw another split finger pitch, this one was up in the zone, about thigh high when it reached home plate. Without any thinking, reacting like an animal pouncing on its prey, I swung at that pitch and made perfect contact.

Physicists say that the optimum trajectory angle for hitting a home run is 45-47 degrees, and when the ball left my bat, it was there...but this park has a SUPER high fence, so I sprinted out of the box hoping to leg out a double if the ball hit it.

Overhead shot of the ballpark at Loyola Marymount U.

But when I looked up, I saw the ball continuing to go up, and up and up, clearing the 90-foot screen, finally landing in front of a house across the street from the houses that backed up to the field, for a three-run home run! We never lost that lead, winning 10-6, and a few weeks later we were invited to the regionals thanks to our play against tough non-conference teams like LMU.

A few years later I was in Puerto Rico during batting practice and saw Darryl Scott who was pitching for San Juan. He walked up to me and asked, "Campy, has your home run at Loyola even landed yet?" We laughed and I admitted that I have never hit another ball even close to as far as that one and really don't know how I did it.

I suppose my fear of failure against this pitcher was the motivator, the visualization technique was the fuel, and the competitive moment was the spark. When all the pieces came together on this one particular pitch, it was the farthest ball I've ever hit. Thank you Google Distance for the visual!

Could it Have Been the Wood?

At the end of my junior year at USC in 1988, we were on the bubble to make the NCAA Baseball Tournament.

School had ended and we all had to move out of our University housing and into new temporary apartments while we waited for the NCAA announcement. We would be there for a couple of nights, or much longer, depending on whether or not we were invited to the tournament.

Since I had a good regular season, I decided to hit with wood bats exclusively that week as we waited to hear. I figured if we made the tourney, I'd start using the aluminum bat again…if not, I had a head start on switching over to wood if I was drafted.

I think we had 3 or 4 practices before we learned we made the cut and were heading to Fresno State. But I continued to hit with wood right up until the first tournament game in Fresno. What happened next was inexplicable!

During our first on-the-field batting practice, I picked my old aluminum bat for the first time in over a week and it felt like a feather! When I started hitting, the ball was simply jumping off my bat like it never had before! What was happening here?

Then I put two and two together and figured out that all of those swings with a much heavier wood bat had strengthen my hands and arms. I also felt like I could wait longer on breaking pitches. The confidence was oozing out of my pores as we started our first game.

We opened the tourney against BYU and in my first at bat in over two weeks, hit a double to right center. That hit helped to solidify my feeling of "being in the zone" and the aluminum bat still felt like a toothpick.

The next day we played Washington State and I took batting practice with wood again…and once again the aluminum bat felt so good in my hands afterwards. I got a couple more hits along with TWO home runs.

It was VERY hot that weekend and after the WSU game, the NCAA official came into our dugout and named five or six guys who were randomly chosen to take a drug test. I was one of them.

I had just caught two games in tough heat and when I got to the drug testing area, I couldn't pee…too dehydrated! I must have drank a gallon of water before finally being able to fill the cup up to the required line. Then I couldn't turn off my bladder for the rest of the night. This is now called "Super Hydrating" and it helped me continue to feel GREAT!

The next day we had a big game against a tough Fresno State team but I was ready, and hit more two home runs! I was so in the zone that I hit a 3-0 CURVEBALL out for a three-run homer! We finally beat FSU that game 18-17 in front of the largest crowd EVER at Beiden Field (5,400+). By winning, it forced FSU to have to beat us TWICE the next day.

When we arrived at the stadium for the final game, the attendance record was broken again (5,600+), a record that still stands to this day!

I was not aware of this at the time but I was only three RBI's away from the USC school record for RBI's in a season. I was still feeling REALLY good but had played hard for the last few days straight.

In my first at bat, I hit a ball off the end of the bat that I should have hit over the moon and yelled "f**k" as loud I could…it echoed throughout the quiet stadium as the ball continued to carry and hit the scoreboard for another HR! I felt stupid for the outburst and sprinted around the bases quickly so none of my buddies would get drilled from my antics.

We battled that game but lost 17-14, forcing a decisive final game.

My first AB of the final game, I hit a long fly and Bret Barbarie scored on a sacrifice fly. I had just tied Rich Dauer for the school record with 92 RBI's that season. (That record still stands!)

We battled that Fresno State team but they kept coming back. Ultimately, the FSU pitcher dug in and was able to hold us down while the FSU offense hammered us a couple innings and we lost 12-3. Fresno State had earned their FIRST EVER trip to the College World Series.

It was a very tough loss for us, one game away from the College World Series.

After the game, the NCAA official kept yelling my name. I figured it was for another drug test, but instead he had me stand with him until the FSU celebration was over. That was tough to watch.

Then just he and I walked out onto the field, and I was announced as the MVP of the Regional where I batted over .400, hit 5 home runs, and had 14 RBI's in 5 games.

Of course, I like to think I was a clutch player who would rise to the occasion. But truth be told, I think it was because I hit with wood the whole week prior.

For you coaches out there, have your players swing HEAVY wood bats in one of your batting practice stations. They will initially struggle with the smaller sweet spot and extra weight in the head of the bat. But then watch as they light up the scoreboard with the aluminums!

PROjans

People ask why I chose USC over the other schools recruiting me out of high school. The short answer is—the tradition of winning and the tradition of making "PROjan" baseball players.

My freshman year, I remember looking into the stands during our first fall league game and noticed at least 20 pro scouts watching us play against a local Junior College team, on a Tuesday, in October, at 8pm. I knew I had picked the right school.

Prior to the start of my freshman spring season, USC held its annual Alumni Game. This particular year many of USC's greatest players showed up. It was like the MLB All-Star Game with Fred Lynn, Steve Kemp, Dave Kingman, Mark McGwire, Bill "Spaceman" Lee, Ron Fairly, Roy Smalley, Rich Dauer, Randy Johnson, and more. RJ was throwing 95 MPH that game…even when he faced a guy from the 1955 team who was in his mid 50's!

When my freshman year ended we had quite a few guys get drafted and signed, including first rounder Brad Brink. Others drafted and/or signed were future Dr. Steve Bast, Dan Henley, Terry Brown, Paul Fuller, Brian Brooks, Don Buford Jr., and John Reilley.

We had a challenging season my sophomore year as Coach Gillespie was making a transition with how we played the game. He was into defense, base running, and had a million signs and signals to remember as the catcher. Gillespie had different signs for when he was standing up and when he was sitting down!

After returning from a summer of playing ball in Alaska in 1987, I felt I had really improved as a catcher, a hitter, and a team leader. I had a GREAT coach in Alaska, Jim Gattis, who taught me about a lot more than baseball; he helped me to begin to mature as a person and a player. I couldn't wait to show Coach Gillespie what I could do when school started at USC for my junior year, in the fall of '87.

We were fortunate to also have some really good baseball players on the football team. In fact, we had three starters playing football, wide receivers John (JJ) Jackson, and Randy Tanner, along with QB Rodney Peete.

When these guys joined us in January for the spring season, we had one awesome lineup.

In all my years of playing baseball, I don't think I played with a better group of human beings and had more fun than that 1988 USC team.

(L-R) Riles, Jackie, Campy, and 'Rillo.

The team chemistry was so tight, even with the new freshman. When I was a freshman there was some pretty harsh hazing going on, but Gillespie had put a halt to it and I was glad. The freshmen like Jeff Cirillo, Jim Henderson, Jackie Nickell, Kevin Farlow, Reid Mizuguchi, Jamie Davenport, Bret Boone, and Damon Buford got off easy!

However, Gillespie did let us keep the batgirl tradition going, so as an upperclassman I was on the committee to select the dozen or so ladies to be on the squad, and that was quite fun, as you can imagine.

When the 1988 season started, we broke the USC record for most wins to start the season, taking 15 in a row. We were ranked #1 in the country, so of course we had to throw a party at Lats' and my apartment.

The parties Lats and I threw at our apartment in Cardinal Gardens were epic.

After every practice or game, there was a collective, "What are we doing tonight?" We always hung out with each other and we were more than teammates, we were good friends...and many of us still are.

Those were some of the best times I had at USC hanging with Chris Billig, Nicole Mendez, Chris Hale, and many more. Even Will Ferrell partied with us!

That year, the Pac-10 South, AKA the 6-Pac, was the best college baseball conference in the universe. A team from our conference had won the previous two College World Series titles and four of the six teams were ranked in the top 10 at one point.

I did the math: Of the 17 guys who traveled with the team in 1988, 15 were drafted. Eighty eight percent of that 1988 team became PROjans!

Some of my teammates went on to big time MLB careers, like Bret Boone (14 years), Jeff Cirillo (14 years), Bret Barbarie (6 years), and Damon Buford (9 years).

That team also produced two NFL players in Rodney Peete and John Jackson, both of whom were also drafted by MLB teams. JJ played in the minors for the Angels and Giants. Rodney was drafted 4 times by MLB teams but never signed. Instead he played 15 years in the NFL.

I sort of expected this type of chemistry to follow me to pro ball teams, but it didn't. Of course I had some great times in pro ball and have lasting friendships from those years, but playing baseball had become a job. It was tough to develop the same kind of team camaraderie, as players would come and go with injuries, trades, and guys getting released.

Right or wrong, my goal when I chose USC was to get drafted, sign a contract and play many years of pro ball, which I did—though not as far as I had dreamed. But the unexpected benefit was meeting and becoming lifelong friends with some of the best people on the planet—people who today still Fight On, just like we did on the field nearly 30 years ago.

Draft Day, 1988

As an amateur baseball player, you work your butt off to improve your game in hopes that someday you get the call from a pro team telling you that you've been drafted.

I found myself in this place two times.

Prior to my senior baseball season in high school I played for the Minnesota Twins scout team run by the local Twins' scouts Jesse Flores and his son, Jesse Jr. This was a great experience.

The Twins team was mixed with other high school players like me, and also pro players who wanted to get some at bats before Spring Training. We would play against college teams so it was very good competition for me.

I remember one game we played at Mt. SAC, and Mark Salas, the starting catcher for the Twins, played for us that day. The Mt. SAC pitchers were nasty and I was excited to get one hit that game. Meanwhile, Salas hit FOUR home runs! I knew that I had a LONG way to go after watching him play.

After my senior year, the Twins offered me a really nice contract to sign based on my play on that scout team.

However, I remember how polished and professional Mark Salas was and knew I wasn't ready yet. My Grandpa Al also really influenced me to go to college and keep improving.

So off to USC I went.

Over three years and two summer ball seasons I was improving, getting stronger, and preparing myself for the opportunity to play in the pros.

From my first Spring Training in 1989.

During my junior season, I was called by at least 15 teams to inquire if I would sign with them if drafted. I said YES to all of them.

The Cincinnati Reds went as far as to have me take an eye exam and answer a series of questions about my physical health. The Giants called to tell me they had me pegged as the top catcher on the west coast and wanted to get me by the third round. The Royals called the most and said they had me in the top 3 also.

Finally…it was draft day, 1988.

I sat around my parent's house and waited and waited and waited. But no call came until later that night, and it was my grandpa Al.

He knew I had been drafted but he couldn't tell me which round or by which team. He said to expect a call the next day from the Head of Scouting from an AMERICAN League team. That's all he would say…

So I remember dreaming of being drafted by the Yankees, or maybe the Twins again, or what if I was an Angel or Tiger? My imagination was running wild thinking of the possibilities.

The next day I finally got the call….from the lowly Seattle Mariners.

At the time, they were, by far, the worst team in the league with the cheapest owner and lousy Spring Training facilities. Sure they had some good players, but of all the teams in the American League I was dreaming of being drafted by, the Seattle Mariners were not even on my list.

Just so you know, when you are drafted you have NO options. You either engage in negotiations with the team that drafted you or you wait until the next time you are eligible to be drafted again.

Right away, the Mariners started jerking me around with the contract negotiations. We tried to threaten them with statements about me returning to USC for my senior year, but they didn't seem to care. They had a package they were authorized to offer and nothing more.

I often joke that being drafted by a bad team can sometimes be a blessing like it was for some of my Mariners teammates. They got up to the bigs quickly or were traded. But the other side of the coin is, if you can't make it up the ladder in a bottom tier organization, the top tier teams think you are damaged goods or not good enough to play for their organization.

And that's pretty much what happened to me…

Today, the Mariners are a much better organization with solid ownership and a future Hall of Famer playing second base.

In June, a player will be drafted as the #71 overall pick like I was in 1988. He will be able to negotiate his bonus starting about $750,000. That's enough for a young player to live off for years and years and was significantly more than anyone got in the 1988 draft including the FIRST PICK!

Then the real adventure begins…

3
Inside the Pro Game

After being drafted by the Seattle Mariners in the 3rd round I was hit with a rude awakening...this was not college anymore.

We played A LOT more games over a much longer season. The grind was absolutely brutal at times. Sometimes I would think, this is what I've worked my life to do? But then the game would start, the adrenalin would begin to flow and the crowd would cheer when my name was announced. That's when I would think, "There's nothing better in the world than playing pro baseball."

I played in the minors from 1988 to my final release in 1995 with a year on the Mariner's 40 man Major League roster. This chapter offers an inside look at life in the minors, and it isn't very glamorous.

Needless to say, if I could do it over again...I would in a heartbeat!

Coach Dick

My first pro baseball manager was a REAL Dick. As a matter of fact, his dad was a Dick, his mom was a Dick, even his kids were Dicks. Why am I being

so harsh? I'm not! His name was Ralph Dick!

Ralph was my manager in 1989, managing the San Bernardino Spirit in the California League, the Single A affiliate of the Seattle Mariners.

Sure, we had a little fun with Ralph's name, but we had nothing but respect and admiration for Ralph, his coaching skills, and his work ethic.

Ralph threw the best batting practice EVER! And he could literally throw all day without stopping. He also had one of the best "Cage curves" you've ever seen. Most coaches can't throw a decent curve in the batting cage because the distance is shorter than normal, but Ralph's curve was nasty and better than some of the pitchers we faced.

I worked out for Ralph's team for a week or so at the end of the 1988 season to prepare for Instructional League. Ralph immediately targeted me for extra hitting.

As soon as he saw me hit, he called me over and said, "Campy, I know you are fresh out of college where you had lots of success. But based on what I'm seeing, you are an easy out, unless you make some changes." I was blown away! No one had ever said things like this to me with the complete confidence that they were right. Quite honestly, it stung to hear this from my first pro coach. But I was determined to improve.

His biggest gripe with my swing was how I used to load all my weight onto my back leg and then "sit and spin." He was a believer in weight transfer from the back leg to the front leg, which was controversial at the time.

I worked hard with Ralph during Instructional League and was able to really drive balls into the gaps by transferring my weight onto my front foot and became a much more balanced hitter entering the 1989 season.

As we began the season, we all learned on Opening Night that Ralph had a fan club just above the visitor's dugout on the third base side, right where he coached third base! They just loved to let Ralph have it. Ralph's fan club would often yell, "Hey Dick, why don't you wear your jersey? Is it because you're a Dick?!" Or other times at the top of their lungs they'd scream and clap in unison, "Hey Dick (clap clap), YOU SUCK!" The other teams just loved this.

Even when Ralph made a brilliant move like calling a hit and run that was perfectly executed, Ralph's fan club would still heckle him.

Our Spirit home jerseys had our names on the back, even Ralph's. But for obvious reasons, he never wore it. So we had a little fun with it. After every home victory, the team writer would name an MVP and interview that player for the next morning's article. That player would don the "Dick" jersey and wear it with pride that night. Ralph always got a kick out of that one.

Ralph's sense of humor is sarcastic and witty. He was also very humble and no one worked harder. He led by example.

Ralph was really tough on me in 1989, and I needed that. He helped to humble me right when my ego was out of control, without alienating me from the team. All he would do was remind me of errors I was making and I had nothing to come back with. He'd say, "Campy, great job in the 6th inning driving in those runs…it made up for the two you gave them in the 5th not blocking those curves in the dirt." He always left me wanting to completely please him—JUST LIKE Coach Gillespie used to do at USC !

I remember hitting a 3-run home run on Opening Night (my first official pro game) on a slider, thanks to Ralph's work with me. I stayed back, recognized the pitch and slightly transferred my weight to the front foot upon contact. BOOM…directly over the T.G.I. Friday's sign in left center for a $50 gift certificate!

After my first season with Ralph, the stats were in. We won the 2nd half but eventually lost in the play-offs to the Bakersfield Dodgers who were led by Eric Karros. Ralph had me catch more games than any other catcher in the minors (120 of 141 games) and my knees felt it! He also had me DH or play first base for another 13 games. I needed the work and appreciated Ralph continuing to put me in the lineup. I ended up with the most HR's of any catcher in the league and made the All-Star team.

In the off-season of 1989, Ralph was promoted to Minor League Batting Instructor. He called me to tell me the news, and also asked me if I wanted to be his catching instructor at a series of baseball camps in Northern Arizona that off-season. I jumped at the chance to make a few bucks while staying in shape. He even let me crash at his beautiful Flagstaff home.

As I climbed the minor league ladder, we saw less and less of Ralph as he worked intensely with the lower level guys in Arizona and Rookie Ball. Then Ralph got an offer to work for the Milwaukee Brewers organization.

By this time, he had legally changed his name to Ralph Dickenson…but he will always be a Dick to me.

I was absolutely overjoyed when I learned that after plugging away as a manager and coach in the minors for over 25 years, Ralph was called to the big leagues in 2014! He was the batting coach for the Houston Astros and proudly wore a jersey with his name on the back! He is coaching some of the best young hitters in the game like Altuve, Singleton, and Springer, and I bet they absolutely love hitting off of Ralph in batting practice just like we did!

Brawling Behind "Blue"

Tensions in baseball can flare up very quickly and escalate into a full-scale brawl. In 1989, I played for the San Bernardino Spirit and we were in Bakersfield playing the Dodgers in the Class A California League.

I happened to know a bunch of players on their team from college and also hanging with a lot of these guys in the AZ Instructional League. Cool group. But on this night, things got crazy.

I have verified the events of the game with several players and here is the story:

Our pitcher was Jim Blueberg (Nicknamed "Blue") from Yuba City, NV. He threw hard with a nasty curve. But his best asset was his competitive drive. He never gave up and demanded the same from his teammates.

Blue was throwing a good game and the score was tight around the 5th inning when the Dodgers started to rally. Blue was pitching well but couldn't manage to get a couple of guys out before a batter hit a home run. Then the batter did a bit too much celebrating rounding the bases for Blue's competitive nature to handle.

The next batter was future Dodgers shortstop Jose Offerman, who could run like the wind. Blue was fuming and didn't even give me time to call a pitch. He just reared back and drilled Offerman in the ribs.

Before I could even get out my catcher's stance, Offerman was charging the mound. He was so fast I couldn't catch him from behind. As a catcher, my job was to protect the pitcher in these types of circumstances, but Offerman was too fast, so Blue was going to have to handle this alone for a few seconds. As Offerman reached the pitcher's mound he went to throw a big hay-maker right hook, but to my amazement, Blue got into a perfect boxing stance. He threw a sharp left jab that stunned Offerman and then Blue dropped him with a right cross straight out of a Mike Tyson highlight reel!

Obviously, Offerman didn't read Blue's bio in the program where it said that he was the Yuba City Community College Golden Gloves Heavyweight Champion!!!

I could see Offerman trying to wake up, but he was just squirming around on the ground with blood coming out of his ear as the Dodgers and Mariners players reached us at the pitcher's mound like a huge wave crashing on the rocks.

The center of the pile is the most dangerous place to be because the wimpy guys sneak up and punch you in the back of the head then run away. I was getting whacked around in the pile but somehow got out from under thousands of pounds of players to see an old friend on the Dodgers, Eric Karros.

I ran over to him. He grabbed my jersey and I grabbed his like a couple of hockey players ready to a fight. We sort of wrestled while looking around for idiots trying to get in a cheap shot until the fight was over.

Finally, the teams went to their dugouts and the umpires started throwing players out of the game. Offerman was thrown out…and sent to the hospital. Blue was thrown out, and he iced his arm and drank a beer in the clubhouse.

I can't remember if we won the game, but we definitely won the brawl!

Minor League Paychecks

When I was drafted by the Seattle Mariners and sent to Fall Instructional League, I was introduced to the realities of minor league pay.

My dad had always told me about how little money he used to earn in the minors but I figured over 25 years later things would have improved. I was wrong.

My first day at Fall Instructional League, they called me into the club-house office to get paid and handed me an envelope. I signed for it and didn't ask how much nor did I count it until I got back to the hotel.

The envelope had the date range of 6 days written on it so I figured it was one week's pay. It totaled $48. When you add up the time on the field along with traveling to games, it worked out to less than $1 an hour!

My first year in 1989 at San Bernardino, I made $700 a month for 5 months, and my portion of rent was $400 a month. The team did not pay for ANYTHING when we were in our home city. We were responsible for housing, clothes, transportation, food, utilities, entertainment…everything.

There was a huge juxtaposition between the perception of fans and reality of the players in the minors. Thousands of fans would cheer for me when they announced my name; kids would line up for my autograph; I would give speeches to hundreds of students at school assemblies; I would have my picture in the newspaper and would give radio interviews to tens of thousands of listeners. Then my paycheck arrived. I did the math. I was making $16.75 a day after taxes!

I had received a decent bonus when I signed, but now that money was quickly getting spent on life basics.

By the time I was married and had a son, I was making $1,200 a month for the 5-month season. We were forced to room with another couple because the bonus money was spent. I received $400-net paychecks every other week and we barely survived. We had $19 in the bank after bills were paid. My wife would be alone for 10-14 days when I was on the road, eating Ramen noodles or rice to save money.

On road trips, we got $7–12 a day in meal money, depending on the level. After a while, we began to get creative. I would pack a hot plate and a big pot so we could save some of the meal money by cooking. When we arrived at the hotel, we'd go to the grocery store and split the cost of buying pasta, sauce, salad, and garlic bread. Not so glamorous, right?

One day I was in our clubhouse in Jacksonville and a letter arrived from my dad. Inside the envelope was a bunch of photos of hitters. He would write comments about their swing for me to learn from and emulate. But one time, between the photos, he slipped in a $20 bill.

So I took that $20 bill and hid it under the insole of my shoe for an emergency. A short time later my wife informed me that we were totally broke and payday wasn't for a few days. I pulled out that $20 and that kept us alive the rest of that week.

After my first year in AA, I was invited to play Winter Ball in Los Mochis Mexico for a WHOPPING $2,500 a month in CASH! That was 2 ½ times more than I received from the Mariners. PLUS, they paid for our hotel room the entire season. This was a God send for us and that money helped us through part of the next season.

In 1992, I was on the Mariners 40 man roster with the highest paying contract on my minor league team, $2,400 a month for 5 months. That's $12,000 before taxes—for the entire season. By the way, that was the most money I ever earned monthly playing professional baseball over the course of 8 years.

I did get paid for a few baseball cards and would occasionally be invited to sign autographs at card shows for a few bucks. That really helped back then, but I wasn't a famous player so I didn't get frequent invites to the big shows.

After a very expensive Winter Ball season in Puerto Rico, we were broke again and living off of credit cards. There were no other options. There simply was not enough money to live.

But my hyper-competitive mind kept thinking, I just need to get to the show and everything will be fixed.

A rookie in 1992 was making $21,800 a MONTH! Plus they would get $110 a DAY for meal money. The big leaguers made more on meal money on the road than I did the whole month!

That off-season, my dad hooked me up selling cars in Anaheim. I had no idea what I was doing but needed money. I used to tell the customers while taking a test drive, "So here's a little secret. I'm not really a car salesman, I'm a baseball player. Also, my dad is the dealership manager, so just tell me what you want to pay per month and I'll try to make it happen." They would give me strange looks, but then one would say, "Well, we want our payment lower than the last loan we had at $350 a month." So, I'd go tell my dad about the deal and he'd come back with $355. Usually the couple would buy the car. I made more money selling cars in 4 months than playing baseball for 8 months.

Ultimately, my decision to stop playing baseball at nearly 28 years old was purely financial. I knew I could still play but I could not afford $1,000-a-month job anymore. Plus, we were thousands of dollars in debt from living off the credit cards. I basically paid to play pro baseball the last couple of years.

If I could do it over again, I would try to stretch out my bonus longer somehow, but don't know if that would have been possible. I played the pro baseball lottery over 8 years, and financially speaking, paid dearly for it. All I have to show for all those years are some old baseball cards and these stories. Of course, I'd do it all again in a minute!

The Baseball Card Racket

When I started playing on Team USA in 1988, the Topps baseball card company was there to sign us to a contract for a USA card. That was my first lesson on how baseball card companies operate.

When I was a kid, my dad was a major league player for the Pittsburgh Pirates. One season, the Topps Company offered my dad an option. As payment for his 1973 card, he could take $500 in cash or a complete set of Black and Decker power tools. He took the tools.

That extra bit of income was always nice for my dad so when Topps had me talk to their executives, I was blown away at their offer…$5. That's not a typo. They literally had a briefcase filled with $5 checks for us to sign.

However, since we were on Team USA, we could not actually cash that check or we would be deemed professionals and therefore not be eligible to play in the Olympics. Crazy!

The Topps photo shoot was at 7 AM on a day off, after I had gotten about 3 hours sleep! I was so tired I didn't bother taking a shower. So when the card came out, I was super greasy and groggy-looking. Thanks Topps!

My baseball card royalty from the generous folks at Topps.

As I began my pro career, I learned quickly that the card companies had a loophole that they used to make gobs of money—minor league cards.

When a card was made of a player in a major league uniform, the card companies were obligated by the player's union licensing agreement. That meant a major league player would receive a minimum of $2,500 per card. But the card companies ONLY made cards of players on the 40-man roster.

I was on the 40-man roster in 1992 so EVERY company made a card of me except one. I was on a Topps prospect card, Donruss, Bowman, and many others. All of them paid me since they included me in the Mariners team set. But one company, the one with the most despicable business practices, used their loophole and made my card in a minor league uniform—f-ing Upper Deck.

To add insult to injury, they used that same card on their national advertisements! When I went to the park one day, there was a new edition of Baseball America laying around with the Upper Deck advertisement on the back cover featuring me in my Jacksonville Suns uniform. Since I was wearing my catcher's gear, you can't see my jersey, but in bold script it says, "Mariners Top Prospect.. If that's not a blatant misuse of the rules, I don't know what is.

The Upper Deck ad also featured Carlos Delgado who I was playing against that night. He was also wearing a minor league uniform. When I got to first base I asked him if he got paid to be on the ad. He said he was offered a $2,500 contract by Upper Deck for that minor league card and use of his image on whatever they wanted.

I decided to call Upper Deck myself and find out what was going on.

I spoke with their head of marketing and expressed my interest in getting a contract with Upper Deck as well. She basically told me that they thought Carlos Delgado would become a star and wanted to contractually lock him up. Then she proceeded to tell me they had no interest in a contract for me. She went on to say I had no rights since the player's contract I signed stated that they could make as many cards as they wanted of me and not pay me since it was a minor league deal. When I questioned the use of my card on their national ad, she laughed and said they used it because it was a good action shot of me throwing from my knees. I continued to complain that this system was unfair and that I wanted SOMETHING for being on the ad. To shut me up, she sent over 100 cards.

In 2006 I found out that Upper Deck made an unauthorized card of my deceased grandpa Al as well. Same deal when I called to complain. They claimed that they were legally allowed to since my dad had given them a verbal OK to print the card, but they never paid us. I requested a reasonable fee but they resisted and said we were welcome to take them to court. To this day, they still haven't paid us for that card.

In late '92 or early '93 I was signing autographs in Puerto Rico and a kid handed me a card of myself that I had never seen from Bowman. Immediately I broke out my best Spanish and asked the kid if he would trade me a ball and a bat for the card. He agreed! I then called Bowman who basically asked where they should send my check. However, I still wonder if they ever would have paid me if I hadn't called.

To this day I get sent at least a card a week to sign. My dad gets even more. The cards are sent to my house even though I've asked every card collector site that lists my address to change it to my office. Almost all the letters I get have a nice, handwritten note saying something like, "You were my favorite catcher" or "I love the Mariners and collect Mariner autographs." I laugh when I see the signed cards for sale on some online store for a buck.

I suppose many players dream about having their own baseball card. I know I did. Unfortunately, the business side of baseball card companies is quite shady, bordering on full-blown exploitation of players names and their images. I'm not sure if the new collective bargaining agreement between the players and owners protect minor leaguers from this predatory system. If I were to guess, I'd say not. Baseball doesn't care about minor league players, their compensation, nor their rights—until they get to the major leagues.

First Ever AA All-Star Game

I've always loved the Mid-Summer Classic!

As a player, your competitive drive extends way past the day-to-day grind of trying to beat a pitcher or throw out a runner. We all want to be ALL STARS!

By the time I reached pro ball, every guy on my team had earned just about every honor there is—All-League, All-County, All-State, All-Region, All-American.... But at the top of the pyramid, there is another pyramid that separates the everyday player from the All-Star.

Typically, All-Star teams are voted by writers, coaches, or league officials. It's very rare for your stats to speak for themselves to receive an honor. Only end-of-the-year titles like batting or home run champions are earned by stats alone. A sportswriter who only sees you play for 8 games a year and then votes on the All-League team is a joke in my opinion. This system makes the All-Star team a popularity contest. It's even that way in the MLB voting system.

One of the greatest travesties I ever witnessed was when Ruben Gonzalez won the Triple Crown in the California League in 1989 yet was not voted by the league writers as MVP. What a JOKE!

By my third year I realized the way the system worked and learned that all I could really do was play hard and hope the writers, the scouts, and my coaches noticed.

In 1991, baseball tried an experiment. It was decided to create the first ever ALL Double A All Star game just like Triple A had been doing for years. This meant that I not only had to beat out the other 5 American League catchers in the Southern League, but also the other 10 from the Texas League and Eastern League.

That season, I was off to good start and was also hitting some home runs. Our team was battling the Greenville Braves for first place and I was catching/throwing well. About two weeks prior to the first ever Double A All-Star game I was notified that I not only made the team but was selected as the starting catcher for the American League team! I was stoked! I still don't know who voted for me but I was grateful.

The only bummer was that the game was in Huntsville, AL which was in our league. It meant that I'd have to drive myself since the distance was under 500 miles...a minor league rule at the time. Over 500 miles and the team was forced to fly you.

When I arrived at the Huntsville hotel, I realized I knew most of the guys on both teams. It's such a small world at that level.

The pre-game festivities were a lot of fun. There was a big luncheon banquet at the hotel then we headed over to the stadium. We took batting practice and then had a home run derby won by John Jaha, future star for the Brewers.

There was also a special baseball created just for our game with blue and red laces—pretty cool! That year my Jacksonville Suns team had FOUR All-Star representatives, tied for the most of any team in AA. We had Bret Boone starting at 2nd base, Roger Salkeld starting at pitcher, I was starting at catcher and Jeff Nelson was the Closer.

I knew that I'd likely only catch for two or three innings and get one at bat. I was fine with that.

When the game started, we were home team and former Giants shortstop, Royce Clayton, led off the game. I knew Royce as a USC recruit. We had a blast the weekend he toured USC. He signed his letter of intent to attend USC but the Giants drafted him in the first round so off to pro ball he went. Anyway, Royce ended up getting on base and I knew he wanted to steal second base.

Roger Salkeld not only threw 100 MPH back then, he also had a quick move to first base. The Mariners were hard-core on pitchers keeping runners off balance and Roger was really good at that. He would occasionally slide step to make sure the runner knew he had that in his arsenal.

With two outs, Clayton took off. Roger got me the ball in enough time for me to throw a strike to Boonie who made a nice sweep tag to get him. A Jacksonville Suns trifecta.

In my only at bat, I faced Mo Sanford from the Reds who had a NASTY curve ball. I battled him deep into the count but ultimately hit a hard one hopper back at him for an out. If he hadn't snagged it, it would have been a base hit up the middle.

Boonie was one of the few guys who played longer and luckily for us he did. In the 7th inning, he doubled in two runs to put us ahead. Nellie came in and it was lights out for the National League team.

When I look back at the players on that team, it's a 1990's who's who. I'm talking Jim Thome, Bret Boone, John Jaha, Royce Clayton, Jeromy Burnitz, Turk Wendell, Mo Sanford, Roger Salkeld, Eric Young, Jeff Nelson, Keith Mitchell, Arthur Rhodes, Javy Lopez, and more.

It was an honor and privilege to play in the first ever Double A All-Star game. It was another boost to my confidence and I knew I could play with the best.

Even though the stats from the All Star game do not count, in AA or the major leagues, something even more important is at stake for the players besides home field advantage in the World Series; it's pride. Even in the era of gazillionaire players, the best are still driven by the will to succeed and to be the best player on the field.

Streaks and Slumps

The famous line from the movie Bull Durham is "Never f**k with a streak." And that is how we lived the precarious life of playing baseball for a living. I believe we all had the utmost respect for the "Streak" because as a player you have so little control over what happens to you and, most importantly, WHY it's happening to you.

For example, as a hitter you may go a few games without getting even one good pitch to swing at, then all of sudden, for no reason whatsoever, you get one every at bat for a week!

This unpredictability manifests in many players as a feeling of helplessness or insecurity. We simply keep trying to control the things that happen around us, but our efforts are completely futile. Baseball (and life) has the tendency to completely humble you—especially when you least expect it.

I have been on some crazy hot streaks and also the other side—slumps!

I compare riding a streak to being strapped to a bolt of lightning. You almost feel like an outside force of nature is controlling your play, and your body is like a puppet, just along for the ride.

I remember hitting 5 home runs in a series and really can't remember the details very well. It was like I was an animal, instinctually hunting my prey and pouncing at exactly the right time. See ball, hit ball, run dummy, turn left in 90 feet.

One time, back at USC in 1988, Coach Gillespie knew I was on a hot streak. So when the count was 3-0, he gave me the hit sign! Usually, he would make us take a strike. The guy threw a 3-0 CURVE and I hit a 3-run home run. That ONLY happens when you are what we called, "Out of your head!"

During that streak, I used the same bat, I ate the same food, wore the same socks, would not get a haircut, watched the same TV shows, etc. all in an effort to keep the magic, and so the streak, alive.

On the dark side of streaks, commonly known as "slumps," I've done the OPPOSITE. Ate at different restaurants, changed up my uniform/undergarments, got a crazy haircut—whatever I could think of doing to mix it up.

In 1990, I was batting .171 after two months and was about as low I could get. I remember calling my dad for advice from 3,000 miles away. He was good at hearing what I was doing and giving me good tips, but even that wasn't working. So he said he would send me something to break the spell. He knew I needed a distraction that would change my attitude.

As I was getting dressed at the stadium before a game, a package was brought to my locker. It was a box with six Eddie Murray bats sent from my dad! The bats were HUGE compared to the ones I was using, but magically, using them I started to turn that season around and was named MVP of the team in September. It just took something as simple as new bats to break me out of that funk.

I started to associate certain things, strange things, to luck and success and employed the tactics to break out of a slump or keep a streak alive.

One such tactic, as weird as this may sound, worked for me, and the only reason it did, as I think back on it, was I BELIEVED IT WOULD WORK!

As soon as I walked onto the field for the first time in uniform, I would scour the field for a feather. Oddly enough, feathers were always on the fields as the birds used the green lawn to hunt bugs and eat the grass seed.

As soon as I located a feather I would do one of two things. If slumping, I'd put the feather in my back left pant pocket, the pocket that faced the pitcher. I convinced myself that every time I did this the feather would have me fly into second base with a double during that game. And damn it if it didn't work when I needed it to! Sounds crazy, but since I believed it worked, it did!

On the other hand, when I was crushing the ball and in the zone, the feather ritual was different. I would again scour the field for a fallen feather, and once I found one, I'd step on it with my right foot and rotate my back leg like I did when I hit, crushing the feather into the grass. Again, I believed that the feather would whip my back leg around and keep the streak alive. Once again, it worked because I believed it.

Many of you have probably heard the term "slump buster." Let's just say it involved having a certain kind of encounter with a certain type of person. Well I tried that early on in college. It didn't work and always caused complications, so that's when I had to get creative. The first thing that ever worked for me to break out of slumps was playing pinball. I rode my bike to the USC arcade and played until it was time to be at the park. It took my mind off my troubles and again, I believed it would help and it gave me just a little extra confidence that day.

Baseball inherently has its peaks and valleys, times when things are "smooth sailing" and others when you are right in the middle of a "storm." But isn't life like that also?

What I've learned from all the ups and downs is, try with all of your might to stay off the emotional rollercoaster. Don't try to control things you cannot. Instead, face smooth sailing and storms equally and with a positive attitude. It is still a challenge I face all the time so I know it's easier said than done, on or off the field.

Aiding the Enemy (and Vice Versa)

During Spring Training of 1993, I knew I was on the bubble, at risk of getting released by the Mariners. They had just sent me down from Triple A to Double A where I had already played two seasons. The organization had some young stud catchers coming up and they even converted Raul Ibanez to catcher that year. I felt like the writing was on the wall, but also knew I had more good years in me.

One night that spring, my old USC roomie, the legendary Dave "Lats" Latter, along with Darryl Vice, who both were playing in the Oakland A's organization, came over to my house in Tempe for dinner.

I knew Darryl from college as he went to Cal and we played several games against them each year. Lats and Daryl had also played together in Santa Maria during summer ball and I hung out with them during a break from Team USA. We became good friends and it was great having them over.

A while after they arrived, Darryl started to tell me that he thought he might not make the cut and get released. I expressed the same concern. So we devised a little scheme. We decided to execute the arrangement the next day when my Mariners Double A team played his A's Double A team.

Darryl played second base and I was the catcher, so here was what we did. When Darryl was batting, if I said ANYTHING to him or the umpire, it was a fastball, and if I said NOTHING to him or the umpire, it was a curve.

Then, when I batted, I would look out to Daryl at the second base position. If his hands were on his knees, it was a fastball. If his hands were between his legs it meant curve.

Desperate times call for desperate measures. And I doubt we were the first two dummies to come up with this kind of a scheme.

That game Darryl went 4-4 and drove in the game-winning run. I hit two home runs (both off top A's pitching prospects) and threw out Darryl trying to steal second base.

We both made our AA teams and met up several times that season in the Southern League. As tempting as it was to cheat during the regular season, we both agreed to only pull out the trick when it meant life or death.

Kangaroo Kourt

When I started playing pro ball I was introduced to a new set of rules, governed by the players themselves, with all infractions brought to the team and heard in "Kangaroo Court."

Court would be held as often as it was needed to be held. In other words, the more the players did stupid stuff, the more often we had court. We had a chart set up in the locker room that was marked up with the various violations. When the list was getting long, a court date was set.

So the first thing you might think is that this system is built around the play ON the field, but it actually extended to the clubhouse, too, and the bus/plane, the hotels, and even our own free time.

Every team had a "Kangaroo Court Ringleader" who would organize the meetings, establish the fine-able infractions, hear the cases, and levy the fines. That was a big responsibility and it usually fell on the eldest player on the team. The "Ringleader" often was experienced in knowing if the alleged accusation had merit and what the penalties would be for the various infractions presented to him in court.

The manager and coaches would get involved and have a list of the on-field crimes such as overthrowing a cut-off man, missing signs, getting picked off, throwing to the wrong base, taking a fastball right down the middle for strike three, or just being late to the bus or practice. The fines were low for most of these offenses, maybe $1 to $3.

But the major crimes were committed off the field and brought stiff penalties. Here is a list of the infractions that levied the heaviest fines:

- **Dick in the spread** – You may NEVER go up to the food area naked and begin to make yourself something to eat. $5
- **Pissing in the shower** – For obvious reasons $3

- **Cock Watching** – Hey, my eyes are up here buddy! We had a multiple offender in Jacksonville and you know who you are! $3 per cock
- **NOT taking a shower after the game** – Usually, the guilty were starting pitchers who sat around doing charts the whole game and wanted to get to the nightclubs as quickly as possible. $5
- **Shitting on the bus** – In such cramped quarters, in the boiling summer sun, #2 needed to wait until we reached a truck stop or the hotel. $10
- **Dip cup with no tissue** – When cups of tobacco spit spill, they make the nastiest mess of all time. This was especially a problem on the bus as guys kicked over the cups and spit would run under the seats. But if you simply stuck some tissue paper in the cup, it wouldn't spill. $5
- **Talking to your wife/girlfriend during the game** - I was guilty of this one when I was in the bullpen. $3
- **Stinking up the entire clubhouse** – This could be accomplished in the bathroom area or by dropping a silent but deadly bomb near the lockers. If the smell peeled paint, you paid for it! $5
- **Rancid smelling shoes/spikes** – If it was nasty enough and two people deemed it punishable…it was. $2 per occasion
- **Miscellaneous Infractions** – Deemed a crime by the Ringleader. For example, one player would immediately dry off after showering, put on socks and shoes ONLY and then walk across the clubhouse to go brush his teeth. $2 for the weirdness factor.
- **More Misc. fines** – I was fined for going out in a rain storm during a delay with a packed stadium and running around the bases in my socks then sliding head first like 30 feet on the slick tarp into home. $5

After a while we all started saying "Oh, that's a fine!" every time we witnessed someone doing something odd, selfish, stupid, or just plain wrong.

When court was in session, the Ringleader was given written offenses by those prosecuting the accused player. Each crime required an accuser and a witness to corroborate the accusation. The Ringleader then would listen to both sides and decide the verdict case by case. Some guys were indicted on numerous charges, while some got off Scott-free. I was always getting charged for doing stupid stuff like the sliding in the rain thing, blowing up the bathroom, spilling chew spit, signing autographs during the game, saying something stupid to newspaper writers, playing guitar too late on the bus…and the fines for these infractions added up!

Overall, Kangaroo Court was just another way to eliminate the tedium of a 6-month long season, and also really help us to come together as a team.

But it was still tough explaining to my wife why I owed $17 to the Kangaroo Court!

Road Trip Reality Check

Part of the thrill of playing college and pro baseball was the travel. These trips were completely paid for by the team or organization, but getting there and the accommodations were sometimes memorable for the WRONG reasons.

A good example was Salinas. It was an eight-hour bus ride to get to a crappy Motel 6. Then the field we played on was an old, decrepit stadium with freezing, wet air coming in off the coast with no clubhouse facilities. Then, by the time the game was over, the town of Salinas had gone to sleep. That meant three nights of Domino's pizza and vending machine cookies for dessert.

In 1990 I was assigned to the Carolina League, home of ultra-sleezy motels. Once, after a home night game, we loaded onto the bus and headed to Lynchburg, VA to play the Red Sox the next day. The ride wasn't that bad and we arrived about 4 or 5 AM. I had woken up when we exited the interstate and it looked like we were in the middle of nowhere. Then, up ahead I saw a flickering neon sign that read, "Harvey's Motel," and I thought that CAN'T be our hotel! But it was. The rooms were big but they smelled like Raid roach killer. The TV only got like 2 stations, and of course, there were NO restaurants anywhere within walking distance, making the experience that much more painful.

When we left Lynchburg and Harvey's Motel and returned home, the trainer called a special meeting to inform us that a few guys had contracted CRABS—from Harvey's Motel! Not from a skanky Lynchburg chick, but from the skanky motel! We were each given a bottle of "Quell" with a mini comb and required to delouse our junk before we could go out for batting practice. Good times!

Then in 1991 I was assigned to Jacksonville in the most notorious bus league in America, the Southern League. I played over 400 games on this team over three seasons and logged tens of thousands of miles on that bus.

We were geographically located in Northern Florida right on the Atlantic Ocean, but we played against teams in South Carolina, North Carolina, Tennessee, and Alabama. Other than our short trip to Orlando (2 ½ hours), the rest were brutal. It was about 7 or 8 hours to Charlotte and 15 hours to Memphis. I actually flew to JAPAN from Memphis in less time than it took to drive on that bus from Jacksonville to Memphis!

Some of the Double A hotels were nice, really nice in fact. The Orlando Hotel was down town, and it was a 5 star Omni with a glass elevator, beautiful views, and room service—even though I couldn't afford it!

At the beginning of every road trip we were given a printed itinerary that included the times to catch the bus to the stadium. Usually it was about 2:30 PM for a 7 PM game.

I remember hopping on the glass elevator to catch the bus and stopping on a floor where other members of my team boarded along with this massive guy.

When we reached the lobby, our first baseman Jim Bowie yelled to the massive guy, "Yo, what are you doing here?" The massive guy said, "You know Boo, just checking out Orlando to see if I like it here." It turned out that Bowie and the massive guy went to LSU together and were buddies.

I was not (and am still not) a big follower of NCAA hoops although I'll play the brackets just in case I'm lucky. Turns out, this guy was well known but I had never heard of him.

We sat down in the lobby of the Omni Hotel where Bowie and the massive guy were catching up on things while we all sat around listening. Bowie asked why he was really in Orlando, and this guy with a fitting name that I thought was his nickname because he was as big as a SHACK said, "The Magic want to draft me as the first pick but I want to be sure I like the town, the arena, the coach, and the players before I agree to sign with them."

We talked with Shaq for a good 20 minutes waiting for the bus to arrive. He was a super-cool guy and I'll never forget how giddy some of my teammates were to have talked with him. I didn't think anything of it until Shaq turned into the SUPERSTAR that he remains to this day.

I have done some basic math and determined that from the time I entered USC in 1985 to my last pro game in 1995 I spent nearly 4 years of my life staying in a hotel/motel, and most of them were flea bags with allergy-inducing air conditioning units.

Nowadays, I still travel for work occasionally. It's funny because I can crash just about anywhere after going through the minor leagues, but my company arranges the hotels for me and they are always very nice.

Recently, my co-worker asked me how my hotel in Houston was since he needed to go there for a meeting. All I could think of was, did I get crabs? No. Did the place smell like roach poison? No. Did the A/C unit smell like a putrid cesspool? No. Were there places to eat nearby? Yes. So I nonchalantly told my co-worker, who had no clue about my hotel experiences, "Yeah…It was pretty nice." But truth be told, that hotel in Houston would have been the absolute nicest hotel I EVER stayed in during my playing days!

Dangerous Medical Substance Option (DMSO)

Like many players, injuries hindered my pro career….that and the inability to hit a slider. But I'll tell you about how far I went to be able to play.

Over the eight years of pro ball, my injuries ranged from a dislocated finger to a separated shoulder to a torn up knee to back spasms to twisted ankles to concussions. But a constant issue was a sore throwing arm—especially in Spring Training.

The Mariners had moved their Spring Training facility way out to the farmlands in Peoria, AZ in 1990. Back then, it was in the middle of nowhere. Literally, there were no stores or gas stations for miles. The only thing you'd see were roadside vendors selling beef jerky, fruit, vegetables, and something called DMSO.

That spring my right elbow was so jacked up that I couldn't bend it more than a few inches. They told me I had a bone spur in the elbow joint that would require surgery. The competition for jobs was intense and players got released every Friday. I knew I couldn't sit out and try to heal, I needed to play and I was desperate to get my arm working. Surgery was simply not an option if I was to survive this Spring Training.

I started trying to mask it with Advil—sometimes as many as 12 capsules a day. It kind of worked, but I knew how harmful that much Advil was for my kidneys and stomach.

Prior to practice one day, I saw one of the older pitchers rub what looked like an underarm roll-on deodorant product onto his elbow. I went up and asked him what it was, and he told me it was DMSO. The same thing I saw the roadside vendors selling on 99th Avenue.

He went on to tell me that he was from Texas and they've been using DMSO on horses and cattle for years as a way to treat injuries.

I may not be a stallion or a bull but I was desperate to be able to throw normally, so the next day I pulled over on the way to the stadium and bought a bottle.

I put the stuff on my elbow, and instantly a horrible, garlic-like taste filled my mouth, like I had eaten a whole clove raw. Later that first day, my teammates complained that my whole body stunk like garlic, like it was oozing through my pores. They avoided me like the plague, but amazingly, my elbow gained greater range of motion.

I repeated the treatment for a few more days and my arm started to actually feel good. Then one of the trainers smelled the garlic reeking from the depths of my soul and knew I was on DMSO, so he told me how it worked.

He said that DMSO is an INDUSTRIAL SOLVENT and goes directly through your skin. It acts as an anti-inflammatory but is VERY dangerous because whatever is on your skin goes right into your bloodstream. Things like bacteria, viruses, germs, etc. He told me that I should not continue with the treatment or I would risk serious side effects. I had no idea this stuff was dangerous so I started weaning myself off of the most powerful product I've ever used to heal a sore arm. In the end, I survived the cuts and made it for another year.

The Campanis C243: Bat to the Stars

The first thing I had to learn once I signed my pro contract was which wood bat model suited me best.

In college, we used aluminum bats that were all shaped the same. You could make the handle thicker by adding tape, but that was about the only modification.

However, with wood bats, I learned there were literally dozens of sizes, shapes, woods, and brands. I asked my dad what he used and he said he settled on the K55 model created by Chuck Klein in the 30's and used by Mickey Mantle. He also told me he had created a bat model early in his career but ended up not liking it.

I asked which bat model and he said the C243. The C was for "Campanis" and he was born in February of 1943. He said around 1964 he was in Louisville for a three-game series and visited the bat factory. That's where he took the thin P72 handle and the large R161 head and had the C243 created.

What he and I didn't know was that the C243 model had become the favorite bat model of some of the best hitters in the game!

I tried the C243 but preferred the M110, the K55, the I13 and the S318 models. They had thicker handles and felt more balanced to me.

After I was done playing ball and was working in radio advertising we flew to San Francisco for a seminar. On the plane one of my buddies, Keith Woods, told me to open the in-flight magazine to an article that mentioned my dad as the creator or the C243! I couldn't believe it! The article went on detail the careers of the players who used the model my dad made. It's a who's who of great hitters: Tony Gwynn, Rod Carew, Wade Boggs, David Ortiz, A.J. Pierzynski, Buster Posey, Paul O'Neil, Kirby Puckett,

Frank Thomas, Cecil Cooper, Mo Vaughn, Jose Bautista, Edgar Martinez, Juan Encarnacion, Tony Armas, Jose Canseco, Derek Jeter, Wally Joyner, Gary Sheffield, and more.

To this day, other companies besides Louisville Slugger have a "C243" model and it remains one of the most popular bat models in the game.

Check out this article from the Smithsonian Magazine about bat models including my dad's C243.

http://www.smithsonianmag.com/history/baseballs-bat-man-62965504/

An Abundance of Accessories

Most occupations use little tools or products that assist the skilled worker to better do their job. Baseball is no exception.

Let's start with an item you won't see on the field. Have you ever heard the term "Bone a bat?" OK kids, you can stop laughing now. To bone a bat is something that has been a part of baseball going back to the beginning.

When using a wooden bat, you should hit with the label up or down—why? The grains of the wood are the hardest part of the wood, so the bat companies intentionally print the label on the soft side of the bat. By hitting with the label up or down, you are allowing the baseball to make contact with the harder grain.

But over a short amount of time, the softer part of the grain gets knocked below the harder grain. By mashing the grains back down onto each other, the bat becomes much harder. Picture a big bone like you'd see watching Tom & Jerry or Bugs Bunny. That was the type we used and is the preferred method for players to harden their bats. Some clubhouses even have bones bolted to work benches to make it easier!

When I started hitting with wood, I went to the grocery store butcher and asked for a huge beef thighbone and he gave it to me for free! I went home, boiled out all of the junk, and used it for my whole career. It's still in my old baseball bag.

Now let's move to the on deck circle. There are several items nowadays for players to get ready for their at bats, starting with good old pine tar. It is exactly what you think—sap from pine trees heated and pressurized that comes out black and sticky. Its original purpose was to protect wood from the elements, but batters quickly learned it was great for getting that extra grip on a wood bat!

In the 70's another sticky item appeared out of nowhere. We just call it "Sticky Stick." The product was found all over the Caribbean in the 70's as way to stop loud, slipping fan belts by giving the belt extra grip on the belt pulley...and it really works! Back then, Manny Mota realized it would be a perfect substitute for the less tacky pine tar most players used. The only downside to the sticky stick is weather. Too hot and the stick melts; too cold and it won't apply to the bat. By the way, the Manny Mota Sticky Stick is STILL the best selling sticky stick in the world and was my favorite back in the day!

There is also a product called rosin. Rosin is a pine-based powdery product that is poured into a sanitary sock. It is used to add additional tackiness to pine tar but it's also that little white sack that pitchers always pick up on the mound. Rosin helps pitchers get a better grip on the ball in sweaty situations.

I caught a pitcher who had some major league years but was trying to get back to the big leagues after surgery. He didn't throw as hard as he used to so he started working on a pitch he called the "Puff." He would go to the rosin bag and load up a whole bunch in his pitching hand. Then he would jam the ball in his palm and throw a changeup. The overabundance of the white powder would shoot out of his hand upon release making a huge "puff," like a white cloud. The batter would get distracted by this puff of powder and usually take the puff pitch for a strike or swing and miss. I still can't believe that pitch hasn't been outlawed. It was nasty and extra hard to see in day games.

Another thing on deck are different types of weighted bats. Some guys like a simple weighted donut. Others like a sledge hammer, or swinging two bats; others even like a device that slips on the end of the bat with big wings that provide wind resistance when swung. All of this was to make the bat feel lighter when it was time to hit.

There are countless practice devices sold in stores and online for training. I'm talking about bats that look like an oar, a metal broomstick, along with mini bats for one arm training. I've used restrictive rubber and neoprene swing aids that insure your arms are doing the right thing. I've hit off of tees that allow you to move the pitch around, and machines that flip you a ball every five seconds, and a tee that uses a stream of air to float the ball when you hit it. I've used mini gloves to increase my hand/eye coordination, jump ropes to improve footwork, lopsided balls to work on fielding bad hops…whatever you need to improve there is a tool out there!

Ultimately, every serious player learns one thing: If an accessory (or combination of accessories) works, keep using them! As you know, baseball players are superstitious and that lends to keeping a wide range of accessories in use. So if swinging a sledge hammer in the on deck circle using sticky stick and rosin for grip helps you get hits, by all means…DO IT!

My Favorite Pitcher to Hit

When you begin to play baseball as a little kid, you start seeing a trend when you have success.

For me, I identified the types of pitchers I hit well—and the ones that OWNED me.

When I say "types" of pitcher, I'm referring to details in that pitcher's game that pegs him into a select category.

For example, tall right-handed power pitchers, who throw straight fastballs right over the top, with a curveball and straight changeup. I hit this type of guy well. Often this was the type of pitcher who was an average starter but threw LOTS of innings for his team.

Another type of pitcher is the right-handed "sinker-slider" guy. You see this guy generally in middle-to-long relief and also in the front of the line getting Tommy John surgeries. But these guys were always tough on me. My old roommate at USC, the legendary Dave "Lats" Latter, was that type of pitcher and I went 0 for 8 against him. He even owned me in batting practice!

By far, the pitcher that absolutely most had my number was the right-handed side arm guy. These guys had a different release point, and just when I felt like I was on a pitch, they'd drop that side arm slider and my ass would be in the third base dugout while I feebly swung with one arm at a slider six inches off the plate.

So thank goodness for LEFTIES!!!! If not for left-handed pitchers, I wouldn't have played as long as I did. And I think I know why.

Here's my theory, and I'd love to hear the critics on this one. I was a right-handed hitter AND my dominant eye was my RIGHT eye. That means that my "back" eye when hitting is my dominant eye.

One's dominant eye can be identified by making a triangle with your hands. Touch your thumbs and pointer fingers together and extend your arms all the way. Then look through that triangle and focus on a fixed object about ten feet away. Now close your left eye. If you can still see the object, you are also right-eye dominant. If the object disappears, keep your triangle in the same place and close your RIGHT eye this time. If the object is in your triangle, you are left-eye dominant.

Most people that are right handed are right eye dominant...same with lefties. This favors guys like George Brett and Wade Boggs who threw right handed, were right eye dominant BUT hit left handed. Therefore their dominant eye was facing the pitcher giving them better vision when hitting.

However, when I faced a lefty, my right-eye dominant self was able to see the ball SO much better. It seemed the visual perspective facing a lefty allowed me to really see their release point, the spin on the ball, and the speed. When you have these factors in your favor, you can do some serious damage. And I did.

I can remember facing lefties more and more as I went up the baseball ladder. There simply were not too many lefties to face until I hit high school. That's when I realized I had this special advantage.

By the time I reached USC, I was having my way with lefties. I can't remember a lefty that intimidated me with his stuff like those damn sinker-slider guys could. It seemed that my swing was tailor-made to hit these guys.

One at bat at USC solidified my love for facing lefties. We were playing Cal State Long Beach and the bases were loaded as I stepped up against a lefty. He started me off with a weak ass curve ball and I hit it a 400-foot foul ball. Then he tried to bust me inside for a ball. Then another curve and another 400 foot strike. Then a changeup and another 400 foot strike. Then with the count still 1-2 he threw an inside fastball that came back over the plate and I hit it 450 feet for a grand slam. I absolutely KNEW I was going to hit this guy, even after the series of long strikes.

I can look back with pride knowing that I crushed lefties that went on to have great careers. Guys like Jaime Moyer, Wilson Alvarez, Arthur Rhodes. Even Randy Johnson even though it was just a simulated game.

But if I had to pick one guy in the world that I OWNED, and he knew it, it was left-hand pitcher, Jason Klonoski. Jason and I were the same age, and I first faced him when he pitched at the University of Arizona. I always hit him well in college and was pleased to learn he was signed by the Twins and I was to face him again in pro ball.

One game in Orlando, I read in the paper that the starting pitcher was my favorite pitcher to face, Jason Klonoski. But I was mired in a nasty slump at the time.

When I took batting practice that day, I still felt awkward and just wasn't in the groove. It's hard to explain, but you just know you are not dialed in. But I kept telling myself that Jason was my slump-buster!

During my first at-bat, we nodded to each other because we had become friends over the years but now it was time to compete. The first pitch he threw looked like a beach ball and I roped a line drive just over his head for single. Then the next at bat ripped a first-pitch double, then another double off of his slider. I ended up 3 for 4, but he threw well that night and beat us.

I faced him a number of times in '87, '88, '92, '93, and although he struck me out ONCE in all that time, the only outs I made were bullets right at someone. It was an incredible and odd thing that we both laughed at over the years.

I continued to crush lefties for the rest of my career and even hit a pinch-hit HR off a lefty. If ALL pitchers were left-handed, I'd have a plaque in Cooperstown!

Fast forward to early in my next career. I had earned an advertising internship at Kamel Kountry 108 radio in Phoenix, Arizona.

When I arrived on my first day, I met all of the bosses. They were super-cool people and I really was excited to see if I could make it doing something OTHER than baseball.

After a couple of days interning, the local sales manager called me into his office. He said he had something to talk to me about. I was thinking, "Did I do something wrong? Did I file something in the wrong place?"

He had me sit down and with a perfectly straight face asked me, "If you had to pick just ONE pitcher you ever faced, who would you say you hit best against?" I thought the question was a bit odd coming my boss, but I instantly blurted out, "That's easy, Jason Klonoski!"

That's when I knew he was having a little fun with me. Turns out his best friend from college was Jason Klonoski. He had spoken with Jason earlier that week, and not knowing the history between Jason and me, asked Jason if he ever heard of me. Jason immediately replied that I was the toughest out he ever faced in his entire career!

The funniest part was, when my boss asked that question, he had Jason on the speakerphone and I didn't know it. When I blurted out his name,

Jason started cracking up on the phone and so did my boss! Jason yelled, "You better have named me! If you hit anyone else as well as you hit me, you'd still be playing!"

Another Chance, Thanks to Joe Madden

On the last day of Spring Training in 1994, after 5 years in the Seattle Mariners organization, including a year on their 40-man Major League Roster, they gave me my unconditional release.

Every Friday was pay day AND cut day. You knew if you made it to Friday with your stuff still in your locker, you had another week to impress the coaches and scouts.

I remember watching guys joking and laughing on the way into the clubhouse until they realized their locker was empty with a note saying "Please go see (insert asshole's name here)." Everyone knew what that meant.

I was tipped off at about 5 PM the night before that I was getting released, so I arrived at the park earlier than the clubhouse guy and packed up my own stuff and left without saying good-bye to anyone.

At the time, I felt like I had gotten a bum rap. For the past two seasons I was hit with devastating injuries that limited my ability to play, including a painful separated throwing shoulder and a broken left wrist. But I knew I could still play and decided I would take matters into my own hands.

As I left the Mariners complex west of Phoenix, I decided I'd drive east to the Angels minor league camp in Mesa and see if they were looking for a catcher. I don't know why I thought of this, but the notion compelled me to to go there blindly.

When I arrived, I walked into the office area and heard someone yell, "Hey Campy! What the hell are you doing here? Shouldn't you be on a flight to Calgary?" It was the Angels' Minor League Director and current manager of the Chicago Cubs, Joe Maddon. He invited me into his office and I explained what had happened.

As I was talking, I noticed he reached into his desk, pulled out some paper and started writing. He told me to keep talking; he was doing some paperwork.

He started asking me about my desire to coach or manage someday. He asked if going into the front office like my grandpa Al intrigued me. He was genuinely interested in my personal story and my career.

Then I discovered the paperwork he had pulled out earlier was an offer to play for the Angels! He added me to the roster and told me to report to the Lake Elsinore Storm in the California League and to sign the contract within 48 hours! What a stroke of luck!

He asked me if I would consider being a mentor/junior coach for one of their top prospects, Todd Greene. I said, "Like Crash Davis in Bull Durham?" He smiled and nodded.

Greeney had just been converted to catcher after having a MONSTER year in rookie ball as an outfielder. They felt that if he could catch as well as he could hit, he'd be an All Star in the big leagues. I agreed to the terms of the contract and to work with Greeney, so off to Lake Elsinore I went.

When I arrived, I realized that for the first time I was the old man on the team. At 26, I was the oldest player and even older than the TRAINER!

I began to work out with Greeney before batting practice every day. He was REALLY rough at that time. However, he was determined to improve and had an awesome attitude.

I remember the manager told me that I wasn't going to play much since he needed to play the young prospects. I understood, but felt ready if a chance to play arose.

Greeney was still learning the details of catching so one game a pitcher asked the manager if I could catch him that game instead of Greeney. The manager agreed to the pitcher's request and had Greeney DH that game while I caught.

The pitcher threw his best game of the year. I threw out a few runners and got some hits. It was a good start, but figured I would be riding pine the next game.

When I arrived at the park the next game I was the DH! Again, I went out and hit the ball well. Plus, I was able to give Greeney some tips on calling pitches during the game and we won again.

For the next few months I either caught or was the DH. In late June I went on a hot streak and was hitting around .300 when we rolled into Rancho Cucamonga. They were our rivals and we needed to win to take over first place.

I caught the first game at their park and in my third at bat hit one off the scoreboard to put us ahead in the 7th inning.

The very next half inning a routine ground ball was hit to our shortstop. I was hustling from catcher to back up the throw as I've done a million times. But the ball short-hopped the first baseman and was heading for the dugout, so I slid on my knees to block the ball like I also had done a million times. But I felt a POP in my left knee, along with a piercing pain. At first I was hoping it was just sprained but it started swelling up immediately.

The swelling was so bad, I overheard the trainer say to the manager "He's done." After all of the hard work battling back to become a relevant player again, this injury was a really tough blow. I was sent in for an MRI and it revealed a torn MCL ligament. The good news was I could rehab it and play the last month of the season.

I had to wear a clunky brace but I worked super hard to rehab that knee and it was getting stronger by the day. Finally, after about 6 weeks, I was cleared to play again.

When I returned to the line-up, I was ready to prove to everyone I could still play...and I did. Over the next week and half I had a 5-game home run streak and drove in a dozen runs. I had to modify my catcher's stance to ac-commodate the brace but the bum knee didn't hurt...too much.

It was at that point that the Major Leaguers went on strike in 1994.

Because we were so close to Anaheim, the minor league brass and major league coaches—including Joe Madden, Rod Carew, and more—started showing up to all of our pre-game practices and games. This was fun but it hurt my chances again. They wanted to see Greeney catch, not me.

Joe Maddon explained the situation and he also commended me for helping Greeney improve, helping the young pitchers develop, and for keeping a positive attitude in the clubhouse. He said that he felt I should keep playing no matter what the Angels decided to do with my contract.

That last three weeks, I barely played, even though I was crushing the ball in batting practice and the limited times I played. I remember hitting a home run on my wife's birthday in Bakersfield and thinking maybe that will help me get more playing time. But how else do you season a catching prospect other than having him catch every day? I was the odd man out.

In the last week, we had a 3-game series against Rancho Cucamonga again and needed to win 2 of 3 or our season was over. We won the first, they won the second and it all came down to the final game.

When I arrived at the park prior to the final game, the writing was on the wall—literally. I was NOT in the line-up. What a telling sign! I knew this was it for me, and it was. We lost the game and the season was over.

Ultimately, the Angels did not renew my contract and I was a ballplayer without a team. At 27 I was ANCIENT and knew that my prospects for making it to the bigs were slim to none.

I've kept in touch with Joe Maddon over the years, I have always liked and respected Joe and consider him one of the best people I ever met in my years in baseball. I am a huge fan of his and will never forget how he gave me another chance in baseball.

4
Minor Leagues, Major Laughs

When you play 30 Spring Training games and then 142 games in a minor league season, you better have a good sense of humor!

Looking back, I really believe that without certain players keeping things light with practical jokes, pranks and storytelling, we would have probably killed each other.

When the built up frustration was so thick inside of me I wanted to scream…that's when I knew it was time to get silly.

In this chapter you will see how we learned to keep our sanity through laughter, even through the all the challenges, and how the humor brought us closer together as teammates and people.

Instructional League

In the Fall of 1988, the Mariners sent me to Arizona Instructional League.

The team was made up of a mix of players from low Rookie Ball all the way up to guys on the fringe of the Big Leagues.

It was my first introduction to these players and I was getting to know each guy one at a time.

We stayed at the Comfort Inn in Tempe where we all ate breakfast before going to the field. After about a week I had met and talked to every guy on the team, or I thought I had.

Instructional League was set up like Spring Training. We would work out all morning, eat lunch, and then play a 9-inning game against other teams like the Cubs, Angels, Dodgers, Brewers, etc.

The morning workouts were mostly defensive so I would go off with the catchers and not interact much with the other players on the team. Then it was catching a bunch of bullpens before lunch.

Lunch was hot soup on a 100-degree day with a PB & J sandwich. For 50 more cents you could get a can of Coke to go with it. Not quite as glamorous as people think pro ballplayers live. And by the way, we were paid $8 a day!

Prior to one game, we were waiting to load onto the shuttle vans when I realized—one of the guys on our team was actually TWO guys!

Our second baseman was Delvin Thomas. He was a well-built, athletic guy who threw right handed, and who I thought was a switch hitter, because I saw him bat left handed also. But it turns out the left handed batter was actually his TWIN brother Kelvin Thomas!

Amazingly, Delvin was a right-handed hitter and thrower and Kelvin was a left-handed hitter and thrower.

Other than that, you couldn't tell them apart.

When I told the brothers I thought they were one guy for a whole week, they cracked up and told me a little secret...if you can't tell which one is which, just check out their grills. Delvin had a gold tooth display with a big star on his LEFT front tooth while Kelvin had the same gold star tooth on his RIGHT front tooth!

Kelvin and Delvin Thomas. Or is it Delvin and Kelvin?

I became good friends with the brothers and ended up playing the entire 1990 season with them. They were so much fun to hang out with and even more exciting to watch play baseball.

Identical twins occur naturally at a rate of 0.04%. What is the percentage of identical twins who played pro sports on the same team? I was fortunate to have played with those two-in-a-billion twins, Kelvin and Delvin Thomas.

Other memories from Instructional League:

- I caught another 6'10" pitcher named Jim Magill built just like Randy Johnson but he threw right-handed.
- I had my first experience dealing with players cycling on steroids.
- I had my first experience living in a hotel room for three months straight.
- I roomed with Ken Griffey, Jr for a week while my regular roommate entertained his lady.

- My dad, grandpa Al, and I had dinner with Vince and Mike Piazza right when Mike was worried he was going to get released by the Dodgers.
- Dan Warthen was our pitching coach. He is now the pitching coach for the Mets.
- I was introduced to "Florida Water" which is water, ice, and ammonia mixed together and put on towels. The towels were super-refreshing in the blazing sun. Of course, it was only a matter of time before someone would accidentally drink a cup and puke for hours.
- Albert Belle hit a rocket off of the liver of one of our pitchers who had to spend the night in the hospital!
- I played with or against future Hall of Famers, future GM's, future managers, future hitting coaches, and future scouts.

Beating On Our Beat Up Car

In 1990, the Mariners sent me to the Carolina League to play for the Peninsula Pilots.

Some of the guys on the team found a nice apartment complex but it was really expensive, especially considering I was only making $850 a month! Instead, we found a 2-bedroom house near the Chesapeake Bay with no A/C, no TV, a couple of beds and a couch—for $275 A MONTH, $55 per guy! Quickly, the place became like Animal House. We drew murals on the walls, had raging parties, jammed live music, got a Labrador who thrashed the place, etc.

The next thing we needed was a ride. We went to the local used car dealer and found a beat up old Buick for $500—$100 per guy.

One night after a game, we loaded into the Buick in a torrential rainstorm to drive home. I was driving about 60 MPH on the busy 664 freeway when everything on the Buick died—the engine, the lights, the power steering, the power brakes—all in the middle of a downpour.

The Buick swerved out of control and across several lanes before I finally steered toward an exit and managed to get off the freeway. We coasted to a stop under a bridge.

This was the pre-cell phone era, so I walked to a pay phone and called AAA who towed us back to the house.

We were so pissed the car had broken down. Then we confirmed it was totaled when we popped open the hood and saw a rod had shot right through the engine. The car had died two months after we bought it.

After several rounds of cursing, one of the guys grabbed a bat and started beating the car with it—smashing out windows and denting the body. Soon the rest of us joined in. Five guys just going to town on this car.

Minutes later, three cop cars and a paddy wagon pulled up with their loud speaker blaring, "Move away from the car and put down your weapons." They shined the spotlights on us and one of the cops said over the loud speaker in a scoffing voice, "Please tell me this is your car," and we all started cracking up.

The policemen got out of their cars and we explained what had happened. The cops laughed and told us to just clean up the glass and go back inside our house. One guy even asked for autographs!

We might not have had the best team in the league that year, but we led the league in having a great time! Just ask the rest of my crew—Jeff Nelson, Bret Boone, Shane Lettario, Ron Pezzoni, Lem Pilkington, and Ron Mullins.

Orlando's "Finest"

In 1992 I was playing for the Jacksonville Suns in Double AA. This particular game we were playing in Orlando.

Being the visitors, we were first to bat. As soon as the game started, a couple sitting in the front row started ragging the umpire BIG TIME. They knew his name, where he was from, and every time he called a pitch a ball, they would yell obscenities at him.

I came up to bat that first inning and said "Hey Marty, I see your fan club is here." He chuckled as the pair continued to hound him. There were only a couple thousand fans at the game so everyone could hear this couple as they laid into the umpire.

As I ran out to catch in the bottom of the first, they stopped ragging the umpire and turned their venom on ME. Again, they knew my family background, the *Nightline* thing with my grandpa; they ripped me when I dropped a ball. The abuse was non-stop! So umpire Marty thanked me for being their new target. But after the inning ended, they went right back to ragging him.

This continued until I went out to catch for the 6th inning, and they were gone. I said to Marty, "Maybe those losers got tired of ripping on us and went back to the swamp." But instead they came back with HUGE 32-ounce beers. What happened next was divine intervention...

The couple propped those massive beers up onto the cement wall between the stands and the field, and the very next pitch the batter hit a super-high foul ball that was on the side of the field where the raggers were sitting. The ball was directly over them but I knew it would end up going into the stands several rows up. So as everyone was looking at the ball, I sprinted as fast as I could right at them, stuck out my elbow and drenched them with 64 ounces of beer.

To my amazement, the home crowd stood up, cheered me for dousing the loudmouths, and started heckling the couple, who, soaking wet, humiliated and pissed off, left the game. Marty said I was his favorite baseball player of all time!

The next time I came to bat, the crowd gave me a standing ovation even though I was on the visiting team. It was the first and last time I was ever cheered for on the road.

By the way, that umpire was Marty Foster, who now has been blowing calls in the big leagues for over 15 years.

God Wanted Us to Win

In 1991 we had a really good team in Jacksonville playing in the AA Southern League—and God really wanted us to win!

That year we had some unreal winning streaks, like 18-1 and 15-2, but the Greenville Braves were also as hot as we were.

We were neck and neck with Greenville heading into the last few games of the 1st half when we went to Huntsville, Alabama for a series with the A's affiliate.

The game was going back and forth...we would score one, they would score one...we would score two, they would score two.

As it was getting late in the game, dark clouds started to fill the sky. Rumbles of thunder started to be faintly heard coming toward the stadium.

At this point in the game, the score was tied. We had a runner at third in the top half of the 9th inning who represented the go-ahead run. I remember being on deck and thinking they will likely pitch around the batter since there was an open base to get to me. But one of us had to drive in this run!

As the batter was preparing for the pitch, the rain started to trickle down. Just a little.

The pitcher stepped off the rubber and rosined up the ball to be sure he had a good grip. He took the sign from the catcher and went into his set position. He was watching the runner on third very closely since that was the go ahead run.

Then, out of nowhere, the hand of God threw the brightest and loudest bolt of lightning at us! It hit the light pole on the third base side of the stadium and made the loudest BOOOOOOOM you've ever heard!

Everyone was screaming and running for cover!

I instinctually went to the ground....we ALL did!

The batter hit the dirt, the catcher hit the dirt, and the pitcher jumped before diving to the ground. But not the umpire, who immediately yelled, "BALK" and our runner trotted home with the go-ahead run! The balk rule states that the pitcher cannot move once he's set or it's called a balk and the runners get to advance a base...even if lightning strikes nearby!

The lightning strike was so close you could feel the static electricity on your arm hair and you could smell the burning of the steel from the lightning striking the light pole.

Amazingly, the lights didn't blow out and the rain only delayed the game for a few minutes. When we took the field for the bottom of the 9th, we got the Huntsville team out 1, 2, 3 and won that game.

After the game, we unanimously voted God as the MVP of the game and gave thanks for that little bit of divine intervention right when we needed it!

The Famous (Formerly Known as "San Diego") Chicken

When I was growing up, a new phenom had begun to take over Major League Baseball—The San Diego Chicken—and I was a HUGE fan.

I remember watching him on TV every chance I could and I loved his antics.

Then he had some kind of dispute with either the team or the radio station where he worked and left the Padres to tour ballparks all over the country as "The Famous Chicken." In 1987, I was on a plane going to Alaska with my team. I was sitting next to a nice guy named Ted who asked what I was going to do in Alaska. I told him I played baseball for the North Pole Nicks and we were going to Anchorage for a game where the Famous Chicken was going to perform.

He smiled and wished me luck.

When we arrived in Anchorage, they had set up a locker for the Chicken near mine. Then all of sudden the guy I sat next to on the flight sat down and started putting on his yellow panty hose. I yelled, "Hey Ted, why didn't you tell me on the plane you were the Chicken?" He replied that he tries to keep it a secret and I understood why.

The Chicken's show used the visiting team catcher and pitcher as his victims for several skits and we had fun that night.

Fast forward a few years and the Chicken had become the #1 draw in baseball. In fact, I learned he had a pay structure based on the league where he performed. The structure was something like; "A" Ball = $4,000 a game, "AA" = $5,000 a game, "AAA" = $7,000 a game and an MLB game was $10,000+ a game…in 1990's money! He performed over 100 shows a year!

One time we went to Charlotte for a game and I learned it was going to be a Chicken night.

He met me in the locker room to ask if I would participate in a few new skits he had come up with since I saw him last. I said I would.

The stadium was absolutely packed to see the Chicken. He started out coaching first base for Charlotte, then went into his new material.

He had this idea to replicate a play like you'd see on TV in instant replay. It started with him rounding third base trying to score. The pitcher threw me the ball and I stood there for a play at the plate with the Chicken. Then he would run me over. But when I hit the ground, we both went into slow motion instant replay. We both went very slowly back to where we were before he ran into me. Then in slow motion, he ran me over AGAIN! It was quite fun and the crowd loved it.

He then had 4 kids dressed in little Chicken suits walk by when I was warming the pitcher up between innings, lift a leg, and pretend to piss on me! Another crowd pleaser. He would also flash a poster of hot girl in a bikini at the pitcher to try to distract him. If the pitch was a strike, he would pull out a poster of a Broomhilda-looking lady in a sexy pose hoping to change the outcome of the next pitch.

The Chicken would also warm up the infielders between innings and make a mockery of it of course.

Over the years I was the butt of his jokes at least a dozen times. Often it was the same gag we had pulled off a few weeks earlier in another city. Ted would call me "Camp" and told me I was one of his favorite victims, though I bet he tells all the catchers that.

Can Players Hear the Crowd?

I get asked from time to time if players can hear what the fans are saying. The answer might surprise you.

While playing, if asked by a newspaper reporter, I would say, "Nope, never hear a word the crowd says. I'm completely focused and in the zone." But that's a blatant lie.

OF COURSE the players can hear fans that are screaming at the top of their lungs from a few feet away. They just pretend that they don't!

However, and this is a BIG however, when I was batting, I heard absolutely nothing. I was so laser focused on what kind of spin was on the ball, where it was going and how fast, that I didn't hear anything. But that moment only lasted for a couple of seconds. Then I could hear everything around me until the next pitch was thrown.

I was conditioned to handle raggers at USC. We were always a target and my sophomore year my grandpa made his infamous *Nightline* comments so I was in their cross hairs. The college raggers did their homework. They knew my mom's name, my dad's name, my girlfriend's name, and seemingly everything about me. They were SUPER witty and some rags were so good I couldn't help but laugh my ass off!

The larger the crowd, the less you can hear individual voices. When I was at USC, we used to play the Dodgers major and minor league players at Dodgers Stadium every January before Spring Training in an exhibition game.

The game was free to attend and some big names were usually there, like Fernando Valenzuela.

One year, Fernando was doing a radio interview and said not only was he going to play against us, but he was going to play right field and hit a home run! So what happened? 56,000 people showed up to see!!!

It was the first time I had played in front of that many people and immediately noticed the fans noise was incoherent—just a big mumble.

My junior year, when I played at Dodgers Stadium for the first time after my grandpa had been fired from the Dodgers, I heard a roar of noise when they announced my name but couldn't tell if they were booing or cheering—there were TOO many people!

When there are that many fans, our verbal signals during a play are useless. I could yell as loud as possible for the third baseman to cut the ball off but he couldn't hear a word, even from only about 45 feet away. When we played at USC, the entire stadium could hear me yell, "CUT! CUT! CUT!"

When I was catching, I was usually the closest player to the stands, and the fans knew it. They would constantly heckle me when I did ANYTHING wrong.

I remember in Modesto, a whole group of drunk fans walked down close to our dugout and decided to rag whomever was on deck. They got a kick out of trying to one up each other but their rags were LAME!

I remember one guy literally screaming at me, "Hey Campanis! Nobody is number 31...I mean nobody!" They would all giggle but I was thinking, is that supposed to piss me off?

Those guys were relentless and after a while some of my teammates started yelling back—EXACTLY the reaction those idiot fans wanted to evoke. Word of advice that applies to all situations in life—never, ever argue with an idiot! That makes you one also. In Double A at Jacksonville I was chasing a foul behind home plate. The wind was howling that day making the ball do crazy things in the air. Plus the ball was hit to a weird corner by where the visitor's dugout met the first row of fans. It was a long run and by the time I got there and tried to get oriented I missed the ball.

A guy sitting in the first row just a few feet away said something I'll never forget: "Come on Campy, you're better than that." That crushed me inside. He didn't yell or scream; he wasn't a dim wit, he was a knowledgeable baseball fan. And that's what hit me so hard. He was right, I should have caught that ball.

Some people only go to games to rag on players. Some guys I played with would get so agitated by these types of fans, but I reminded them that they PAID to see us work! I had to justify the fan abuse somehow and to me that was the ultimate way to look at it. You paid your $15 to yell at me. So let it all out blow hard!

When Tony Gwynn Jr. played his first game after his father passed away, the usually obnoxious Phillies fans gave him a standing ovation when he was introduced as the pinch hitter. The fans cheered him for a good 30 seconds… and he heard it all. He commented after the game that he was getting choked up with emotion from all of the love he felt. Ballplayers are people too.

Yes, fans who like to yell at players, we can hear you, and we probably think you're an A-Hole!

Minor League Road Trip

I know a lot of you take time off and hit the road for vacation.

I thought I'd share what a typical road trip was like when I played baseball in the minor leagues back before the internet, Facebook…a time when no one had cell phones…and dinosaurs roamed the earth!

Let's say it's 1991 or 1992…

There was always a game schedule hanging on the bulletin board in the clubhouse. The days would often drift together and suddenly you'd realize the next day was a travel day.

I played three years in the Southern League for the Jacksonville Suns. The geographic location of Jacksonville put us on the eastern side of the league and hundreds of miles from the rest of the teams. That meant epic bus trips.

When we arrived for the last game of a home stand we would have to bring everything we needed for the road trip because we would leave directly from the stadium after the game. Our clubhouse was small to begin with but on road trip days it was extra cluttered.

Some guys would pack like we'd be gone for months. Some guys brought video game consoles. Some guys brought guitars (like me) or golf clubs or huge coolers. It was a mess!

After we played the "get away" game, the GM of the team would go all out for us—and serve us the left over hot dogs. Occasionally they would even bring in a bunch of cups of flat beer to wash it down. Or we had to pony up 50 cents for a Coke out of the vending machine.

I would then take a shower and get dressed. Before loading up my stuff on the bus, I would find my wife and son and kiss them goodbye. Usually there were lots of fans hanging out so I'd spend some time signing baseball cards and talking with people. Then it was time to load up my junk onto the bus.

My baseball bag weighed nearly 100 pounds. It was loaded with 6 bats, my catchers gear, two pairs of spikes, three catchers mitts, three pairs of batting gloves, thumb pads, tape, jocks, cups, shoelaces, aspirin, Advil, vitamins, a batting helmet, and of course my trusty bone to keep my bats rock-hard. I used to get a bunch of kids to volunteer to carry my bag…one little perk of the job.

Then I'd take my guitar and Walkman onto the bus and set up in my seat. Because I was the catcher, I was awarded a full bus section of 2 seats. The starting pitcher also was given a full section, and the rest of the guys had to rock, paper, scissors for the rest of the full section seats left. The losers had to sit with someone else for the next 9 hours. That sucked.

As we drove off from the stadium, waving goodbye to our loved ones, there was almost a party-like atmosphere on the bus. Often times, someone was bumping a boom box and guys would dance and sing. At the same time, the trainer would go from player to player handing out meal money for the trip.

Meal money was different based on what level you were playing. The big leaguers got $120 a day when I played. We got $12 in Double A. Quite a difference!

When the meal money was handed out, it was still early in the evening for us. Most of us were used to going to bed at about 3 AM every night and waking up around noon. We were nocturnal beasts and midnight was too early to go to bed.

This was the time the team broke off into cliques. Some guys switched seats so they could play cards; some guys huddled around the TV's and watched Top Gun for the 900th time; some guys came to the back of the bus where I was jamming out live karaoke for the closet singers on the team; some guys put on their headphones and starred out of the window, likely thinking about the game we just played.

By 4 AM, everyone was asleep. Guys who couldn't handle sleeping next to another dude brought pool rafts and slept on the bus floor or in the overhead luggage compartment.

Inevitably, the bus driver needed to fill up and take a break so we'd pull into a truck stop in the middle of nowhere.

I would often wake up and go into the truck stop for something to snack on. I would also find rare gems at these random truck stops like compilation music cassettes from Muddy Waters, BB King, and Howlin' Wolf, or a Classic Rock cassette with a bunch of one hit wonders...for $1.99.

These were the truck stops that sold pickled eggs, pickled pig's feet, pickled chicken feet, beef jerky, buffalo jerky, turkey jerky, pork rinds, BBQ pork rinds, Flaming Hot pork rinds, boiled peanuts, and random sodas like Cheerwine and Big Red.

I used to like to do crossword puzzles so I'd often pick up a local newspaper from some small town in South Carolina or wherever we were. It was always interesting to read about these small communities, their triumphs and their tragedies. Often times, the local sports pages included at least our box score or a related story about teams in our league.

We would usually arrive at our hotel before 11 AM or so and check in. This was the most volatile time between players because everyone was tired and irritable. Arguments would often occur because someone spilled their chew spit cup on someone's bag or someone was being inconsiderate and blocking the narrow aisle on the bus. Tempers flare when you are around the same guys every day and don't get a good night sleep, especially when you are 24 years old.

Once we checked in our rooms, we usually took a nap for a few hours before it was time to get back on the bus and head to the stadium. This was my favorite time and I used to visualize playing on that field and facing the pitcher I knew was throwing that night. I'd visualize catching a pitch and perfectly executing the ball transfer, shifting my feet and throwing out the runner on perfect throw to the bag.

Most hotels were located near fast food, and since we only had a very limited amount of meal money, we were forced to eat cheap and unhealthy fast food before and after games.

Once back on the bus and heading to the stadium, there was this calm-before-the-storm feeling. Most guys started to focus on the game. You'd see guys stand up on the bus and get into their batting stance. Pitchers would start stretching their arms or warming up their shoulders doing exercises.

When the bus arrived, we'd dig our baseball bags out, carry them into the visitor's clubhouse, and find a locker. Some visiting clubhouses were fully equipped and there were plenty of lockers for everyone. In other clubhouses your locker was a nail on the wall with no bench to sit down.

After the game, we had to wait until EVERYONE was on the bus, which took at least two hours. Most guys had long distance calling cards back then. I would call my wife about 2 AM each night to see how she was doing and let her know how I played.

When we woke up on the last day of a road trip, the trainer notified the lucky guys who had been assigned as "get away rooms." There were usually three get away rooms chosen. That's where the rest of us had to take all of our belongings once we checked out of our own rooms by 11 AM. We'd have a few hours to kill before the bus would leave, so guys watched soap operas or game shows while other played cards or slept.

When it was time to leave, we'd load up the bus and head off for the last game of the roadie.

Once the game was over and we tipped the visiting clubhouse attendant, most of us were broke. We'd combine our funds at times to buy a 12-er or some dip and pile back onto the bus for another 9 hour ride.

As the bus pulled into our home stadium, there would be a bunch of cars randomly parked around the clubhouse entrance. We'd unload our baseball gear and take it into the clubhouse and hop in the awaiting car to go home for few hours before we had to come back and play another game.

The smell of diesel fuel still reminds me of those days. It was a grueling lifestyle yet I really enjoyed it. I liked waking up in a strange town and exploring as much as I could during the limited free time we had. I discovered Beele Street in Memphis, Chapel Hill, Georgetown, Graceland and many more places on road trips. I also met the Ramones, Hootie and the Blowfish, the Vandals, Bruce Hornsby and was snubbed by Oprah, who quickly closed the hotel elevator door when she saw us coming!

Get out and explore! To me, there is nothing like getting in the car and rolling to find a new adventure. As a matter of fact, I think I'm going to head up to Big Bear this weekend for a road trip!

Jacksonville Stadium SUCKS!

Growing up, I traveled quite a bit as we followed my dad from team to team.

Most times these travels were to areas with a totally different weather pattern than the mild Southern California climate I was used to. I remember we had regular tornado warnings in both Overland Park, Kansas and

Charleston, West Virginia. It was quite scary as a kid and often times my dad wasn't around because he was on a road trip. We had some close calls over the years but made it through.

When I was seven years old, my dad retired from baseball after playing for 15 pro seasons. We had settled into our new house in Yorba Linda—a brand new development built inside an orange grove flanked by the old Union 76 oil fields. About the only bad weather we would get was a nasty Santa Ana wind event with dozens of tumbleweeds littering our back yard.

I became accustomed to the mild SoCal weather, but it still gets hot here. However, there is much less humidity with a reliable afternoon breeze coming in from the ocean most days. I really took it for granted until I started playing in other states.

I remember my first trip to play in Vegas. We had a DAYTIME doubleheader in JULY! The temperature was near 120 that day and I was catching the first game and playing third the second game. Sure it was hot, but the "Dry Heat" thing is true. You can simply pour water over your head and feel a temporary sense of refreshment.

A few years later I played in Baton Rouge, Louisiana and Memphis, TN in the Summer. WHOA! Now that was AFRICA hot!

I remember catching a day game in Memphis in unbearable humidity. By the 2nd inning my jersey was absolutely drenched in sweat. I literally took it off in the dugout and rang out several pints of sweat. That next inning when I went into my catcher's stance. Sweat oozed out of the shoelace holes on my spikes and made a sloshy sound when I walked. There was no relief from any cool afternoon breeze like in SoCal, but after a while there was another kind of relief—thunderstorms! In SoCal, we occasionally get some flash lightning, but rarely get visible bolts of lightning followed by loud bursts of thunder. In the south it was quite common.

When it rained that day in Memphis, the relief from the heat was so refreshing. The occasional cool breezes that blew the rain sideways was something I had never experienced before. Then the lightning started. I was so awestruck I stood under the covered dugout to watch the spectacle…until I was forced by team officials to get INSIDE. They had seen the devastation left behind from these storms, including the flash flooding that often occurred following massive downpours.

From 1991 through 1993 I played for the Jacksonville Suns, the Double A affiliate of the Seattle Mariners. The joke around the clubhouse was that I was the Mayor of Jacksonville since I played there so long. I was on the team for 423 games over the course of 15 months, April – August—the hottest time of the year.

One nice thing about Jacksonville was the afternoon ocean breeze—just like SoCal—but the humidity was still very high for me. It seemed like in Jacksonville we were hit with a thunderstorm every day.

I remember one particular day, the thunderstorms came in about noon and POUNDED the stadium. It was raining as hard as I had ever seen for close to an hour. I imagined the amount of water on the field must have turned it into a swamp. But to my surprise, when I went to the stadium, it was PERFECT! But how???

When I was dressed and walking out to the field I had to make a detour through the bullpen because the dugout was about 4 feet deep in water.

So I asked our clubby why the dugout was under water, and he told me about the field pumps.

It rained so often in Jacksonville during the baseball season they had to come up with a permanent solution to handle the water. They told me that turf was too hot for the players and a dome was not in Jacksonville's budget so they did the next best thing.

The field in Jacksonville was built like the old Astroturf fields with cut outs around each base, but the rest of the field was grass, including the areas the shortstops and second basemen cover. The field was equipped with massive underground water pumps buried under a thin grassy layer covering tons of water-absorbing sand. The sand sent the water downward and into chutes where the water was collected and sent to the pumps. The pumps then shot the water though hundreds of feet of underground pipes into the home dugout where it poured like a raging river into a massive drain under the bench.

The system was unbelievably efficient except for one small detail. Baseball players chew seeds, gum, dip, Red Man, and litter the dugout with cups, wrappers and tape…all of which clogged the main drain.

I remember one game where the rain hit during the game. I was on the field and the umpire kept trying to finish the inning, but it was pouring so he was forced to call a delay.

The umpire locker room was up another tunnel from our clubhouse so both the umpire and I ran toward our dugout for shelter. But the pumps were already turned on and the drain was clogged making a four-foot deep soup of brown nastiness.

I pulled a big yellow plastic trashcan over the fence from the box seat section and took out the half-filled trash bag. Then found an old bat. I instructed the umpire to put the trashcan into the water-filled dugout…and get inside. I handed him the bat, and like a pontoon going down a lazy river, the umpire drifted over to the tunnel where his locker room was located. The other umpires followed. I wish I had a photo of that just to prove that the Southern League umpires were garbage after all! I know FOR A FACT the pumps helped us win games. How? The opposing teams would be at their hotel when the storms would roll in. They would walk outside and see massive flooding and automatically think—a glorious day off! On several occasions I was catching after a big storm and when a player came up to bat I could smell booze.

One time I asked a guy, who I knew well, if he had been drinking. He said, "After watching all the rain coming down we all started pounding pitchers of beer at the bowling alley. We thought for sure the game would get banged. But somehow this field doesn't flood…WTF?" I laughed and told him about the field pumps. He just shook his head as he tried to hit a 95 MPH fastball while wasted.

Adapting to what life throws at you was a big part of the baseball experience, and the weather always played a major role. When I started coaching, the kids would complain that it was SOOOO hot when it was even a little warm, maybe 85 degrees. I tried to explain how lucky they were to play baseball in SoCal, when it's way hotter in so many other places. They would just look at me like I was an idiot and yell to their mom, "Get me a Cherry Snow Cone, I'm dying of heat exhaustion here!"

Minor League Promo Nights

When I started my pro career in the minor leagues I was instantly introduced to the crazy world of baseball promotions.

In San Bernardino in '89 I hit my first pro home run over left field. As I was circling the bases the announcer was going crazy saying that I had just won the "TGIF Home Run Feast" by hitting the ball over the TGIF sign and through the goal post.

I learned that I won a $50 gift certificate and was stoked!

The GM of the team started to explain that TGIF was a paying sponsor of the team and also had this special extra promotion for the "Home Run Feast." I had never heard of such a thing.

That's when I started noticing all of the crazy antics the teams would perform in order to bring in more fans.

Over my career, I caught the ceremonial first pitch from Ms. California, Ms. Florida, Ms. Virginia, Ms. Tennessee, Ms. Alaska, Ronald McDonald, the Burger King, The French's Mustard Man, The Radio Ape in Jacksonville, plus tons of actors, politicians, musicians, and athletes in other sports!

I saw some funny promotions like these:

1. "The UPS Truck Headlight Smash" in San Jose: A fan chose a Giants player to throw a ball at a UPS truck. If the player knocked out both headlights with two throws, the fan won a big prize. If the player missed on his first throw they usually

threw the next one right through the windshield, which was always fun to watch.

2. "The Birmingham Mother's Day Diamond Dig" in Birmingham, Alabama: Every mother who attended the game on Mother's Day was given a soup spoon. After the game, all of the mothers were invited onto the dirt infield to dig up a 3-carat diamond that was slightly buried under the field. There were like 2,000 ladies in their Sunday best down on their knees digging in the dirt!

3. "The Sumo Showdown" in Lake Elsinore pitted two fans wearing a 100-pound Sumo wrestler body suit complete with a gargantuan belly, designed to bump the other guy out of the ring. This promo was a blast and some of the duels were epic. But my favorite was when they both fell on their huge belly and couldn't get back up no matter how hard they tried.

4. "The Supercut Cutfest" in Jacksonville FL: A few times a year, prior to the game, we would get trimmed up, on the field. We made a bit of joke out of it by requesting the wildest haircuts of the day. Yes, I am sorry to admit, I rocked the "Mushroom" cut for a while.

We also had traveling baseball personalities that brought in extra fans, like the world famous San Diego Chicken, Max Patkin, and Lady Dynamite. Sometimes things didn't go as planned...

In Chattanooga, they always did the "Bat Races" near the home team team's dugout. The "Bat Races" are when two people put their foreheads on a bat and circle the bat ten times before they have to run and touch the hand of a team employee. This time one of the contestants was belligerently drunk but they let him participate anyway. This guy made it through his 10 bat spins when he started running sideways, then more sideways, then ran straight into the metal pole supporting the home team's dugout and puked up gallons of beer, hot dogs, and ice cream! I could smell it from home plate! The home team had to go down to the bullpen while it was being hosed down. NASTY! The drunk guy was laying there like he was dead. They had to call an ambulance!

If you get a chance to visit a minor league game this summer, DO IT! They often have special giveaways, concerts, fireworks, and more. It's so much fun, SUPER inexpensive, and you'll see some very good baseball, too.

A Rare Day Off Enjoyed

When Spring Training started, the only day we would get off would be the day we flew to whatever city we were assigned to start the season. That would mean for me 60 straight 12-hour days of getting up at 6 AM, catching a dozen or more bullpens, defensive drills, bunt defense drills, first and third defense drills, batting practice, situational hitting, afternoon games, eating soup in 100 degree weather, and living in a hotel.

Once we landed in our hometown that season, we would start games right away. Then, about 6 weeks into the season, we'd get our first REAL day off, but it was often a travel day where we'd end up in a place like Memphis at about 3 PM with 24 hours to kill. When this happened, I liked to get spontaneous and check out whatever new town we were in.

I had played for Team USA near Memphis and spent several nights on the famed Beale Street hanging out at BB King's Blues Club. So one year I convinced a bunch of the guys to join me. We ended up closing the place down and saw some of the best blues musicians in the world. I started going to Beale Street for LUNCH just to catch the artists jamming at Open Mic. It was a great education for me as an aspiring guitar player. I stole so many of those guys' licks and made my own little style out of some the sounds I heard on Beale Street.

At USC, during one of the rare days off in Hawaii, we rented cars and went to Hanauma Bay where we found a natural formation that at high tide is quite a ride—literally!

It's called the "Toilet Bowl" and is a 10-foot wide and 6-foot deep hole. It was carved into the rocks from millions of years of erosion as the waves squeezed through holes in the reef. When the waves come through the reef and into the toilet bowl, it fills the hole with high pressure water and shoots 20 feet in the air! We tested the ferocity of the "flush" by throwing a Styrofoam cooler in the hole. When the pressurized water hit the "Toilet Bowl," it shattered the cooler in a million pieces and shot it 15 feet into the air!

There were about six of us and we were nervous. Should we do this or move along to the next thing? Suddenly, one of the guys jumped in the hole, so the rest of us followed.

When the first wave started funneling through the reef, I started thinking, "You DUMBASS! Let me out of here!" But before I could do anything, the toilet flushed and shot us out of the hole like we were little bathtub toys, even though together we were over 1,000 pounds of flesh and bones! It was so fun, we all jumped in again, and again! The only scary time came when the undertow caught one of our guys and we had to pull him out of the hole where the water went back out to sea. Had he been sucked in, he would've been in BIG trouble!

In Mexican Winter Ball, the schedule was similar, only a few days off during the whole season, so we made the most of them when we could. One day, our friend Cesar invited us to the beach for lunch and swimming. Immediately I thought of relaxing like we used to at Newport or Huntington Beaches. But I learned this was not a "Developed" beach.

The beach was called "Topolobampo" and was about 45 minutes from Los Mochis. It looked the same as it did in 1492 when Columbus discovered the New World. There was not one home, not one store, not one lifeguard tower. Even the sand was more like river sand and not the white sand I was used to. But there was a restaurant and that's where Cesar had us go for lunch.

The restaurant had no walls. It was on a dirt floor with palm tree leaves as a roof. They had a HUGE homemade BBQ and used wood charcoal to cook fresh fish that were still ALIVE! The waiter had us go to a massive tub of live sea bass and pick the ones we wanted. I knew that in Mexico, if it's still alive you would likely not get sick, so I was very happy to see this.

We selected two massive sea bass and headed back to our table in the shade.

About 20 minutes later, the waiter walked over with two large platters wrapped up in tin foil. As he opened the foil, the best smell hit us. They cooked the sea bass to perfection in butter, garlic, and lemon.

To my surprise, Cesar's kids literally jumped up on the table and started pulling off the fish fins and devouring them. They started fighting over the last one! They said they loved the crunchiness, like a "papita" or potato chip. It was no different from our family meals when someone wants the turkey leg. But crunchy fish fins?

My wife Lisa was pregnant at the time and odd smells would make her nauseous, but this fresh fish and the outdoor environment made for a very pleasant meal.

One of the best days off came in Puerto Rico during Winter Ball with our good friends, Frank and Sue Bolick. Bo and I were (and still are) great friends plus both Sue and my wife got along very well. When we both were sent to Puerto Rico we decided to share a home to save on costs. We also shared a minivan rental.

One of the players on our team, who grew up in the southern part of Puerto Rico near Ponce, was telling me about this cool little town that is like an amusement park on the ocean so we decided to check it out on an off-day.

We spend the early part of our off day hanging out at our house which was on a calm, little bay in Mayaguez. I'd go to one of our 6 coconut trees, cut open a ripe specimen using my newfound machete skills, revealing the juice. Then, of course, a couple shots of Barcardi right into the coconut that I used as a cup. Very refreshing and quite tasty!

About 5 PM we left for this town called Lajas about 30 minutes away.

Just as our teammate had described it—Lajas was a cool little oceanfront town with all kinds of restaurants, small carnival rides, and games—plus it had something I had never heard of—a Phosphorescent Bay!

At first I thought that the bay lit up at night when the moon shined down on the dark sections, but as it turns out, there are billions of tiny plankton in this bay that, when agitated, put off a rather bright greenish glow.

We boarded a ship that had a number of buckets attached by ropes and we motored out in to the Phosphorescent Bay. Once we reached the prime spot, the crew cut the lights on the boat and threw the buckets into the water. Then they pulled the buckets back up into the boat and spilled them onto the dark deck. It was the most amazing sight. The water was glowing like it was radioactive. You could put your hand in the bucket and just by moving the water around, it would light up the whole deck!

After the cruise, we found a quaint little seafood restaurant right on the water and enjoyed lobster, crab, shrimp, and a few Medalla beers.

As I continued to play pro ball, we spent days off doing more fun activities like hitting Disneyworld, Epcot Center, Disneyland, camping, fishing, jet skiing, golfing. And sometimes we did absolutely NOTHING AT ALL!

It's a long and arduous season that puts a tremendous burden on players both physically and mentally. We learned quickly to take advantage of these days to let some steam off, recharge, and relax. We tried our best to take full advantage of every minute of that day off because we knew it was going to be another 35 days straight playing before the next one!

Salem Bugs and Thugs

Two things that never surprised me in the minor leagues were the sub-par stadiums along with how idiotic people can become when drunk and belligerent.

It was hard enough to just survive playing minor league baseball, but sometimes things at certain cities were just a bit tougher. Case in point, Salem, Virginia.

First of all, there was NO clubhouse! This is a tough thing to deal with because most players have to get some kind of medical treatment before a game. Many players have nagging injuries and need to get ultrasound on an aching joint, or ice a knee, or get taped up, or whatever. Some guys need a rub down just to throw a bullpen. With no training room or clubhouse, it made everyone work extra hard.

We also had to dress at the hotel before the game and shower at the hotel after the game. That also meant the overworked trainer would have to wash and dry our uniforms after midnight at some local laundromat.

Another crappy thing about that old Salem ballpark were the light poles. They were actually in FAIR TERRITORY, as was the scoreboard in left field!

Not only were the light poles in fair grounds, they put a HUGE Marlboro Man ad on one of the poles in left center and it was in fair territory, too!

I remember facing a Salem Bucs pitcher who was just converted from playing first base. They were giving him one last chance to play pro ball as knuckleball pitcher. His name was Tim Wakefield. He floated one of those knucklers up there and I absolutely crushed a shot to deep left center. I knew it was way out, but as I looked up the left fielder was running IN. That's when I realized the ball was going to hit the Marlboro Man's head and the left fielder was in perfect position to throw me out at second base. That ball would have left ANY MLB stadium but in Salem I got a damn SINGLE!

I have to admit that during another game at Salem I hit one off the end of the bat and thought it was a routine fly out, but it cleared that short porch in left for a lame Home Run. Of course it looked like a BOMB in the score-book!

The following events happened all in one game in Salem in 1990…

We were playing on a humid night with a packed house. It was a Salem Bucs give away night so people came in droves for the free item.

Then, in about the 3rd inning, it started SNOWING, even thought it was about 85 degrees that night. Then we realized what was going on—it was snowing dead moths that were floating down after flying into the powerful field light that was directly above our dugout.

There was nothing the field maintenance people could do to stop them. The moths were attracted to that light and flew into the high wattage bulbs and killed themselves! They were falling into our dugout at such a rate that the grounds crew guys had to shovel the carcasses out once an inning or there would have been mounds of dead moths in our way.

We were winning the game and the local belligerents decided they need-ed to help their hometown team. The dugout and bullpens at Salem allow for any drunken fool to walk right up and deliver their slurred rants from just a few feet away through a chain link fence. That night there happened to be an army of them.

The drunks were so ruthless, they were about to cause a brawl. They continually used the "N" word on several of our players and guys were ready to jump the fence with a bat. That's when our manager, Jim Nettles, called time out to inform the umpires that we needed police security or we would protest the game.

After a while, the police did arrive and secured our dugout/bullpen areas but the thugs were waiting at our bus after the game. I knew we had to walk through the crowd to get to our bus so I made sure I had a few baseballs in my hand in case we needed some extra firepower. Plus, I had three bats in my bag if things got crazy.

The police "kinda" escorted us to the bus but they were too busy laughing at the locals ragging us.

Finally, we made it through the gauntlet and were all on the bus, though sitting there, most of us wanted to go kick the locals' asses. That's when Nettles completely defused the situation with this comment: "Come on guys, we won the game, that's what's important. Remember, when jerk-offs like these finish taking a crap and wipe their fat asses, they always get shit on their thumb! Never argue with idiots, especially drunk idiots!" We all cracked up and that laughter helped us relax and enjoy the victory.

I'm sure these bad apples do not represent the average Salem VA resident, but that night they might have been the WORST fans I ever played in front of in 10 years of college and pro baseball—even worse than Arizona State!

Today, Salem has a modern stadium that opened in 1995, complete with clubhouses, light poles BEHIND the fence along with modern dugouts, and bullpens AWAY from the crowd. I wonder if the drunken idiots still come out in droves on the free seat cushion give away night!

Getting Through Game Delays

Some of the funniest and coolest stuff happened when there was a delay in the game.

Sometimes we had rain delays that lasted hours, and sometimes there was a malfunction and we had to stop and wait until whatever it was got fixed.

When bored, we would play cards, dominos, clubhouse putt putt, watch TV, sleep, do a crossword, play guitar, read the paper. But on occasion we would get creative.

When we arrived in Jacksonville in 1991 they had put in a new dugout bench that was elevated to see the field better. It was made of these long planks of heavy wood, but they were only fastened on the ends with bolts. Due to this construction, we figured out we could play killer bass and drum lines by hitting the bench!

During a rain delay, shortstop Jack Smith and I went off. I was hitting the bench with the side of my fist making a subwoofer bass rhythm while Jack was slapping out a drum beat. Then some of the guys started rapping. We could change the pitch of the beats by moving closer to the end of the bench. It was freakin' cool—Gangsta Rap during a rain delay!

Another game in Jacksonville, the light tower by third base went out. While we waited for the electric company to fix it, I had an idea. I went inside the clubhouse and stuffed like 10 towels inside my jersey to form a massive beer gut and another 10 towels in the back of my pants to form a huge badonkadonk ass. I then grabbed a 7-foot novelty baseball bat from the office and went out on the field where 10,000 people were anxiously waiting for play to resume.

The announcer saw what I was doing and started to do a joke play-by-play. I stepped up to the plate, took a big swing with my big ass and gut and then proceeded to rumble around the bases. When I reached home I did the biggest belly flop right on home plate. The crowd loved it, but my manager wasn't amused. I was fined $20.

Another incident of boredom killing was in Durham. The field is OLD, and they have their PA announcer sitting at field level, unlike most parks where the announcer is up in the press box.

If I recall, there was an issue with the sprinklers coming on so we were waiting until they could turn them off. That's when an idea came to mind.

I quickly scribbled down a note and had the batboy run it over to the announcer, just as our starting pitcher walked by with his jacket on, leaving the game for the clubhouse to ice down.

My note said the pitcher needed the Mariners' doctor to report to the clubhouse immediately...so this is what was said.

"YOUR ATTENTION PLEASE, WILL DOCTOR HUGH JARDON PLEASE REPORT TO THE MARINERS CLUBHOUSE, DOCTOR HUGH JARDON PLEASE REP...."

That's when the announcer knew he had been pranked. But he got me back later in the game by intentionally mispronouncing my name "NOW BATTING, CATCHER, JIM CUUUUUUUMP-ANUS."

Making a Tough Job Even Tougher

When it comes to playing a very difficult game like baseball, sometimes the facility makes it that much tougher.

I don't want to sound like a cry baby, but I'm going to vent a bit about some of the places I was forced to play. I sure hope most of them are old relics by now.

There are so many factors players deal with during a game. Sometimes it's a terrible locker room, sometimes you can't see the ball at twilight or the lights are dim, sometimes there are tons of rocks on the infield. It all affects the game and how you play.

Amazingly, the fields and facilities at most of the college parks were very well maintained. Many didn't have clubhouses, but it didn't matter since we were accustomed to dressing at the hotel or driving to the local away games already dressed. But in pro ball, the clubhouse was like our home away from home.

One of the WORST clubhouses I ever dealt with was under a really nice stadium with a major league-caliber field in Kinston, SC, home of the Kinston Indians in 1990. It looked like the visitor's clubhouse was an afterthought of the architect, as it was not connected to the dugout like the home team's was. We had to walk around the dugout and under the stands to get there.

Inside this closet they called a clubhouse were about 10 lockers with a bunch of nails hammered half way into the wood. Those were to hang up our clothes on! There was no AC, and as you know, South Carolina can get quite hot and humid during the summer.

To make matters worse, the showers could only accommodate six guys at a time, with water pressure so high it left a mark, and the friggin' drains were CLOGGED!

It was so gross showering with dark brown, nasty water half way up to your knee while being pelted by a firehouse. The floor of that clubhouse was also filthy, so no matter how hard you tried to put your socks on with clean feet, you couldn't. And it felt like you had rocks in your shoes the rest of the night!

When I played in the Cal League I noticed two parks that should have NEVER hosted pro games—and many players paid the price for it: Bakersfield and Stockton. These parks were decent in every respect except one very important factor—the sun sets directly over the center field wall. Even during batting practice, it was nearly impossible to see certain pitches even with just the coach pitching.

As a catcher, I got blinded both ways, when hitting AND catching! Due to this problem, at least Bakersfield didn't start their games until 8 PM. But Stockton started at 7pm.

There have been more guys beaned in Stockton than any other park I know of simply because of the blinding sun. I never understood why they would build a field that faces the setting sun.

When I was chosen to play in Alaska after my sophomore year at USC, I was excited. We started the season off with five games in the beautiful Aloha Stadium in Hawaii and then headed home, landing in Fairbanks, which was about 20 minutes away from our little town of North Pole. And yes, our logo was Santa Claus swinging a bat!

The issue with our field up there in Alaska was that they literally cleared out a section of the forest, threw down some sod, put up a fence and said, "There it is…play ball!" There were no bleachers, a short backstop like at an elementary school has, wood dugouts that could only hold half of the team, no raised bullpen mounds, and rocks and rocks and rocks EVERY-WHERE!

After a couple of days practicing on this field, we begged the GM to allow us to do some work to improve the conditions. He agreed, so we had a "Rock Party!"

We literally spend hours and hours hauling rocks of all sizes off the in-field and dumping them into the woods behind the third base dugout. By the time we were done, we moved thousands of rocks and the field was start-ing to shape up.

That field also had the worst infestation of pterodactyl-sized mosquitos anywhere on earth. We used to call them the state bird! It seemed like the mosquitos migrated right through the forest that was carved out to make the field and then learned to chow down on baseball players and fans.

My favorite all-time rain out remedy came on that field a couple of months later. We were battling our cross-town rivals from Fairbanks for first place and needed to get one of the last home games in before the season ended. But it had rained all night and the field was a total mess. The short-stop area was so flooded you couldn't even see the dirt. Home plate was the same thing, but thick in mud. That's when the local U.S. Air Force base took matters into its own hands!

As we sat and watched in disbelief, Air Force personnel started pouring gasoline all over the field, including gallons at shortstop and around home plate where the flooding was the worst.

Then those crazy guys LIT THE FIELD ON FIRE! We all ran out of the dugout and straight to the parking lot because the flames were so high and the heat was unbearable.

Just as we exited the dugout and found some shelter in the parking lot, a MASSIVE CH-47 Chinook helicopter with two huge propeller blades swooped in from over the outfield wall. It was like a movie! The Chinook was there to dry the field and put out the gasoline-induced fires! After about 10 minutes of hovering just a few feet off the ground, the Chinook took off, and to our amazement, the field was ready to go! Except for one little detail. The stench of gasoline was so strong it made many of us sick, including me, as I sat behind home plate half the game inhaling the fumes. But we did win that game and we took the league title.

Overall, most stadiums lacked SOMETHING, kinda like the Goldilocks story. This one is too big (Blair Field in Long Beach, Birmingham), this one is too small (Salem, Adelanto). But sometimes, it was just right.

My favorite was in Charlotte. I loved everything about that stadium—the clubhouse, the dugout, the condition of the field, and the bullpens; it was the right size and there were sold out crowds every time we played there. Plus, we stayed in a nice hotel near places to eat.

I also liked Orlando, Rancho Cucamonga, Frederick, Huntsville, Nashville, Prince William, Lake Elsinore, and even that old park in Reno.

Today, the minor league players have it made. Nearly every park in every league is either completely revamped or recently built. They play on fields as nice as the old big league fields!

I bet my grandpa's generation and my dad's generation of players felt the same way about the parks my generation played in. They probably would say, "You guys had it made…we all shared one nail on the wall! Plus, you had hot water and towels! The grounds crew used to hose us down after a game and we had to use our street clothes to dry off!"

5
Distant Diamonds

Most players do not get the opportunity to play all over the world like I did.

Many of my childhood winters were spent in Venezuela, Dominican Republic, and Mexico following my dad around. Years later, I played on Team USA in High School and College. I traveled the world in 1985 and also in 1988. Then, a few years later, I found myself playing winter ball in Mexico during the 1991-92 season and Puerto Rico in 1992–93. My teammates and I experienced special moments at a young age many never do, playing the wonderful game of baseball.

Many times, the only thing we had in common with the native people was baseball. They took us in like family and introduced us to their local cuisine and customs, especially Cesar Ascencio from Los Mochis, Mexico. I believe these years really opened up my eyes to how most of the world lives. We have it pretty good here in the US.

My teammates and I saw extreme poverty, crime, corruption, and a total lack of the basic things we take for granted in the US, like safe drinking water. But the mood of the people we encountered was always so upbeat. Their positive spirit amidst all of the chaos is something I'll never forget.

The Japanese Twinkie

In 1988 I played on Team USA prior the Olympics.

It was a goal of mine to play on the Olympic team since watching the 1984 Olympic baseball team led by Mark McGwire and Will Clark.

I had a really good season at USC in the spring of '88 and was invited to attend the Olympic tryouts in Millington TN.

Soon I was on the travel team and we had 60 games scheduled prior to the World Championships in August then a final roster cut before the Olympics.

From the Team USA Program in 1988.

The Mariners had drafted me in the third round and made sure I was VERY aware that they did NOT want me to play on Team USA but wanted me to sign and start playing in A ball in San Bernardino.

I didn't really even think much about it. I wanted to play on the Olympic team!

Soon Team USA was on a 16-hour flight to Japan to play seven games all over the country.

When we arrived at the airport there were HUNDREDS of reporters and photographers to greet us.

The first night I went exploring Tokyo and was checking out the ladies. I'd walk by and say "Hi" and they gave me weird looks. Then another girl walked by and I said "Hi" Same weird look. The next day our interpreter told me "Hi" means "YES." Wow did I feel stupid!

That week we played to packed stadiums and the fans seemed to follow us everywhere.

After a game in Sendai we had to be escorted by the police to our bus. Once we were on the bus the fans started shaking it and banging on the windows in an effort to get us to come out and sign autographs.

In Japan there is a tradition where if you sign something or grant an interview they give you a present.

We all went out and for at least 45 minutes signed everything they had, took pictures and they gave us a bunch of presents.

I had a whole shopping bag full of gifts and started looking through it on way to our next stop.

The fans had given me good luck charms, commemorative pins, hats, pennants, and a bunch of food, including a TWINKIE!

It had been like 10 days of nothing but Japanese food so a Twinkie was going to hit the spot. I stood up and announced to the team that I had a Twinkie and everyone was jealous. Guys were willing to trade just about anything for it.

As I examined the Twinkie closer up I noticed the Twinkie guy was replaced by a purple octopus guy. I just figured that was the cultural equivalent to our Twinkie guy wearing a cowboy hat.

I slowly unwrapped my prized possession and thought that I should savor this treat all the way to the end.

As I took my first bite, the delicious spongy cake reminded me of home. But as I got to the creamy filling, something was wrong. It was purple!

It was at that moment I put two and two together and realized it was stuffed with OCTOPUS tentacles and a purple OCTOPUS gravy of some sort!!!! NASTY!!!!

Later on that same trip, our interpreter asked if we wanted to watch the Tyson-Spinks fight. We thought they were going to pull over and take us somewhere to watch it, but instead, the TV sets on the bus all turned on and we were watching the world heavyweight championship, on a bus, stuck in traffic somewhere in Japan. That was unheard of in America back then!

We finished our tour of Japan and flew back to the US with games in the Northwest and the South.

As we continued to play through July and into August, I was called into the coach's office. He told me that there was a 50% chance I was going to be an alternate on the team and 50% chance I would be a full team member. Including me, we had three catchers but I would DH against left handed pitching so they were still trying to decide what to do.

I can't remember being more angry at the circumstance I was in. Leave now and the last few months were a waste of time. Stay and risk being sent home with nothing. I had to make a decision.

Since the Mariners were so adamant that I sign a contract, I called my scout who said they had a roster spot ready for me in San Bernardino.

That night, I resigned from Team USA to start playing pro.

When I arrived in San Bernardino the head minor league guy from the Mariners was there to deliver bad news. They had changed their mind and I had to sit out the rest of the season since it would count as a full year of play for me...BASTARDS! What a way to start off a career. The Mariners were mad at me for holding out signing, playing on Team USA and took a year of play away from me to insure they had more time to decide what do with me after my third season.

Since I had signed, I couldn't go back to the Olympic team either.

In September, the 1988 Olympic team won Gold in Seoul Korea.

The silver lining: In September the Mariners sent me to Tempe AZ for Instructional Ball where I met my wife.

Things always seem to work out the way they are supposed to....

Campan-EE!!

In 1991-92 I played winter ball in Mexico. Flashback 20 years earlier…when I was about 4 or 5 my dad played in Mexico and we would go down there to visit every year.

My dad had played for several teams in Mexico over his 10 years of winter ball including my team in Los Mochis. When I arrived in Los Mochis, I was instantly a fan favorite because of my dad. He was very popular as a player but then I was told by dozens of people other things he had done. Here's what they told me…

My dad had a pocketful of US coins on him all of the time. The kids in these towns knew the ballplayers and where they stayed. So when my dad walked out of his front door he was met by a small army of street kids who wanted to carry his baseball bag and his bats.

The kids didn't go to school, lived in terrible poverty but had such an optimistic attitude about life. He would pay the kids in US coins to carry his bag and bats. The kids made more from carrying my dad's gear than their parents did trying to get work. He would also buy them food and sodas.

Many of these kids (who were now adults) found me to tell me how my dad helped them and their families survive in those years. That was very special to hear.

But my favorite story from Mexico happened on a road trip.

My dad played for several years in a small town called Guasave (Wa-saw-vey). This was a farm town and life was very challenging for the people. But baseball was their escape and they would spend more for a ticket than they had made that whole day working!

My dad bought an old motorcycle one year and that was how he drove to the field every day. At Christmas time, he went to the local market and purchased several dozen toys and put them in a big sack. He then purchased a Santa Claus outfit, hopped on his motorcycle carrying the huge sack of toys, and rode into the poorest part of Guasave.

As he rolled up, the kids started screaming "Campan-ee, Campan-ee!" They recognized him! He handed out the toys and went back to the hotel.

This act of kindness didn't go unnoticed in Guasave...the kids told the newspaper reporters what my dad did and they wrote stories about "Santa Campan-ee." He became a local legend.

When I played my first game in Guasave, I had heard the Santa story, even from my manager, Aurelio Rodriguez, who was my dad's teammate back then. But what happened next was unexpected. As they announced my name as the batter, the stadium went crazy. The crowd of over 10,000 was standing and cheering and chanting "Cam-pan-ee! Cam-pan-ee!"

The umpire called time out, walked over to me and said "Your father was a very good player but more importantly he was very good to our people, we still love him." I couldn't believe it! It still gives me the chills thinking about that moment.

Before we left for Los Mochis, my dad gave me $100 in quarters and he told me about the street kids. I half believed him, but figured I'd learn for sure when I got there.

That winter, after a few weeks and few dollars in quarters given out, we had our own little army of street kids who followed us everywhere. They were a huge help to us teaching us about where to go, and where NOT to go in Los Mochis. They even kept us entertained by singing and dancing for tips.

Hopefully, we enhanced their lives as much as they inspired us with their positive spirit amidst such poverty. I only wish I could have helped more.

Senor Relleno

In the early 90's I played winter ball for Los Caneros de Los Mochis. Yes, we were the "Sugarcane Cutters!" The team was made up of 15 Mexican League players plus 6 American players. The same with every team in the league.

Because I knew Spanish, I became the "American Players Union Rep" when it came to communicating/negotiating with the owner of the team.

The team owner, who is now Governor of the state of Sinaloa, and his family were good people and often invited Lisa and I to fancy parties just to show off their American player who could tell stories to their guests in crappy Spanish.

One day I went to the team office to pick up my paycheck but something had happened.

The owner explained to me that the Mexican peso had just dropped like 33% in value. I thought no big deal because we had negotiated to pay the Americans in US Dollars. Then he told me the real problem.

He said that the average Mexican citizen didn't trust the government to keep the financial system stable. He continued saying that the people were standing in long lines at the banks to convert their pesos to the stronger dollar. This meant that we were not going to get paid that day...because there were NO MORE DOLLARS AVAILABLE IN LOS MOCHIS!!!

With as much respect as I could muster, I told the owner that the American guys would not play that night unless we received our pay. He understood and promised me that we would be paid prior to the game, but I had my doubts.

I went back to the hotel where all the American guys were staying to tell them the news. We liked our owner and he had always been cool, but we knew we had to stand our ground or this might become a regular thing.

When we arrived for batting practice we told the manager, Aurelio Rodriguez, the situation. He understood, but trusted our owner would come through.

After batting practice, the owner was nowhere to be found. We told Aurelio that we were not going to play unless there was a miracle and the owner paid us.

With about 10 minutes until game time, the owner burst into the locker room and escorted us to the ticket office with armed guards. I remember we all had on our metal spikes and the sound of us walking on cement echoed under the stadium as we were rushed through.

Once in the ticket office, the owner brought each of us into the money room and counted out our pay—in $5 and $1 bills ONLY! He paid us with the money the fans used to buy their tickets!

My pay was $1,250 for that period. They paid me in like 200 $5 bills and 250 $1 bills. The stack of cash looked like a scene out of Scarface!

I started thinking, should I give this wad of cash to my wife? No, too dangerous to have that much in the stands. Should I hide it in my locker? No, can't trust the people who were always coming in and out. Finally I came up with the only possible solution. I folded the 3-inch high pile of cash in half and shoved it into my jock on top of my protective cup. No one could steal it there!

When Aurelio saw me, he cracked up. He knew what I was holding down there.

When I went to bat, the catcher started laughing also. He asked me in Spanish if I was "caliente," which means "Horny." Yeah, yeah, funny stuff. When the game was over, I wore my uniform back to the hotel keeping the cash safely tucked away.

The next day I went directly to the local Western Union office and wired the slightly damp wad of cash to our bank in the US.

Later that season I told that story to the owner's friends at a party. They nicknamed me "Buen Paquete" or "El Relleno," which translates to something like "The Well-Endowed One."

The Pickup Truck Cowboy

Playing Winter Ball in Mexico for five months was an awesome experience, thanks to the wonderful people we met. As the 1991 baseball season was winding down, I received a call from one of the Mariner's minor league coordinators informing me that I was invited to play for the Caneros de Los Mochis in the Mexican Pacific League. I knew of this team because 20+ years earlier my dad played for them. My manager was also a former teammate of my dad's, the late, great Detroit Tiger third baseman, Aurelio Rodriguez.

Soon after arriving down there, we were introduced to a guy who was a friend of the team owner and super fan of the Caneros, Cesar Ascencio. He was a very successful pig farmer with a great sense of humor and outgoing personality. He was in his early 40's and starting to bald. His wife jokingly liked to call him "Pelon." We all hit it off right away.

Cesar became a good friend and we trusted him. We used to hang out a lot after games and eat huge shrimp cocktails at the team owner's house parties where I would tell baseball stories in my best Spanish.

One rule the team had was no wives on the team bus, so Cesar offered to drive a couple of wives to nearby games like in Fernando Valenzuela's home town of Navajoa.

It was about a 2-hour ride to Navajoa so I figured we'd see them arrive an hour before game time in Cesar's full size, white Dodge pick up.

When you play on the road, your team takes batting practice after the home team. I kept looking up in the stands but didn't see Cesar or the wives yet. I thought they must have gotten a later start than they had said.

Then it was our turn to take BP…still no sign of them. When it was 20 minutes prior to the game starting, I went down the left field line to start warming up the starting pitcher in the bullpen.

At the Navajo stadium, the bullpen had a chain link fence that had a view to the parking lot outside of the stadium. Every now and then I'd look out to see if the white Dodge pickup truck was there, but it still wasn't, and I was starting to worry. I had heard some of the nightmare stories of highway pirates and unscrupulous Federales who blackmailed drivers to pay them cash.

Right as the starting pitcher was finishing his warm up pitches I saw an amazing sight. It was Cesar driving into the parking lot in his white Dodge truck. But something was very odd!

Cesar was standing in the back bed of the pickup truck holding a long rope. My wife was in the driver seat and the other wife had the window down and was leaning out talking to Cesar. I couldn't figure out what was going on, but they were there safe and sound so I focused on the game we were about to play.

After the game, I walked out to greet Cesar and my wife and asked why he was in the bed of the truck while my wife was driving. They both laughed as Cesar began to explain.

It turns out the accelerator cable from the gas pedal to the carburetor broke so they had to pull over while he tried to fix it. After about an hour, Cesar realized the cable could not be repaired but luckily he had a rope and an idea.

About 5 months before we went to Mexico I had to teach my wife how to drive a stick. She had always driven an automatic but my car was stick and she needed to drive it occasionally so she reluctantly learned. Luckily she did.

Cesar's truck was a stick shift also. His plan was to tie a rope to the carburetor where the gas pedal cable had broken. Then he strung the rope through the back of the hood and over the cab. Then he jumped into the BED of the pickup truck and pulled on the rope revving the engine. My wife set the truck into first gear, and right as Cesar pulled on the rope, she gently let out the clutch and they were moving. They had to work together to shift to the next gear so the other wife would hear my wife say, "shift" and she'd yell "shift" out the window to Cesar who would slacken the rope just like taking your foot off the gas pedal. Then my wife would shift to the next gear.

This went on until they were in 5th gear and rolling 65 MPH down the highway with Cesar holding the accelerator rope for dear life. He had NO protection from the wind or the dozens of bugs that he swallowed on that one-and-a-half hour trip.

By the end of the game, the handy Cesar had fixed his truck's accelerator cable and it was good to go again. He drove us to the hotel where we had dinner and laughed about "Cesar, El Caballero del Camion" (Cesar, the Pickup Truck Cowboy).

A couple of days later, on the drive back to Los Mochis with the wives in tow, he was pulled over by a Federale who demanded $80 from them or they were all going to jail!

Tough trip for Cesar, but like most things in Mexico, all you can do is laugh and thank God you survived another day!

El Dentisto Longhorn

During the 1991-92 season in Los Mochis, Mexico I bit down on a damn Jujy Fruit and pulled out a crown from my back molar. To make matters worse, the crown was porcelain and cracked into a bunch of pieces as I bit back down

So I asked around and found a dentist in town. Being far from home, I was nervous going there as getting any medical treatment in a third world country can be quite dangerous. But his office was just like any dentist in the US with all of the modern equipment and amenities. To my surprise, the dentist was half Mexican and half Chinese, but spoke perfect English with a Texas drawl. I found out he was a former Texas Longhorn and learned English Texas-style.

As the dentist began to treat me, he asks, "How'd y'all manage to break that there crown?" I told him about the Jujy Fruit incident and he says, "Well I reckon I could glue it back together, but it would be best to install a new one, know what I mean?" I started thinking, how much is a crown in Mexico—$400? $600? More than that? And does this guy know what he's doing?

I returned to his office with all the cash I had, and, very nervous, put the fate of my teeth in his hands as he began to install this new nickel crown. I didn't know which I was more nervous about—my teeth or the bill. I figured I could maybe negotiate with him—you know, offer free tickets, autographed balls, uniforms, etc.

After I was done, he sent me to the office manager for payment. The manager says "180,000 pesos por favor." I quickly did the math and realized the whole bill was just $60...$60!!!

Decades years later, I've never encountered a single problem with that crown!

Starting Ahead of Hall of Famers

After a season-ending injury in 1992 (more on that later), my wife, son Alex, and I went back to Orange County, CA to stay with my parents during the off-season. My dad set me up selling cars and I was working out nearly every day to stay in shape.

A few weeks later, I got a call from the Mariners—they had a winter ball gig for me! The Mariners had negotiated with the Mayaguez team in Puerto Rico to sign me as their starting catcher. They told me to pack and leave right away.

Once I landed and got my locker set up, I noticed a couple of other catchers were on the team. But I didn't worry; I was guaranteed to be the starter.

During our first practice, one of the catchers came up to me to let me know he was going to DH and maybe play first base, but not catch. It was as if he were saying, "I would be the starter, but lucky for you, I don't want to catch." And I was totally fine with the arrangement. He was cool and we got along just fine. Plus, I learned a lot from watching him consistently crush balls to the gaps.

The other catcher was very young and in his first pro season. He met me in the bullpen and immediately wanted me to show him all of my tricks. Things like how I received the ball, how I transferred the ball from my glove to throwing hand, how I used angles to block pitches in the dirt, my foot-work when throwing out runners, etc. He was very inquisitive and thankful for all of my tips. He was also quite respectful and I enjoyed sharing what I knew with him. Then I saw him take batting practice from both sides of the plate and knew this kid was destined for the big leagues, but never dreamed he'd do what he did.

As the winter season wound down, these two catchers played sparingly, leaving me to catch most of the innings that season. I batted about .260 in a tough league for hitters. The league was so tough to hit homers, I ended up tied for 3rd in the ENTIRE league with ONE home run!

I may not have made it to the majors, other than being on an MLB 40-man roster, but how many guys can say that they started at catcher over future Hall of Fame catchers Ivan Rodriguez and Jorge Posada?

Lisa's Wild Horse Ride

In the winter of 1992-93 I played baseball in Mayaguez, Puerto Rico. All of the American guys and our wives decided to find a big house to rent and live in together. We found a cool place right on the water and just off the main road to town.

Before each game, we'd go to the back of the house where gentle waves from a crystal clear lagoon rolled up on our little beach. My oldest son, Alex, was not even a year old but LOVED getting in his floaty and wading in the water for hours. We could walk about a ¼ mile out in the lagoon and still be only waist deep in water. It was truly a paradise. I LOVED to pick coconuts from our tree, cut them open as the locals had shown me, and drink that fresh milk. It was even better with a splash of Bacardi!

The house itself was super lo-tech with no TV, but had a big grassy front and side yards, with steel gates, and even bars on the windows. We felt safe there.

Late one night we were playing cards and kept hearing something outside. Then we heard it again, then again. So like the dumb guy in a horror movie, I walked outside to find out what it was.

It turned out to be a horse running up and down the main road in front of our house. I quickly ran inside and told everyone. Out of nowhere my wife threw the rental van keys at me and said, "We have to go save him!"

We all piled into the Ford Aerostar minivan with the sliding side door to chase this horse down.

As I pulled up next the horse, he spooked and took off running at like 25 MPH. I chased after him and pulled up at his side, when suddenly my crazy wife opened the sliding van door and JUMPED from the van onto the horse BAREBACK, holding nothing but the horse's mane!

She had told me many times about her horse riding background working with horses but I never dreamed she would try a move like that!

Like a pro, she turned the horse around and rode it back to our house. Once inside the gates, we were able to pen the horse in our lush front yard.

It was about 2 AM by then so we decided the horse was safe and we could go to bed.

When we woke up, my wife went out to check on the horse. Suddenly, she yelled, "Jim, you better get out here." So I ran outside to see what was wrong. The horse had not only eaten every blade of grass on our lush lawn, but also all of the rubber molding from the bumper and doors on the damn minivan! All I could think was "Horses eat rubber?"

While I was trying to wrap all of this around my little brain, a lady walking by called us over to tell us it was her horse. It had escaped its pen the night before. She went home and came back with a bridle to take the horse home. She strapped that bridle on the horse and walked it home. No thank you (or gracias) even when we told her of the lengths we went to save that horse.

In the end, we were glad no one was hurt and the horse was safely back at its stable. But I was charged over $300 for new rubber molding on that Aerostar minivan, plus we were out one lawn! I guess the old saying is true: No good deed goes unpunished.

Road Trip Road Kill

In 1993 my wife Lisa and infant son came down for a road trip to Orlando while I was playing for the Jacksonville Suns.

Our center fielder, Darrin Bragg, shared an apartment with us about 45 miles from Jacksonville near the famous Ponte Vedra Golf Course. The team manager allowed us to drive home with my wife instead of on the team bus to save us a bunch of time.

Lisa was driving with my son Alex in his car seat in the front seat. Darrin and I drank some beers after the game so we were chilling in the back seat.

From the time when I first met Lisa, she has been the biggest animal lover of all time. When she sees a dead dog that was hit by a car she quickly gives the sign of the cross, says a little prayer, and sheds a tear for the deceased animal. That was Lisa, and it still is. In fact, she runs a charity called Leashes of Love Rescue, Inc. LOLR.org that rescues dogs, fosters them, and finds qualified families to adopt them. That's how much she loves animals.

It was getting late as we drove up the A1A highway on Florida's East coast past St. Augustine. Lisa had to turn on the bright lights to see on this dark stretch of highway in the middle of nowhere.

As we passed Vilano Beach, the landscape turned to coastal swamps with the highway running right through the middle of lush forests near the ocean.

All of the sudden we came upon THOUSANDS of armadillos crossing A1A from the forest toward the ocean. They were totally focused on getting to the beach like they were in a mating frenzy or something. It was literally a sea of white armadillos!

My wife was swerving to avoid the first few dozen but finally, KA-BOOM, she hit one, then another, then another, and another. She slowed down to try to weave her way through them, but when afraid, armadillos instinctively stop and roll themselves into a ball for protection, so she couldn't avoid hitting one after another. It was complete CARNAGE!

Lisa was hysterical and crying as she pulled over, crushing a few more as she finally reached the side of the road. Of course Darrin and I were just cracking up in the back seat as we got bounced around from all of the armadillo impacts.

I got out to inspect the devastation. In all, she must have run over 20 or 30 armadillos which lay strewn on the highway like a bunch of random little speed bumps.

To this day, she still hasn't forgiven me for making fun of her armadillo mass-murdering rampage.

An Average Day in Puerto Rico

Puerto Rico was arguably the Winter League with the most talent, and when I arrived I knew we had a damn good team. The first thing I noticed when I unloaded my gear at the clubhouse were the number of major leaguers on my team—and not just scrubs, starters! We had Alex Diaz, Coco Cordero, Jose Tony Valentin, Ivan Cruz, Roberto Hernandez, Ivan Rodriguez, Jorge Pasada, and more.

When we arrived I also learned that I knew some of the American players, so we decided to find a house together to split the rent. It was Frank Bolick and his wife, pitchers Roger Smithberg and Matt Grout, along with my wife, our 10-month-old son, Alex, and me.

When we started playing our first games, I was still trying to shake off the cobwebs from not having played for about a month.

It was the first time in my career where I was thrown right into the line of fire with very little time to get into "baseball shape," and expected to perform. I was struggling BIG TIME! I tried to focus on being a GREAT defensive catcher, but I was simply trying too hard to impress my coaches and teammates and I was totally stinking up the place every time I stepped on the field.

After a tough week, when I was obviously stressed to the max, my pitching coach called me over during a game. He said, "Campy, you look like you've never played baseball in your life. You look lost, scared, and stressed out. So go into my locker. I have a cooler full of beer. Pound one of the beers right now and you'll finish this game strong. You need take the edge off—trust me!"

So I did just that, and amazingly, I did feel more relaxed. In fact, I got a base hit my next at bat and started to get my confidence back.

Our pitching staff was stellar but so were the batters in the league including Juan Gonzalez, Carlos Baerga, Carlos Delgado, Bernie Williams, Edgar Martinez, Sandy and Roberto Alomar, Jim Thome, and many more.

Turned out it was the year of the pitcher and for one major reason: Crappy baseballs! We stored our game balls in a humid closet under the stadium. Just walking in there caused you to pour sweat, and made the leather on the balls loosen up from the seams. Some of the balls were so sloppy you could pinch the laces! This made hitting them even tougher since they didn't travel like a normal ball.

I remember absolutely crushing a fastball to left-center thinking it was going to clear the fence, but watched the center fielder dive and rob me of a double. The ball should have been long gone!

A few games later, I hit a home run on a curveball from a lefty. It was one of those that I hit perfectly. But I knew it still could stay in the yard so I hustled to first but this one went over. I was so relieved. My first HR since the injury.

As I entered the dugout for congrats from my teammates, I realized no one was standing up, no one was looking at me, and no one was shaking my hand after that rare home run. That's when it clicked in my head—I was getting the SILENT TREATMENT! I blurted out a general, "Ohhh, f**k you then!" and they all started cracking up. That's when they mobbed me with hugs. It was a very funny moment that I will never forget.

As the season progressed, I started hitting better and my wrist started to heal. It felt much stronger but was still not 100%.

About that time there was an unprecedented event in baseball—the first expansion draft in my generation. There were two new teams entering the league, the Tampa Bay Devil Rays and the Colorado Rockies. The rules were set; all of the MLB teams were allowed to protect just 15 players and the rest were available for the expansion draft.

Our closer, Roberto Hernandez, lived in Mayaguez and also was protected by the Chicago White Sox. He had a satellite dish, which was very rare in 1992. He told Frank Bolick and I we were invited to his house to watch the draft live in case we were chosen. I was so excited at the thought of being taken from Seattle Mariner hell to greener pastures with ANY team. But an expansion team could be even better as I would be higher up the ladder among the catchers on the team.

Bolick and I arrived at Roberto's house right when the draft started, but we had to leave soon for our game that was 45 minutes away in Ponce. We watched the first several rounds and saw a bunch of guys we knew get picked. I hoped those guys knew how lucky they were to be chosen. Unfortunately, neither Bolick nor I was picked. Then I realized we were running late! We ran to the car and I drove like 85 MPH on the highway, only to get pulled over by Highway Patrol.

I spoke to the officer in Spanish and explained that we were just at Roberto Hernandez's house watching the expansion draft to see if we were chosen, and now we had to get to Ponce for the game. He asked me in Spanish who was in the car with me and I told him it was third baseman, Frank Bolick. Turns out he saw Bolick hit a home run two nights earlier and was star struck. He kept saying, "Oh, Frank Bolick, Yes, Frank Bolick, very good batter!" Then said to me in perfect English, "OK, just drive the speed limit and good luck tonight in the game." And he let us go!

Even after explaining everything to our manager, he was still pissed at us for being late, but we won that night and Bolick had another great game.

A week or so later, Bolick was traded from the Mariners to the Expos. The Expos GM called Bolick at the stadium and told him to pack up his stuff and go home. They didn't want him getting hurt playing in Puerto Rico. I was so happy for Bo but knew one of my best buddies and one of our top hitters was leaving. His absence hurt us as we were heading towards the final few weeks of the season.

As the season was winding down, we were tied with Juan Gonzalez's San Juan team. On our last regular season game a huge tropical storm rolled into the area and we weren't sure we would play. Batting practice was cancelled but the tarp was down so the grounds crew was able to fix up the field enough to make it playable. I'll never forget how hard the wind was blowing in from left field—probably close to 60 MPH!

In his first at bat, Juan Gonzalez hit a ball to left field that would have gone out of the universe, but the wind held it back. Our left fielder turned to try to catch it by the wall but it just went over, and that was all the offense either team could muster under those conditions. San Juan won, resulting in a one-game tie-breaker the next day to see who was to go to the playoffs.

Roger Smithberg was designated the starting pitcher for the one game play-off. He and I spoke in detail for hours about how we were going to pitch to the San Juan team, and we felt we had a solid game plan.

When we arrived at the stadium, Roger went absolutely crazy when he saw I wasn't catching him as I had all the rest of the games that season. He was livid and barged into the coach's office to demand that I START OVER IVAN RODRIGUEZ!

Remember, Ivan was the starting catcher for the American League All-Star team that year, but didn't want to catch in Winter Ball! Roger and I had a very good pitcher-catcher rapport that he was trying to sell to the manager. The manager simply said, "Come on Roger, Ivan wants to get ready for Spring Training and has decided now is the time. He's an all-star in the major leagues. You'll be fine."

We ended up losing that game by one run. It was a tight game that either team could have won. But the season was over.

When I looked back on that season in Mayaguez, I was happy with what I had accomplished. I hit well against the best pitching I had ever faced. I had caught some of the game's best pitchers, who complimented me for helping them though challenging innings.

I am so glad to see that Mayaguez has continued its commitment to baseball and built the team a brand new stadium. Someday I'd love to return and have some ballpark pinchos, washed down with a local concoction called Juan 23 (Veinte Tres)!

6
The Game Behind the Plate

I was a shortstop growing up and didn't switch to catching full time until my junior year at USC. But when I did, I knew I had found my "home." Catching was very natural for me and I absolutely loved everything about the position. I have to admit, it kinda sucked getting plowed at the plate, but that was part of the gig back then.

In this section, I delve into some of the insights and techniques I picked up over the years for playing the position of catcher. I also share my unique view of the game as seen squatting as low as I could get, waiting for the pitch I called with a guy wearing blue squeezing his face right next to mine for nine innings.

The Catchers Union

When I was converted to a full time catcher, it was like joining a fraternity. First off, I was excited to catch because it felt natural to me. I liked running the game and keeping pitchers focused on getting outs. I liked being the field general and relaying the plays from the coach to the team. I liked everything about it.

Put simply, being a catcher is the single most physically and mentally demanding position in baseball, and one of the toughest in all of sports.

1. The catcher starts his day by catching four or five pitchers for 20 minutes each prior to batting practice.
2. The catcher helps the pitching coach make adjustments to the pitchers' delivery by offering feedback.
3. The catcher calls every pitch, so he has to study the other team's batters and match the pitcher's strengths against the batters weaknesses.
4. Catchers have to establish a positive relationship with the umpires.
5. Once the catcher identifies a pitch in the dirt, he must quickly throw his body in front of it and block it any way possible—but not deflect it away allowing the runners to advance.
6. The catcher makes the calls on which base to throw to on a bunt.
7. The catcher constantly looks at his manager for defensive signs and communicates those signs to the team.

8. The catcher races to back up first base on every ground ball hit to the infield when no one is on base.

9. The catcher gets hit in an unprotected area of his body nearly every game. As soon as one bruise heals you get another one.

10. A catcher's left hand index finger gets so swollen every game it ends up looking like a bratwurst.

11. Catching puts enormous strain on knees, ankles, the lower back, and throwing arm.

12. Catchers throw the ball more than any other player on the team.

13. Catchers must be able to put on all the gear in under 60 seconds to ensure not disrupting the pitcher's warm up routine.

14. The catcher calls the pitch to drill the batter to send a message to the other team.

15. The catcher is the manager on the field.

One game a catcher came up to bat for the other team. He said "Hey Campy, Catcher's Union rules today, OK?" I would always say "Sure!"

Basically, since all catchers are gluttons for punishment, we band together and treat each other with respect. There is a code that was passed down from my dad to me. He explained that the mutual respect catchers have for one another is because what we do is so specialized; only 2 or 3 guys on a team are catchers. That means the Catchers Union is a very elite group of guys who uniquely know what it's like to play the most punishing position in the game.

We followed this unwritten code of conduct most of the time, unless the other guy broke it. Then all bets were off. The Code entitled catchers to receive a first pitch fastball during their first at bat, but not later when the game was on the line. Another Catcher's Union rule was to not run over the other catcher, unless the game was on the line. We would also let other catchers use our gear if theirs was broken during the game.

Some call them the "Tool of Ignorance." I call them the "Tools of Intelligence." Today, 10 of the 30 MLB managers were former members of the Catcher's Union!

The Bob Boone Funnel Technique

One night I was hanging out with Bret Boone at his parents' house when his dad (Bob) and uncle (Rod) asked us if we wanted to go on an all-night Vegas run. Of course we jumped at the chance. Bret and I hopped into the back of Bob's pickup truck, equipped with a nice shell, and Rod drove the whole way from the Boone's house in Orange County.

We arrived about midnight and I proceeded to do the typical Vegas thing—lose money, go to the ATM, get free drinks, lose more money, go the ATM again, get more free drinks. But Bob wasn't drinking since he was driving home, and he was also winning!

We gambled until about 6 AM and headed out to the truck for the return trip. This time Bret and I were up front with Rod crashed out in the back. At the time, Bob was an All-Star, Gold Glove winning, World Champion catcher—one of the best in the game, with a reputation of stealing strikes with the way he caught pitches.

I was still learning the many details and nuances of catching. I had only been catching full time for about one season at that point. As we drove, I started nodding off as did Bret. Bob pulled over after a while for gas so I woke up and grabbed some snacks and coffee.

As we started driving again, Bob asked us to keep him company so he could stay awake. We small talked for a while then I asked Bob, "What's your secret to framing pitches and how do you steal so many strikes?" His eyes lit up!

Using the Bob Boone Funneling Technique catching future major leaguer Jeff Darwin in Jacksonville.

For the next three hours he went into detail about how he caught. He talked about his basic stance, the gloves he preferred, angles, footwork, throwing and even a detailed lesson about stealing strikes using his "Framing Funnel" technique.

This one I found particularly interesting because it was so different than what other coaches had tried to teach me. Basically, the standard way a catcher would try to fool an umpire was to catch the ball out in front and then with the wrist, "frame" the glove around the strike zone. But umpires had grown wary of this type of framing because they could clearly see the catchers trying to deceive them, and it wasn't working that well anymore.

Bob's technique was quite the opposite. He showed me how he did it. First, he crouched into the smallest stance possible so the umpire's view of the corners was not obstructed. As the pitch came in, if it was a strike or close to a strike, he kept his head perfectly still. He believed that when umpires saw catchers' heads move it indicated they were reaching and would call the pitch a ball. Then, if a pitch was on the corner, he would intentionally catch the ball in the webbing of the glove and quickly funnel the glove close to his chest instead of holding out there like so many other catchers did. He didn't "frame" the pitch, but rather "funneled" it to his chest.

By catching a pitch on the outside corner (to a right-handed batter) in the webbing, it was like an optical illusion to the umpire. The pitch would appear to be 2-3 inches closer to the strike zone than where Bob actually caught it. Then he would funnel the glove to his chest, NOT leaving out there for the ump to see. If you remember him catching, he often missed pitches off the tip of his glove (with no one on base) trying to steal an extra inch or two.

On the inside pitch to right handed hitters, he would never point his thumb to the sky. Instead, he would keep his thumb pointed down and catch the ball more in the palm to once again create the illusion the ball was more over the plate than it was.

He continued with his lesson by sharing his footwork technique when runners were stealing. He showed me with his hands the way most catchers just rotate their feet 90 degrees and throw. He told me his technique required the catcher to take a very short step with the right foot FIRST. I had never heard that before. Then the left foot should land just to the left of the point of the plate. At that time I used to step all the way OVER the plate and that ate up valuable time.

Bob talked to me for three straight hours, and although I had been up all night, I was wide-awake listening to a legend teach me his craft.

When we got home, I immediately wrote down everything I could remember about the lessons. I kept that paper in my baseball bag and worked on the "Boone Framing Funnel" technique the entire fall season at USC.

When I was able to finally use it in a real game situation I was blown away by all the strikes I was stealing. I watched some video of me catching and could tell that I was making borderline pitches look so good the umpires called them strikes. I also decreased my time throwing to second base by about 0.2 seconds, which is like six feet of the base stealer's stride.

Ironically, in 1991, Bob and I were both at Spring Training with the Mariners competing to make the major league team. Bob was very kind to me and continued to tutor me on the "Boone Framing Funnel." My defense improved dramatically that Spring. As a second-year player in the organization, I was a long shot to make the Mariners and Bob was 43 by then but was still major league caliber.

Ultimately, neither of us made the team. I was sent to AA that season with his son Bret, and Bob officially retired to later manage both the Royals and Reds for three years each. Bob now runs the minor league system & player development for the Washington Nationals.

I was drafted as a good hitter/average catcher, but thanks to the lessons I learned from Bob Boone during a sunrise drive from Vegas, plus my hard work learning the skills, I turned into a really good defensive catcher that extended my career by several years.

Calling the Game

When I started playing pro ball I realized that how I CALLED a game was almost as important as how I CAUGHT the game. To prepare, I would watch the other team take batting practice. By doing that I could tell what types of swings the batters had and start to see where their weaknesses were. I would focus in on their front shoulders. That told me A LOT about how to pitch to them.

Picture a right-handed hitter like Trout, Cabrera or Puig and watch how long these hitters keep their left shoulder tucked in. You can actually see the number on the back of their jerseys from the centerfield camera angle. These were the toughest guys to call…they could cover the strike zone, stay inside the ball and drive it hard to any field.

Conversely, the batters who pulled their front shoulders out too soon were outs waiting to happen. I could call fastballs in and curves/sliders away and the front shoulder pullers had no chance.

Another thing I looked for was bat speed. I learned to call fast pitches to slow bats and slow pitches to fast bats.

This one works!!! When a batter stepped up to the plate wearing a guard on his front leg that was a HUGE signal to me. The guard was there because the batter hits around the ball and sometimes off his own leg. These hitters are usually dead pull hitters but they pull pitches out over the plate. These types of hitters could NOT keep an inside pitch fair with this "hit around the ball" swing so I'd try to bust them inside.

Switch hitters were extremely vulnerable to the fast-slow pitch calling. I roomed with Frank Bolick who was one of the best switch hitters I ever played with. He was the one who told me switch hitters HATE changeups. Fastballs, curves, sliders…no problem, but changeups screw with their swings. So I made sure to use this information when calling pitches to switch hitters.

The Mariners had one rule for catchers to follow when calling pitches. No sliders from right-handed pitchers to left-handed batters after the 7th inning. This was Lou Pinella's rule and it was a smart one. Lefty hitters could just drop the head of the bat and hammer those low and in breaking balls to right field.

So in general, calling pitches went like this:

- Fast Bat – Call the opposite pitch. In other words…call curves, changeups and sliders in fastball counts like 0-0, 1-0, 2-1, 3-2.

- Slow Bat – Pound them with the heat. I would call fastballs in or out, up or down based on the pitcher. A slow bat should never beat you by hitting a slow pitch.

- Straight Away Hitter – This is the upper 5% of batters and the toughest out. They are balanced, keep their bat in the strike zone for a long time, and have good patience. I would try to outsmart them by calling fastballs in curve counts and curves in fastball counts. Also, I tried to show them changeups every at bat if the pitcher could throw one for strikes.

All in all, I loved the chess game aspect of calling pitches. When the pitcher and I were dialed in, it was like playing great music in a band. We had a rhythm and mentally were connected on how to pitch to each batter. To me, this was the most fun and rewarding part of my game and I still watch how catchers call pitches.

Catchers' Intuition

Growing up, my grandpa Al would often tell me to sit next to him when we were watching baseball on TV or at a Dodgers game. It was time for baseball lessons!

These were some of my fondest memories of my grandpa because he showed me so much about the game at a very young age. Especially, how to identify certain qualities and quirks in hitters that later served me very well as a catcher.

Often times these quirks were easy to see, like watching the batter step in the bucket. You can see how the batter's front foot goes toward third base (for a right-handed batter) when he strides to hit. When batters do this, it leaves them extremely vulnerable for low and away fastballs and sliders. However, they can be dangerous and inside out a fastball middle in. Good lesson learned, and I used that tip for the rest of my playing days.

When we would watch games on TV, it was easier to see these quirks or problems in a player's swing. I remember watching a lot of TV games with my grandpa in the early 80's as he decided not to travel as much if the Dodger games were televised. He could sit in his La-Z-Boy recliner and pick apart the swings of every batter, Dodger players included. He would comment on how to pitch each batter and would get fired up when the Dodger catchers didn't recognize the holes in the opposing batters' swings. Plus he had advance scouting reports for the pitchers and catchers to study.

When I was a kid, I thought the players were PERFECT. I had no idea that even major leaguers had problems with their swings, but my grandpa proved to me that they were humans too. They had to work hard every day to maintain their hand-eye coordination and the proper approach to hitting. Of course, baseball is so mental it's important to recognize routines and quirks when an opposing batter steps up to hit—and that's how I became really good at calling a game.

By the time I was in pro ball, I was being judged just as much by how I called a game as by how I played the game. Pitchers would often tell my managers that they wanted ME to catch them because they knew that I would get batters out any way possible.

Keep in mind, these were still pro batters who had made it as far as they had for a reason. Despite the glaring holes in some of their swings, the pitcher still needed to deliver the pitch I called in the location I called or the batter would crush it.

Watching for holes in a batter's swing was the first step in setting up a plan of attack but some opposing batters would still get hits so I'd have to go to "Level 2" and mentally jack with him. I would do every single thing I could to get into the batters head, and sometimes I had to get creative. I would try to get a laugh from the super intense guys or I wouldn't say anything to the guys who liked to talk and joke, just to get them out of their routine.

Executing a rundown between home and third.

Another way to get in guys' heads was the deceptive shake off. This is when I would flash a sign intended for the pitcher to shake off simply to get the batter to question himself. If the count was 2-1, for example, a lot of batters would sit on a fastball. But when a pitcher shakes off three signs, the batter starts thinking, "Hey maybe he's going to throw a slider, or maybe a changeup," and I had him.

I remember one batter who LOVED the batter's box to be completely clean, no spike marks or anything. It was a quirk bordering on an osbsession—so I used it to my advantage.

If this batter hit a little foul ball that could be fair of foul and he had run down the line, I took the opportunity to make dozens of spike marks in his ultra-clean batter's box. It was like throwing a bag of trash onto a neat freak's living room floor. The guy FREAKED OUT, and I knew I had gotten inside his head. My intentional defacement of HIS batter's box continued when he stepped out of the box to get a sign I would walk into his box and yell to the infield the number of outs, then take a knee in HIS box to adjust my shin guards, all in an effort to get him out of his routine.

There was another guy who played for the Cubs who hated when ANYONE touched his bat. I found out about this quirk from a guy on his team when we were hanging out after a game. When this guy batted, I would ALWAYS pick up his bat after a foul ball and hand it to him. He would then drop the bat and pick it up himself, thinking my bad luck touch would be erased. But instead it just messed with his brain.

One time in 1989 I took this tactic to the extreme. I was catching in the Cal League for the Mariner's Class A affiliate in San Bernardino and we were playing the Bakersfield Dodgers featuring future star, Eric Karros.

I knew Karros well as we roomed together in Alaska one summer and we also played dozens of games against each other when I was at USC and he was at UCLA. In fact, he and his buddies would meet up with us at USC on Thursday nights to party and we'd go to Westwood on Friday. They introduced me to sushi.

But on the field, my job was to get him out any way I could.

Eric had a long swing, and if the pitcher could get a hard sinker or fastball on the inner third of the plate, Karros couldn't extend those big arms. But that's easier said than done and he was crushing us one series, so I had to take drastic measures. I told him what pitches were coming!

I literally said to him when he stepped up to hit, "EK, you are killing us, so I might as well just tell you what's coming. OK here comes a fastball low and away." He said, "Campy, shut-up man, I'm trying to hit." So I said, "No really, fastball low and away" as the pitcher was winding up. I knew he would question if I was telling him the truth or if I was messing with him. But I never once lied, and he NEVER got a hit when I told him exactly what was coming!

In the bottom of the ninth with a chance to win the game, Karros stepped up and immediately said, "Come on Campy, just let me hit!" So I shot back, "OK, here is, a get-it-over slider for your first pitch," and he watched it go by for strike one. Then I said, "Watch your lips, gonna bust you inside on this pitch," and he took a mighty swing but missed for strike two. Meanwhile, the umpire was cracking up as I had told him earlier what I was doing. Finally, with the count 1-2 and the game on the line, I told Karros a slider was coming. He glanced back at me like "You Dick" and flew out to right field to end the game.

As we were celebrating the victory on the field, Karros ran by and yelled, "F**k you Campy!!!" Words said in the heat of the moment. But the next day we went to a matinee showing of a new baseball movie that had just come out called "Field of Dreams," and all was forgiven.

Some of this stuff didn't always work and I'm sure I was drilled a few times over the years for being a prick but it was part of my overall catching skill set, and I think it kept me in a uniform for a few extra years.

When I started coaching my boys in little league, I couldn't help but steal the other team's signs, watch the catcher set up differently for a fastball or a curve, see the pitcher tip off his pitches, see huge holes in opposing batters' swings and know how to exploit them. But my biggest lesson in my life coaching kids was learning how to put away the nasty, hyper-competitive side of me and just let the young kids have fun and play the wonderful game of baseball. That said, when they reach high school, it's time to pull out that old bag of dirty tricks and win!

The Art of Stealing Signs

My dad coached me when I was young and taught me the art of stealing signs, pitches, and how to communicate the information to the rest of the team.

I remember when I was 10 or 11, a few pitchers started to throw curve balls. That was something new to me and I would chase bad curves in the dirt.

After striking out against this one pitcher, my dad walked over and said, "Do you want to know what pitch is coming?" I said, "How do you know what he's going to throw?"

He then showed me a little trick that held up through pro ball.

When some pitchers are in the wind up they tend to hold the ball in their throwing hand behind their back or leg. When they do that they are forced to bring the ball into their glove at some point. When that throwing hand holding the ball goes to the glove, MANY pitchers tip the pitch. How?

When they begin the wind-up they literally show you either the fingers on top of the ball or on the side of the ball. It's a subconscious thing based on the different grip for the different pitches. When their fingers are on TOP of the ball, it's a fastball. When on the SIDE, it's a curve or slider.

I will tell you that knowing what's coming makes hitting so much easier.

Another way my dad taught me to steal pitches was from the catcher. In little league and even high school, some catchers would flash the signs so either our first base or third base coach could see them. Then we would have a verbal cue like first name fastball, last name curveball. I'd listen for the coach to yell "OK, Campanis, line drive here" or "Come on, Jimmy, base hit."

I was converted to a catcher at USC and one of the first games I started as a freshman was on the old Prime Ticket TV Network. It was against UC Santa Barbara.

That game was fun. I threw out my first college runner and hit an RBI double to score the go ahead run in the 8th inning.

But the next day, at practice, the USC coaches called me into their office. Coach Dedeaux said "Tiger, we were lucky to win last night thanks to your clutch hit, but I just learned that the UCSB team knew what pitches were coming." I asked how they figured it out. Did they use the TV monitors to steal the signs? No, he replied. They were picking them up off of ME!

It turns out, after I gave the pitcher the sign I stepped with my left foot first for fastballs and my right foot first for curves. The UCSB coaches picked up on this and relayed the signs to the hitter somehow. I forever changed the way I set up after hearing that.

Fast forward a couple of years, and I was now facing future major leaguer, Scott Erickson, in the California League, where he was pitching for Visalia. That's when our shortstop, Bryan King, noticed that he had a tic that tipped his pitches.

Erickson would do this tic in the wind up AND out of the stretch. It was subtle, but prior to throwing EVERY pitch he would straighten the pointer finger that stuck out of his glove for a fastball or squeeze his pointer finger down for a slider.

Facing a really tough guy but knowing what was coming was AWESOME! I had 3 hits and hit the ball hard every at bat. Erickson quickly made it to the big leagues so I called and left a message for Tino Martinez about the "Erickson finger tip off." The Mariners pounded him that series. Eventually he became aware of the problem and stopped tipping his pitches after his rookie season.

During one of my Big League Camp Spring Training games we were playing the Giants and I was catching. I started hearing Dusty Baker yelling first name/last name to the batters and I figured out that he was calling LOCATION, not pitch, based on where I was setting set up.

I remember a foul ball went near their dugout and I ran over by him chasing the ball and said, "Dusty, c'mon man, stop relaying location to the batters!" He grinned at me with a toothpick in his mouth and said, "All right Little Campy." But it was MY fault; I was setting up too early. Watch catchers on TV today. They set up at the very last second for this very reason.

There is a saying in baseball—if you're not cheating, you're not trying. I rest my case.

Home Plate Collisions

I grew up watching catchers like Steve Yeager and Mike Scioscia throw their entire body in front of home plate, even when they didn't have the ball, in order to block it from the runner. That often led to getting blasted by the runner in a massive home plate collision.

As I started catching more and more, I was involved in more plays at the plate, and I started to get run over, too—or runners TRIED to run me over.

When the rules were changed, making it illegal to both block the plate as a catcher and to run over a catcher as a baserunner, I thought it was about time. But I had been guilty of both, blocking the plate and also running over catchers.

The thing about a play at the plate is, if the catcher has the ball, there is very little the runner can do. As a catcher, I could punish a runner who tried to go high and run me over, by jamming my glove with the ball tightly gripped in my right hand directly into their face. This would knock their legs out from underneath them and flip them on their backs. Then I would spin off of the contact like a running back who just escaped a linebacker, allowing me to be in position to throw if needed.

Blocking the plate **with** the ball. This is now illegal!

But on those occasions when it's a bang-bang play at the plate, a catcher is left completely exposed, just like I was when Joe Randa from the Royals plowed me worse than anyone ever had or would again.

We were in a tie game and Randa was on 2nd base with two outs when the batter hit a shot up the middle. Randa had a bowling ball-type body, built like a running back, and had good speed. Our center fielder Darrin Bragg caught the ball and threw a bullet to me at home plate, but it was just to my right. As I caught the ball, Randa just crushed me. I never saw him coming. When I looked to catch the ball, I didn't even have enough time to turn my head before he hit me, and I heard a loud POP. It was my throwing shoulder and it was badly separated. I missed over 60 games and didn't play again that season until the very last game. That shoulder is still messed up and it tells me when it's going to rain by shooting a sharp pain right where the separation occurred.

The new rule definitely makes the game safer, but I'm still adjusting to seeing one of the most exciting plays in baseball turn into yawner of an out.

One thing I can say with complete certainty—head first sliding into home plate is a BAD idea! Even with the new rules, a runner is asking for trouble sliding head first. I recall a few times when a runner tried to sneak in that way.

One time during instructional league a top Cubs prospect tried to score that way on a little grounder to shortstop with the infield in. I caught the ball and saw him diving for the outside corner of the plate. That's when instincts took over and I jumped to block his hand from hitting the plate. Instead, his left shoulder took the blow and I heard and FELT his collarbone break on my shin guard near my knee. I felt horrible, but my catching coach told me I did everything right. The Cubs coaches also let me know that it wasn't my fault; he should not have slid head first into home like that.

Although the rule is set up to protect both catchers and runners, it does take away the most exciting play in baseball—the bang-bang play at the plate. That mentality, however, is barbaric, and reminds me of what the Romans must have demanded from the gladiators to entertain them. I suppose it is time for me to evolve and favor this rule, but it's tough when I see a runner who is able to hook slide home past the catcher these days, when before he would have had no chance.

The Hardest Throwing Pitchers I Caught

Catching is a skill that takes years to develop, but I was thrown right into a crash course at USC. The first thing you deal with is catching the FASTBALL. It's relatively easy to catch the other pitches, but when a guy can crank it up into the mid 90's, you'd better be ready! At that speed the ball gets LOUD as it cuts through the air and makes a huge BOOM when you catch it perfectly in the pocket of the glove.

My freshman year, I caught some of USC's upperclassmen when I first was converted, and was getting used to catching some serious cheddar from pitchers like first rounder Brad Brink and third rounder Steve Bast. But I didn't catch much that season in games.

My sophomore year we had a catcher who was really good on defense. He could block balls with the best of them and had this keen ability to recognize the pitch early and get his body in front of the ball. That was the hardest thing for me to learn—seeing the pitch that would not reach me in the air and getting ready to block it with ANYTHING, including my bare hand if need be.

That catcher's name was Brian Nichols. But he did something very few players have ever done. He was also our CLOSER!

I was the starting first baseman that season, but when we were leading by less than three runs, Nichols would take off the gear and pitch!

When the switch was made, I ran into the dugout, strapped on the "tools of intelligence," and ran out to warm up Nick-dog, who threw about 95 that season!

Our team didn't offer Brian many save opportunities, but he ended up leading the conference and earning All-American honors that season. Unfortunately, he blew out his shoulder and only played one season of pro ball before hanging it up.

When I played for Team USA I was introduced to some SERIOUS pitching. We had 5 or 6 guys bringing it in the mid 90's. The tough part of catching a ball that fast is its late movement. Late movement occurs when the pitcher has the ability to over-pronate upon his release. That causes the rotation of the ball to have a slight angle, so when it catches the air, it sinks. If you are not prepared for the late sink, your thumb gets pounded.

The Team USA guys had BIG TIME late movement. Especially Ben McDonald, Jim Abbott, and Andy Benes. They could bring it, and also had excellent breaking pitches to back up their heat.

People often ask who was the hardest throwing pitcher that I ever caught. There are a few. Catching these guys was a thrill, and also painful! They would blew up my left hand, handcuff me, short hop me, not to mention causing 100 MPH foul tips off every part of my body. But I loved catching and it was the price I had to pay to play.

1. **Roger Salkeld**: When I first caught Roger, he was a young pup just a couple years out of high school in Double A Jacksonville. He was the first pitcher I caught who had a legit fastball in the HIGH 90's. In fact, I have a photo somewhere of Roger's follow through as the hitter swung and missed while I caught it, taken from behind a speed gun that registered 100 MPH. Roger should've been called up that season, but in the Mariners' infinite wisdom, they didn't. Then Roger had shoulder problems and a surgery. He pitched a couple of years with the Mariners and was traded to the Reds.

2. **Jim Converse:** Jim was a little dude by pitcher standards. He was just 5'9" and weighed 180 lbs. But somehow he could throw a ball through a brick wall! I caught him in Double A Jacksonville as a starter. He threw every fifth game, and like Salkeld, had this late movement that punished my left hand. But Converse was the one and only pitcher to punish me in the worst way possible. One game in Huntsville, he was absolutely dealing. He would start a guy off with a slow curve for strike, then pound a 95 MPH fastball on the corner, then another one just off the corner that I could steal occasionally from the umpire. I got so confident in his control that game, I got cocky and went into what I called the "Tony Pena Stance." That's where I would straighten out my right leg and sit on the ground with my left leg bent like a hurdler running track. This gave Jim a super low target and allowed the umpire to see the corner I was trying to hit much easier. Jim was cruising into the late innings when I called a 1-2 fastball on the outside corner to a right-handed hitter and assumed the Pena Stance. But this time Jimmy's control was just a bit off; the ball had more sink on it that usual. As I saw the sink, I went to pick it with my glove like a first baseman, but the dirt on the field was loaded with a product called "Diamond Dry" to dry it up from recent rains. The ball did NOT bounce up like it should have and I completely missed it with my glove. That 95 MPH fastball hit me square in the cup—and CRACKED it! Yes…I was in some serious, serious, serious pain! But instead of laying there and delaying the game while the trainer pulled on my belt buckle or whatever he would do in that situation, I limped off the field and straight into the training room. I was given a bag of ice and looked at the trainer like, "Are you serious?" He said, "I'm not gonna do it!" My cajones swelled up so much they were smooth like a damn cue ball so the trainer

insisted I ultrasound my junk at the hotel that night. That was more painful than the ICE was! I had to miss the next game, due to SWELLING! Jim was called up to the Mariners soon after that and had a nice career pitching for Seattle and Kansas City.

3. **Roberto Hernandez:** In 1992 I was sent to Puerto Rico and caught the White Sox closer Roberto Hernandez quite frequently. He consistently threw harder than any pitcher I ever caught. Granted, others were usually starters like Salkeld, Converse, and even Randy Johnson, but Roberto had the luxury of throwing one inning a few times a week so he ALWAYS had gas in his tank. One thing about catching him was that I took so many foul tips off my head when he pitched. It was like my head was a freakin' ball magnet. I started to wonder why and I came to this conclusion. His ball appeared to RISE when the hitter saw it, so batters hit under the ball more than they didn't. Often times, when the batter just barely tipped the ball off Hernandez, you could smell burning wood from the bat grazing the ball. Now that's serious HEAT! Roberto lived off of this visual deception and it served him well for many, many successful years in the big leagues. But I saw the lights go off when a ball crushed my mask every time he pitched!

Today, it seems EVERY pitcher is throwing 95 MPH. I believe the radar guns are to blame. However, there are a few who are legendary already, including the closer, Aroldis Chapman, who has hit 105 MPH on the new guns. That would still be over 100 on the older guns.

My dad used to tell me that hitters can tee off on anyone's fastball if they are looking for it. It's true, batters gear up for 95 MPH and if the pitch is low in the zone can catch up and hit BOMBS.

But when a pitcher can get up there closer to 100 MPH, they are damn near unhittable.

Foreign Substances

Over the years, stories come out about pitchers getting caught with some kind of foreign substance on them.

As a former catcher, I can tell you that pitchers who cheat get caught about 1% of the time. The rest of the time their subtle movements allow them to load up and the umps are clueless.

For example, I caught this one pitcher who used to slick his hair back with tons of gel. By the time he had warmed up in the bullpen and threw his five warm up pitches he was sweating.

Right before his first pitch, he would casually take his hat off and hand brush his hair back with his throwing hand. The gel and sweat was a good combination that added grip and this pitcher felt it improved his curveball.

Other pitchers (many) asked me to put pine tar in the pocket of my catcher's glove. As a pitch was caught, the ball would make contact with the sticky pine tar. When I threw the ball back, they could feel the sticky area and would be ready for the next pitch. This was the only time I was left holding the bag so to speak and there was a chance the ump could hear the ball stick to the pine tar when I pulled it out of the glove and I'd be busted. For this reason, I didn't like the pine tag in my pocket, so I would load up the thumb side of the glove and rub the ball on it when I threw it back to the pitcher.

On the other side of foreign substance pitching were the slippery guys. They didn't want grip but rather slip.

If you remember, as a kid you probably took watermelon seeds and pinched them between your fingers. You could shoot them out pretty far. That's how these pitchers threw what is called a "spitball." However, what will surprise many baseball fans' is spit is NOT the fluid of choice for spitballers.

I only caught five or six guys that relied on this type of pitch but here's how they got away with it.

1. Vasoline/KY jelly – The pitcher would put a healthy amount of their favorite jelly way down below the cup area where it "taint" gonna be checked, if you know what I mean. After delivering a pitch, these guys knew if they needed to load up a spitball so they would follow through their motion and grab a little of the slippery stuff when everyone was watching the flight of the ball.
2. Snot – This was gross but very effective. The pitcher would shove jalapeno juice up his nose right before he went out on the mound. Some guys ate one on the way to the mound. As you know, jalapenos make your nose run like crazy. So these pitchers would shoot a snot rocket into their glove when no one was looking and use the slippery snot to squeeze out the spitball.

A good spitball is hard to control, catch, or hit. The late drop and almost knuckleball movement is wicked as the pitch was thrown hard like a fastball.

I don't think pitchers will ever stop trying to get that advantage of grip or slip until there is a major investigation and fines/suspensions are increased.

In my informed opinion, a lot of the benefit for guys who did this was psychological. The extra grip or slip gave them more confidence, but didn't necessarily make their pitches any nastier. Well, except that one guy's snotball!

Jacked Up Left Hand

When I started catching full time in college, I quickly realized that my catching hand was being severely abused every day. Not to mention my knees, ankles, and back!

Catchers' gloves are designed with a very small area to catch the ball known, of course, as the "pocket." This small pocket design means that if you are even an inch off, the ball pounds your hand or index finger, or jams your thumb.

To this day, I have not found a pad sufficient to absorb the punishment a 95 MPH fastball can unleash onto your left hand. Some pads worked for a few games, but most just got in the way.

After catching a three-game weekend series in college, my left-hand index finger would be so swollen my finger prints were gone! It didn't hurt in the heat of the game, but it sure throbbed afterwards.

When I got to pro ball, the pitchers threw a lot harder. I remember my first season in San Bernardino, we drafted this young buck out of Wichita State, Jim Newlin, who threw the HEAVIEST ball I had ever caught. A "heavy" ball is a term used when describing how it feels to catch (and hit) certain pitchers. The heavy comes from late movement—and it HURTS! Newly was throwing so hard that year that he actually knocked me out of a game. I thought he broke my hand it swelled up so bad. I still have calcium deposits in that area!

In 1990, I was catching in the Carolina League when our pitcher threw an outside sinker to JT Snow who was batting left-handed. He swung and foul tipped the ball off the pinkie area of my left hand and all of sudden this

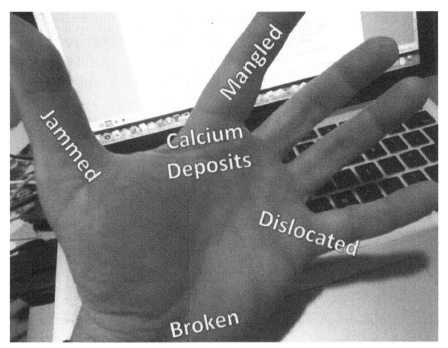

Paying the price of catching.

burning sensation hit me. I pulled my hand out of the glove and realized my pinkie knuckle was completely dislocated! I slapped my hand on my leg a couple of times to set it back, but it kept dislocating the rest of the game so I had to go on the DL while it healed.

I caught 1,000+ games over the years and for all the damage to my body that came from the job, my left hand shows it the most. I haven't even mentioned the other nagging injuries associated with catching. My throwing arm was constantly in need of care. I had a sweatshirt I wore even in the heat of the summer that covered just my right arm to keep it warm. My wife thought I was crazy but it really helped!

Plus, my ankles were a mess, my left knee barked, and I needed chiropractic care every couple of weeks just to be ready to play. All of these ailments for a guy in his early 20's! You can always tell the old catchers at the Old Timers Games or reunions as they hobble up to say hello.

With all that complaining out of the way, I'll add that I consider catchers to be the smartest guys in the game. But there is no denying there is a good reason the equipment we strapped every day to play is called the "tools of ignorance," because even after we are done playing, we continue to pay the price.

Sliders—For Better or Worse

Let me tell you about my favorite pitch to call when I was catching and my least favorite pitch to hit as a batter…the SLIDER.

Like many decent players, I pitched in Little League and a bit in High School. I quickly realized that if you can throw a curveball for a strike, you will be successful. But if you can throw a slider for a strike, you will be NASTY.

Here's the baseball definition of the slider. It's a pitch that when released is spun like throwing a football spiral. A properly thrown slider will have a red dot right in the middle of the ball from the spinning laces. That's the cue when hitting to recognize the pitch being a slider…that red dot. A curveball is spun differently. Whereas a slider is spun sideways, a curve is spun from top to bottom, or as we call them, a 12-to-6 curve. The 12 and 6 represent their positions on a clock so a 12-to-6 curve spins vertically and drops down. The slider is thrown harder and cuts just a few inches. That faster speed and late break make it difficult to recognize and hit hard. That's why so many pitchers throw a slider.

I remember my grandpa talking to me about the slider. He had a rule with the Dodgers back then. NO ONE was to be taught a slider! Can you imagine? If a player was traded to the Dodgers and had a slider, it was allowed. But for newly drafted players, they had to ditch the slider or the Dodgers would not play them.

Why did they do this? The slider is the #1 reason pitchers got hurt then and it's the same today.

The slider puts so much stress on the UCL ligament in the elbow, it is responsible for countless Tommy John surgeries along with painful tendonitis.

My old friend and former roommate at USC, the legendary Dave "Lats" Latter, had one of the best sliders I ever caught. He also had control of the pitch and would sometimes throw it five times in a row.

As Lats progressed, he started to learn a sinker to compliment his slider. Scouts would watch him pitch and were not impressed by his radar gun speed. His sinker came in at about 88 MPH. But as a catcher, he was bitch to catch. The ball was always running one way or another and it was HEAVY from the late movement.

Lats snapping off his nasty slider at USC.

Lats was drafted by the A's and surprised everyone with his rapid rise through the ranks. He was living off that sinker/slider combination and was becoming a major league caliber set-up man when disaster struck—torn UCL in his pitching elbow.

He spent over a year rehabbing the elbow and staying in shape. The A's gave him very little opportunity to come back. During the time off, the A's found new pitchers to fill the void left by Lats, and he was released before he could really get it going again.

To Lats' credit, he persevered and played another three seasons in the Independent Pro Leagues, tossing hundreds of innings after the TJ surgery, but he never made it back to where he was before the injury.

Lats' story is not very different from the dozens of pitchers you've heard of who had TJ surgery. Why are there so many Tommy John surgeries these days? The SLIDER! EVERYONE is throwing harder than in years past PLUS throwing a hard slider that puts enormous strain on the elbow.

Occasionally a pitcher will throw for years with no elbow problems despite snapping off a nasty slider, but that's a rare bird.

The only other pitch that even comes close to ending so many careers are the deceptive ones like the changeup and split fingers. Both of those pitches, if not properly thrown, will tear a UCL just as quick as throwing hard sliders. Ask Stephen Strasberg how he blew out his elbow and he'll say changeups.

The reality is, pitchers have NEVER been getting injured as much as they are today. I believe it's the combination of stronger bodies delivering considerably more torque to the small ligaments in the elbow. Although the rate of pitchers recovering and returning to the majors is high, most never regain the same stuff they had before. Some pitchers blow the elbow out AGAIN and find another ligament to sew in there, like the Beardman, Brian Wilson.

I've heard people say that MLB should go back in time to when UCL injuries were at a minimum and figure out why. I bet you'll go back to a time when most pitchers threw a four-seam STRAIGHT fastball, a 12-to-6 curve, and a circle changeup. But would those types of pitchers have a chance in this super competitive world of pitching when it seems everyone is throwing 97 MPH with a wicked slider?

A new generation of baseball training and conditioning specialists like Bill LeSuer are addressing this problem before it happens. Bill is a flexibility coach and has had great success in limiting the number of UCL injuries using his proprietary flexibility palpation techniques...and he is booked SOLID.

I'm afraid pitching today is a double edged sword: Throw hard with a wicked slider and make it for a couple of years before TJ surgery, or throw straight fastballs with a curve and never even get a shot at playing pro ball. You know what most pitchers would choose. So I believe UCL tears and Tommy John surgeries will continue to be rampant. I simply don't see an end in sight to this problem.

Catching a No-No

One of my baseball dreams came true on June 16th, 1990. I caught a NO HITTER! As a catcher, you dream of few things like jumping into the stands to catch a foul ball, diving to catch a foul bunt, throwing a guy out on your knees...and catching a no hitter. I had already done all of those, EXCEPT the no hitter, going into my second year of pro baseball.

In 1990, I was sent to the Carolina League to play for the Peninsula Pilots in Newport News, VA. It was old park, so old, in fact, my Grandpa Al had managed one of the first teams in that stadium nearly 50 years earlier. The drab stadium was home to our drab team, and in the early part of the season it was fitting.

Thru June, we had the WORST record in all of pro baseball. I was hitting under .200 and it was downright miserable to come to the field every day. We had a great group of guys but we simply didn't have the firepower needed to win.

As the second half started, the Mariners sent down a few pitchers, including future Yankee great Jeff Nelson, and also sent us a recent draft pick out of USC named Bret Boone.

Immediately, these players started making an impact and helped our team gain confidence, especially one of our starting pitchers named Rick "Bally" Balabon. Bally was originally drafted in the first round by the Yankees and was involved in the trade with Jay Buhner coming to the Mariners in 1989. I had caught Bally the year before but he had had arm problems most of that season.

On this day in 1990, we were playing the Frederick Keys (A Ball affiliate of the Orioles) featuring future major leaguers Pete Rose, Jr. and Ricky Gutierrez. They were leading the Carolina League's Northern Division at the time.

Bally was not a specimen. He had a normal build at about 6'2", 180. I never saw him in high school but he told me he hit 96 MPH on the gun. Then, in his second season with the Yankees, he hurt his shoulder and had to have it scoped. He was struggling to return to the same form that he had before and was getting knocked around as a result. He couldn't just blow the ball by hitters anymore. He needed to learn how to "pitch".

We talked before the game about working location. I was emphasizing location because his velocity was still under 90 MPH and hitters would tee off on him when he left it over the plate. He also had a curveball and changeup, but no slider. I had limited pitches to work with so Bally really needed to hit his spots.

As the game began, I noticed that he was really in command of his fastball. I would call a low and away fastball to a right-handed hitter and Bally was painting the corner. Occasionally, I would call for a high fastball to get batters to chase, but that day, his killer pitch was his curveball. I must have caught Bally 20 times and his curve was never so wicked.

After an inning or so, he was in a groove and we both were mentally clicking on the pitch selection. I remember Ricky Gutierrez batting, who was an outstanding fastball hitter. We started him off with a low and away fastball for a strike, then another that Ricky fouled off, then a waste pitch up and in, and finally Ricky chased a curve in the dirt for strike three. That became the formula for the rest of the game. It worked, and we were getting player after player out.

Around the 5th inning Bally was cruising—two fastballs on the corner, a brush back pitch then the hammer.

Of course, to throw a no hitter, you need to be LUCKY! And Bally must have been living right as our defense made play after play to keep the no-no alive. One play, there was a soft grounder hit to third but the throw was off line. But first baseman Lem Pilkington came off the bag to tag the runner and keep the no-hitter alive. Later Bally made a mistake and the batter crushed a ball to center field, but Jesus Tavares ran it down making a diving catch. But the one play that saved the no-no was a great backhand play at shortstop by Bobby Holley who quickly planted and fired a strike to first, just getting the runner by a half step.

Bally was throwing a PERFECT game until he walked the lead off hitter in the 7th. Then he struck out the next batter and I threw out the runner trying to steal for a strike 'em out, throw 'em out double play.

On offense, we were getting our hits but not scoring so going into the later innings, it was a 0-0 game until we rallied to go ahead 4-0. During our half-hour rally, Bally went to the very end of the dugout and sat all alone. He didn't want to hear ANYTHING about a no hitter. As you know, that is a major baseball superstition still in play today.

When Bally went out for the last inning, he knew it all came down to these last three outs. Since our formula was working so well and he had not lost any velocity or snap on his curve, I kept it going. Fastballs away, waste pitch up and in, then curve in the dirt.

You could cut the tension with a knife.

As the catcher, I felt even more pressure and tried to not out think myself, but I worried the hitters would start guessing location or pitch based on my pitch pattern. I also knew Bally was aware of the no-no so I had to be confident and continue to pump him up and keep him focused.

Any catcher can tell you, there are times when you wish you could have stuck you glove out for catcher's interference instead of letting the batter get a hit. This was one of those times as I squatted down to give Bally the sign.

Out of desperation, the Frederick team was intentionally trying to get into Bally's head saying things like, "Come on guys, no way this guy throws a no-no against us!" But to Bally's credit, he kept his composure.

Appropriately, Bally went 0-2 to the last batter. I called for a curve in the dirt, but instead, he placed it perfectly on the outside corner for a called strike three. Bally had just thrown his first no hitter and I had caught mine!

After the final out, we mobbed Bally like we had just won the World Series! It was pandemonium. We really needed this to boost our spirits after the tough season we'd had so far. The GM of Frederick was so impressed by the no-hitter, he brought bottles of champagne into our clubhouse for the celebration.

Unfortunately, Bally's arm problems continued to plague him and by the end of the next season in Double A, he was out of baseball. Another promising career cut short due to injury.

I caught several hundred more games after that one and came close to catching more no-hitters, but so many things have to go right for it to happen, just like that night in June of 1990 when all of Rick Balabon's planets lined up and he threw the game of life. And no one can ever take that away from him...or me!

Mound Meetings

One of my favorite scenes in one of my favorite movies is the meeting on the mound with the pitching coach in Bull Durham. That scene went something like this:

The players are deep in discussion and Larry the pitching coach runs out to the mound to see what's going on. "Excuse me, what's going on here," he asks. It turns out they're talking about everything BUT the game – getting a live rooster, grappling with finding the right wedding present, etc. Rather than blow up at the players, Larry rattles off solutions to everyone's problems, pats them on the rump, and says "Let's get two!"

There are legitimate reasons for catchers to visit the pitcher on the mound during the course of a game. Typically, I'd run out there if the manager asked me to stall while a relief pitcher needed more time to warm up. Also, I'd run out to make sure we had our signs straight with a runner on second base. But I was really good at knowing when to visit the mound during the heat of battle.

I've come to the conclusion that there are basically two types of pitchers, those who are super intense and laser-focused, and those scared shitless. Sometimes, the same pitcher is BOTH guys throughout the course of a game, and as a catcher, it was my job to keep the pitcher in the best mental frame of mind.

I remember catching my old friend, the late Kevin Foster. He was a fairly quiet guy with a tremendous work ethic. The Mariners picked up Kevin in a trade from the Phillies and he was sent to Jacksonville to join our staff. When I caught him in the bullpen, I was impressed. He threw hard with a nice changeup, could hit his spots and had a hard 12-to-6 curveball.

I was just getting to know him so I wasn't sure how he reacted to the stress of a game yet...but I was going to find out. The first game I caught Kevin he was getting hit around pretty good in the early innings so I ran out to the mound to give him a chance to relax for a minute.

When I got out there, he said, "What do you want? Get back there and call the game!" I was taken aback. He had been such a nice guy to me since his arrival. Then it dawned on me, he was one of those "super-competitor" types. He completely transformed when he hit the mound and became ultra-focused on getting outs.

It was at that moment that I spontaneously said, "Kev, just wanted to let you know that there's a super hot chick in row 5 just to the right of home plate. See her?" He looked at me with this scowl. Then it turned to the biggest grin in the world. He knew I was there to calm him down and distract him for a moment so he could regroup.

I used a similar tactic with Kevin anytime he was a bit too intense to pitch effectively. One time I ran out to calm Kevin down and said, "Hey, where do you want to grab dinner after the game? There's an Applebee's by the hotel. If you get this guy out, first beer is on me!" Kevin was getting used to my ploy but it was working.

Truth be told, most of the time I was a cheerleader. By that I mean my job was to either instill confidence in the pitcher or fear...or both.

As I said, EVERY pitcher gets into trouble. It's how they reacted to the stress that mattered to me. I could literally see the fear in the eyes of tired pitchers who knew they were not at 100%. So I would run out there and hit them with a little pep talk. I'd say things like, "You're throwing great, focus on the glove and hit the spots. You can do this...come on! Get us out of this jam!" Many times, this pep talk helped to get us out of an inning.

In extreme cases I had to get hard-core. I'd say, "Come on you f**king pussy, pull your tampon out and give me your best shit. You're throwing like a f**king girl! What would your dad say if he saw this performance? Huh? He would be embarrassed to call you his son!" This worked very well and snapped a scared pitcher out of his shell, probably because he wanted to kill me after what I screamed at him. You can't use this tactic on every guy, only the ones that you know needed a bit of negative reinforcement to give them a boost.

Although most of our mound meetings were about mundane baseball strategies like bunt defense assignments or first and third plays, other times I was like a sports psychologist trying to evoke the best performance from that pitcher at that given moment. I've had many pitchers come up to me after the game to thank me for keeping their head together or calming them down during a critical inning. To me, those were some of the most satisfying moments in my career—helping a pitcher through tough times. This didn't end up in my box score or on a report my manager sent to the major league club. But in the big picture, it was more important than getting three hits and knocking in a few runs.

7
Great Players, Great Guys

It blows my mind to think that I played with or against several Hall of Famers. But whether they were famous or not so famous, there's no question one of the best parts of being a ballplayer is the people I met, the great times we had together, and the friendships we made, many of which are going strong to this day.

Ken Griffey Jr.

Over the years I learned that I am a horrible gambler—the hard way.

One of my first roommates in pro ball was Ken Griffey Jr. He was the first pick in the draft just one year earlier and was just 18 years old at the time. He and I became very competitive. Whether it was video games or football, we liked to make bets with each other. I think this competitive thing was fueled by the fact that we both came from baseball families. I didn't back down to his taunting or his posturing so naturally, he tested me.

One day during Instructional Fall League, he bet me $50 he could hit more home runs in batting practice to left field, which was my power field, than I could. I jumped on the chance to make $50 the easy way!

We each took our 10 swings and then rotated two more times, 30 swings total. I hit a few in the first round and felt like he would have to put on a show hitting all his homers to left field only. By this time, a crowd of coaches and players had gathered around to watch our little contest. Well, it wasn't even close. He hit like 15 out of 30 way out of a HUGE spring training practice field, all to LEFT!!!

After batting practice ended I had to go the bullpen and catch several pitchers. There were Mariner scouts in the bullpen with radar guns that day as they were clocking some of the new draft picks. Griff had just finished outfield work and was walking by the bullpens when he yelled out that he would bet me another $50 he could throw over 90 MPH on the mound.

The scout aimed his radar gun as Griff reared back and threw. He hit 93 MPH on the first pitch. Damn—another $50!

Finally, practice was nearly over, but we had to condition by running 90-foot wind sprints and walking back to the left field foul line. As we were walking back, he said, "Damn Campy, you are slow as hell. I'll bet you triple or nothing I can beat you running BACKWARDS!"

So after being humiliated by his athleticism and unworldly talent on two other bets, my stubborn thick-headedness got the best of me and I agreed to the race. We had one coach by us to make sure we had a fair start and two coaches at the finish line.

The coach barked out, "One your mark, get set, GO!" and we were off. I took an early lead, but he clicked into another gear, passed me and won by a couple of steps BACKWARDS! Unreal, and I never lived that one down. That day I lost $150 and I only made $90 that WHOLE WEEK!

Even though he was only 18 years old, we all knew Ken Griffey Jr. was destined for greatness. The kind of greatness that only comes around once or twice in a generation.

If you ask any player from the 90's who the best player they ever saw was, most won't even hesitate and blurt out, "Ken Griffey Jr.". I agree 100%

Cesar Cedeno

When I was around 15 I used to go to Dodgers Stadium with my grandpa Al during summer break. When we arrived at the stadium, he would go to his office and I would go down to the clubhouse and strap on a batboy uniform.

I had a bunch of duties assigned to me by the head batboy, who was like 20 so technically he was a bat "man." These duties included getting old game balls and throwing them into a big barrel filled with pink school erasers. Why? The barrel was hooked up to an electric motor and when turned on, it spun the barrel and caused the erasers to literally erase all of the blemishes off of the baseballs. Then I would put all of the whitened baseballs into several bags for batting practice.

Next I had to get all of the stuff the players used on their bats—pine tar, rosin, tape, sticky stick and the donut weights they used to warm up. Next I would help one of the coaches hitting grounders to make sure he always had a ball to hit. Later I would help clear the gear off the field after batting practice and make sure all the bats were in the bat rack.

When game time came we would rotate innings running out to get the bat. Sometimes I would run extra baseballs out to the umpire. All in all it was fun and I loved being that close to the game.

Then, one game one of the main batmen couldn't make it to the game so they assigned me to be the right field ball kid. How cool, I thought!

They told me that I had one main job besides chasing foul balls that ended up on the field. I was going to warm up the right fielder from the visiting team between every inning they were on the field.

This particular game was against the Cincinnati Reds and the right fielder was Cesar Cedeno, who was known for having one of the best throwing arms in the game.

When he came out for the first inning, I threw him the ball, but kind of lobbed it to him. Then he fired back it to me and yelled in broken English "Throw the ball man, let it go!" My next throw was still lame as I was nervous as hell I might throw it over his head. He literally ran in and yelled at me to gun one at him…so I did. He yelled back, "Atta Boy, throw hard again like this!" He took a running start and threw one at least 95 MPH at me.

I had never seen a ball going that fast. It was also the loudest ball I had ever heard as it came whizzing toward me. But as the ball got closer it was clear that it was over my head. I jumped as high as my 15-year-old body could jump, but I just couldn't reach it. As I turned to follow the ball, I realized it was going to make it to the stands in the air and I yelled "Heads up! Heads up!"

This ball traveling in the mid 90's ended up drilling a woman spectator who wasn't paying attention, right in the side of the head. BOOM—she was out like a light. I was mortified! But Cedeno was laughing his ass off and yelled to get another ball. This time I got a running start and fired it as hard as I could. For the rest of the game I threw every ball with 110% of my ability.

Later in the game, as he was running in he stopped to say to me, "Don't ever be timid, understand? When you step on this field, you go all out or go home."

I never forgot that.

Charlie Hough

Growing up around the Dodgers, I was very fortunate to not only meet the players, but I hung out with many of them. One of my all-time favorite people from that era is Charlie Hough. Charlie is one of those charismatic, high energy, jokester kind of guys with an infectious personality. EVERY-ONE who meets him feels the same way.

When I was batboy for the Dodgers in the 70's and 80's, Charlie was throwing his knuckleball—and he kept throwing it until 1994 when he was 46 years old! He pitched 25 years in the big leagues and never broke 85 MPH! My dad and Charlie maintained their friendship even after Charlie went to the Texas Rangers in 1980. They often golf together as they still live near each other.

When I was drafted and signed my pro contract, my dad suggested that we contact Charlie to see if he wanted to work out in the off season. My dad knew Charlie had dozens of balls in his garage and needed to throw to hitters. We went over to Charlie's house to chat about it. I had been there many times. It was like a shrine to Elvis. Elvis booze bottles, Elvis statues, Elvis clothes, Elvis coffee mugs, Elvis Blue Suede Shoes… Elvis EVERYTHING!

Charlie started telling us that he never throws a knuckleball until the week before Spring Training. Before that, he throws nothing but fastballs off the mound. That sounded perfect for batting practice. He suggested I call some of my other buddies to see if they wanted to work out also.

I called old friend, Bret Boone, who had just signed with the Mariners the year before, along with Bob Hamlin, who I played against when he was at UCLA. He had just signed with the Royals. (A few years later Bob earned Rookie of the Year honors in 1994). Charlie liked the fact that there was three of us insuring he could throw a lot of pitches, plus Hamelin was left handed so Charlie was able to practice against batters from both sides of the plate.

Hamelin knew the coach at Santa Ana College and arranged for us to use the field, the batting cage, and the L-screen so Charlie wouldn't get nailed by a line drive. That first workout, we started by playing catch. I noticed Charlie chewing a big wad of Red Man AND smoking a cigarette at the same time. He joked that he needed to kick start the ticker! After warming up we set up the field and Charlie took the mound.

When I got in there to hit, I was absolutely crushing the ball, and so were Booney and Bob. Charlie threw absolutely PERFECT batting practice. We must have hit 40 balls over the fence by the end of the practice and as I started walking around the field to get the home run balls, Charlie yelled to leave them; he wanted to take us to lunch.

We continued working out at Santa Ana College for a few more weeks and he would keep bringing dozens of balls to replace the ones that we lost in the street. The kids who lived near the park must have collected a hundred balls by the time we were done!

Then, as we were getting closer to Spring Training, he asked me to bring all my catchers, gear and catch him throwing a full bullpen. I was so excited. He was going to finally bust out that famous knuckleball! But he didn't! In fact, he only threw a few breaking pitches over the 40-pitch bullpen. Then, on the last two days we were going to work out before camp, he started throwing his signature pitch. And it was WICKED!

He had three types of knucklers. One broke away from a right hander, one broke away from a left hander, and one just floated up there. The way he threw his floater, you could actually read the label on the ball. No spin whatsoever!

Charlie must have thrown 80 of them to me that day. Once in awhile, he would stop pitching, pull out an emery board, and file his fingernails to a point. Every now and then he would throw an absolutely uncatchable knuckler and I used the Bob Uecker technique…wait until it stops rolling then pick it up. I would completely miss some of those dancers with my glove and catch it with a piece of flesh. Pretty embarrassing, but some of those pitches moved at the last split second. He kept telling me to imagine catching a butterfly: Wait until the last second then snare it out of thin air. That worked well.

Charlie always carried a massive catcher's mitt designed to catch knuckleballers. I tried it during my first bullpen with him, but after I figured out the "Snatch the butterfly from the air" technique, my smaller but much lighter glove worked better and I started to consistently catch his nastiness. Afterwards he said to me, "You can catch me…and I don't say that to every catcher." That was a real honor.

Over the course of my career I caught several knuckleball pitchers and even developed a pretty nasty one myself. But nothing even close to the awesome Charlie Hough.

25 years in the majors leagues, 216 wins and 216 losses, 3,701 innings pitched, 2,362 strikeouts, with a respectable career ERA of 3.75. Charlie is the ONLY pitcher to ever start over 400 games AND relieve in over 400 games. I doubt that record will ever be broken.

Remembering Bobby Welch

I remember going into the coach's locker room at Dodgers Stadium one game in 1978 when I was 11 years old to get dressed. I was going to bat boy that night. At that exact moment, Ron Perranoski, the Dodgers' pitching coach was sitting there talking with Mark Cresse, the Dodgers' bullpen coach about the new, young phenom pitcher just called up from the minors named Bobby Welch.

I remember them discussing the issue of Burt Hooten needing to miss a start due to a nagging injury. They felt the rest would help him get back into the groove. Then they started discussing who should replace Hooten as the starter that night.

They kept throwing around ideas like having Rick Rhoden start on three days rest...or relief pitcher Charlie Hough could start that game...maybe Terry Forster? And for some reason, Cresse said, "So what do you think Little Campy? Who should we start tonight instead of Hooten?" I instinctually blurted out, "Start the kid!" They both cracked up.

Then Perranoski said, "Why the kid and not one of the relievers?" I replied back that the hitters on the other team had already faced the relievers but had not faced Welch so he would have an advantage.

To my amazement, they started Bobby Welch that night and I had a front row seat. He went on to start 13 games that season with FOUR complete games as a 21-year-old rookie.

Later that season Bobby and Reggie Jackson went head-to-head in an EPIC battle during the 1978 World Series. I was at the game and you could cut the tension with a knife. Reggie was Mr. October and Welch was a little-known rookie being asked to close a 4-3 World Series game. Welch showed no sign of fear or intimidation. He simply blew away the game's top home run hitter, sealing the victory for the Dodgers.

Unfortunately, even at that young age, Welch was already a functional alcoholic, hiding his addiction as best he could. But now he was under the big league magnifying glass and it wasn't long before people started to talk. My grandpa took a lot of heat protecting Bobby and later Bobby told me how much he loved my grandpa for supporting him through such a tough time in his life.

A year before his passing, I had the pleasure of speaking with Bobby for about 20 minutes at my dad's golf tournament. He told me about his kids, his desire to get back in the game, and how he had never been happier in his own skin. He still had that ultra-competitive streak in him that made him a winner and was damn good golfer as well.

RIP Bobby Welch…your legacy will live on for a long time.

The Merchant of Menace— Mark Merchant

In 1989, I was sent to play for the San Bernardino Spirit in the California League. We had a good group of guys on that team but things were going to get a lot more fun. The Mariners made a trade and were sending us a new player.

That new player was Mark Merchant.

Merch had an interesting backstory. He was selected by the Pittsburgh Pirates out of high school as the #2 pick of the 1987 draft behind Ken Griffey Jr. Players who get drafted that high have ALL the tools and so did Merch—switch hitter with power, great arm, base stealer, and an all out gamer.

Merch and I became friends right away and started rooming on the road. We constantly talked about batting techniques, situational hitting, how to hit certain pitchers, etc. Plus I learned a lot about his stint with the Pirates.

As it turned out, Merch had already suffered several injuries and at only 19 years old was battling to get back to his previous form. All of his injuries could be attributed to the way he played…ALL OUT!

He'd run into walls, dive for line drives, plow over catchers, and constantly put pressure on the other team with his base running. But my favorite Merch move was when he batted. On 2-0 or 3-1 counts he would swing harder than any player I ever saw. Occasionally, he'd even throw in a loud grunt or fall to the ground after a massive hack. That was the only way he knew how to play the game.

I remember he told me that he had slammed into an outfield wall and separated his throwing shoulder the year before with the Pirates and it hadn't healed. From personal experience, I know that is one of the most serious injuries a player can have. I couldn't even comb my hair for 6 months after I separated mine. Merch was determined and kept working to get his throwing arm back to even 80% of what it used to be.

But the thing I remember most talking to Merch late night after games was the extreme pressure he was under having been drafted so high. In fact, in 1989, 19-year old Ken Griffey Jr. made his major league debut while Merch was just getting to A ball. I think Merch knew that I had personal pressure also coming from a baseball family, so he knew I could relate to his situation.

Put yourself into Merch's shoes for a minute: you get touted by EVERY baseball expert as the next Mickey Mantle while still in high school. You are the High School Baseball Player of the Year in the ENTIRE state of Florida. You have Nintendo-type stats your senior year. You are offered scholarships to every school you'd want to attend. You live in a small town that has very little to focus on but YOU. EVERYONE in Oviedo, Florida knows your name and is counting on you to put their small town on the map. Now that's true pressure!

Coincidentally, I roomed with Griffey before I met Merch and knew Griff had similar pressures as well. If you ever met the teenage Griffey you'd know that he hid his insecurities from others behind a giant wall of cockiness. But the difference was that Griff was able to stay healthy as he catapulted to the show.

During that 1989 season, I could sense the pressure starting to affect Merch. Whenever he would get a bit discouraged, I used to try to lighten the moment with a joke or gag. He has an infectious laugh and I could usually shake his funk if my joke was funny enough.

I remember we had a three-game series in Reno and before we even left for our first game, Merch had blown his meal money and maxed out his ATM gambling. After the game, I agreed to buy him dinner at the hotel. When my change came back from the waitress I flipped Merch a dollar bill and told him to go win a million bucks. He put the dollar into the nearest slot machine and hit 7-7-7! He won like $250!

We played on different teams the next year, but by '91 he was an every day player on my AA team in Jacksonville, FL. He was crushing the ball that year, but unfortunately I hit a ground ball to the shortstop and his injury bug bit him again. As he slid in hard to break up the play, he broke his ankle. Another world-class tool had been damaged.

I ran over to see if he was OK with the trainer but it was a nasty break. He said to me writhing in pain, "Camp, this is it. It's over. I'm done as a baseball player." That was the hardest thing for me to watch as a player and a friend. Here's a guy who really LOVED the game who feared that at 22... he was done.

By this time, Griffey was a 3-time MLB All Star.

But to Merch's credit, he kept going. Eventually, he settled in with the Reds organization and had some monster years for them in the minors. But now, Merch was not the young phenom anymore, he was just another really good player trying to make it. He was no longer the "Bonus Baby" who was going to get a million chances to succeed. He now had to hope and pray that a slot opened up in AAA or the big leagues for him to sneak in. And just like my experience late in my career, it simply did not happen. He kept playing for a few more years with the White Sox and KC before playing in Mexico and Independent leagues.

I'm sure he felt like I did toward the end of my career: I can't quit, I haven't made it yet! Then the questions…What else can I do but play baseball? What am I going to do next? How am I going to be able to transition into "Real Life?"

Most challenges are there to teach us, and that's how it was for Merch. Today, he's a successful real estate/appraisal professional along with a high school baseball coach. Interesting note: His former minor league manager, Jim Leyland, gave Merch's first real estate boss a glowing letter of recommendation, and that helped him start his new life in the "Real World."

But I know one thing for sure—Merch is still going ALL OUT!

Jim Henderson

Baseball is a game of failure. The BEST fail 7 out of 10 times, so as a player you are constantly dealing with challenges and adversity. The reason most players reach the elite levels of baseball is not from their God-given abilities but it's their mental fortitude and toughness mixed with a massive competitive streak. Good baseball players are driven to succeed and are hardwired to NEVER give up!

When the game is on the line, the players who are mentally able to cope with the pressure and even THRIVE on it are the ones who make it, not the 3 PM batting practice hitter or the pitcher who has unreal stuff in the bullpen. It's those who perform their best when it matters most.

This trait is not exclusive to the baseball field and MANY of my former teammates have used their work ethic and competitive drive after their careers have ended to become doctors, sports commentators, investment bankers, executives, accountants, business owners and even lawyers. But every now and then, some guys have to deal with an extra amount of adversity in their lives. This is when their true character shines the brightest. Case in point…Jim Henderson.

Jim and I met when I was a junior and he came to USC as a catcher. He was a big dude for a freshman—like 6'3" 210 pounds and had serious pop with that Easton Black Magic. He grew up in the Valley and had played with some of the best players of that area on a summer ball team. His teammates included Jeff Cirillo, Matt Franco, Mike Leiberthal, and more. He excelled his senior year and was drafted in the 33rd round out of Westlake HS by the Brewers. But he chose to go to USC instead.

As a freshmen, Jim came in with a bum elbow that needed surgery about half way through the year, but he kept catching bullpens until he went under the knife.

I remember in '88 we had a 7-day road trip over Spring Break taking us to New Orleans and Mobile. Back then we didn't have laptops or cell phone apps that make writing a term paper easier. We had to punch them out on a Smith-Corona typewriter using Liquid Paper to blot out mistakes. Before Spring Break one of my masochistic professors assigned us a term paper based on a book he wrote. Yes, he made us all buy his book and then use it as the basis of the term paper representing a quarter of our grade for the semester.

By this point in the season in '88 I was already getting quite a bit of attention by the media, agents, and by pro scouts. Nearly every night I got a call from someone interested in my future plans. This attention was quite a distraction to me, but at the same time it completely motivated me to want to continue the success I was having.

Right before our road trip I ran into Jim in the clubhouse. I mentioned that I was going to blow off the term paper and hoped I got drafted and signed. Since he wasn't on the travel team, Jim said, "I'll do your term paper while you're on the road...for $50." I couldn't pull my wallet out fast enough! I gave him the book and he said he'd have it done when I got back.

True to his word, Jim wrote a fantastic 15-page term paper for me and I got my first "A" in that class! A month later I was drafted in the 3rd round by the Seattle Mariners and knew my time at USC was over.

Jim Henderson also had a revelation: He was going to need a fresh start somewhere else to get a chance to play. Jim had a full academic ride AND was a top-notch player so he knew most any college baseball program would want him. He finally identified Arizona State as a perfect place for him to go and he transferred there for what would be his redshirt freshman year in 1989.

Jim started playing every day his sophomore season and began to show the scouts he was pro caliber. He made the All-Regional squad on a really good ASU team featuring future major leaguers Fernando Vina, Mike Kelly, Kevin Higgins, and Eric Helfand.

As the '92 collegiate season was winding down, Jim was getting the attention of scouts, especially former Dodgers' GM, who was then scouting for the Montreal Expos, Kevin Malone. As Jim told me recently, Kevin saw him play about 10 games and Jim hit a home run in 9 of them. Nearly every home run that season was witnessed by Kevin! Naturally, Kevin thought he was scouting the next Johnny Bench and recommended the Expos draft Jim in the upcoming June draft, and they did.

Jim was contacted by Kevin, told of the news, and signed a contract a few days later. The Expos assigned him to Rookie Ball in Jamestown in the New-York-Penn League. They had a few practices, Jim was awarded the starting catching duties, and the season began.

By this time, Jim and I had lost contact with each other as we were both chasing our dreams of becoming major league catchers. On opening day in Jamestown, his Expos team opened at home. Jim was excited to be playing professional baseball and in his debut went 1 for 3 with a double, a walk and drove in 3 runs—a nice start for Jim and the team.

Their trainer was the only guy on the team who had a car and he also knew the area. He invited a group of guys to join him at a local bar to see a killer rock band that night after the first game. The other players including future major league pitcher, Rod Henderson (no relation), rock/paper/scissored to sit in the front seat for the drive over to the bar.

Jim won and buckled up in the front seat for the ride. When they arrived at the bar, a sign on the bar door said the show had been cancelled so they decide to call it a night and go home.

As the Expos trainer drove toward the interstate, a few drops of rain started falling. As they entered the interstate, it was pouring. All of a sudden, the trainer panicked with all of the rain coming down and oversteered the car causing it flip…SEVEN times! Jim was the only person in the car with his seatbelt buckled.

Amazingly, everyone else was thrown from the car and landed safely in the soft, grassy median along the interstate, except for Jim who was strapped in by his seat belt. None of the guys thrown from the car was seriously injured and some even walked away from that horrific crash. But Jim suffered a C3 & C4 compression fracture! He BROKE HIS NECK!

Now Jim was going to have to fight for more than a base hit, more than a win for his team…he was in for the biggest fight of his life.

When he was officially diagnosed at the hospital, he had an incomplete spinal cord injury. The doctor told him it was the worst neck break he had ever seen. The doctor continued to say that the only reason he wasn't a quadriplegic or dead was that Jim had the biggest spinal column he had ever seen. Jim's survival was already a miracle but they still were not sure if he'd ever walk again.

Kevin Malone called Jim at the hospital in complete tears. He felt terrible, not because his prize draft pick was hurt, but because he really cared for Jim as a person. The Expos minor league director also flew into town but it was really for legal reasons. Jim had been injured while being driven by an Expos minor league employee.

Jim started rehabbing in that hospital, and to everyone's surprise, he took his first steps after just four weeks using the parallel bars for assistance. That was a BIG deal for Jim and the doctors were elated at his rapid progress.

At that point, Jim decided he could improve quicker at home with the help of friends and family while in rehab. He hit the pool every morning and the gym in the afternoon to just to be able to walk unassisted once again. Then just six months after the accident, Jim got a letter from the Expos.

The letter was a standard release form—no explanation—no we're sorry our employee did this to you—no concern for his well being as a human. It was just a document discharging him from his employment as a professional baseball player with the Montreal Expos.

As I would have, Jim assumed that the Expos would concede to his worker's comp claim since it involved a team employee. Yet, the Expos decided to contest Jim's injury, and the worker's comp claim was ultimately denied because it was not an official team function. Jim did not receive even ONE PENNY from the Expos for this career-ending injury that wasn't even his fault.

The only thing that the Expos did was not likely the Expos' idea—an autographed bat with words of encouragement from the then starting catcher for the Expos, Gary Carter, who had a heart of gold. Jim really appreciated that gesture from Gary.

Jim was at a crossroads in his life. Just 23 years old and in less than a year went from being a highly touted major league catching prospect to a man struggling to be able to do the basic things he took for granted before.

This is when winners kick it into high gear, and Jim is a winner! He decided he was going to walk again and also was going to be a success in another field where he could use his wit and intelligence. So just as his dad had done, he enrolled in law school while he continued to rehab.

After 3-and-a-half years he surprised everyone by not only graduating from Arizona State Law School but by being able to walk unassisted. He lost some of the mobility in his right arm but he continued to work hard to improve while he set off on a new career as a lawyer.

I was not aware of Jim's accident when it happened, nor did I hear of it until we had reconnected on Facebook a few years ago. It was quite heartbreaking for me to hear what happened and I bet several of our mutual friends may not have heard of the accident until now either. Jim didn't go around advertising his condition, he just kept fighting to improve his health and grow his law firm.

When we met up for lunch the first time I'd seen him in years, he looked great. Sure I noticed that his neck was a bit stiff, but considering what happened to him, he was in excellent shape.

Within minutes I also noticed Jim is still the same wise-ass guy he's always been. He's the smartest guy in the room who uses his sharp wit against helpless fools who try to outdo him. This trait served him well in the clubhouse and has served him even more so as an attorney.

Today, Jim and his dad run a successful law practice in Santa Monica. Jim represents several clients, including off shore gambling entities, and he is constantly traveling the globe on their behalf.

I'm sure he has mentally dissected the events that led up to that fateful night in Jamestown: What if he lost that rock/paper/scissors? What if he told the trainer he was tired and went home? What if he was drafted by ANOTHER team that never would have put him in that situation to begin with? What if? What if?

But Jim is a winner. Winners don't ask what if. They go out and forge a new path. They strive for success and work tirelessly to achieve it.

Today, Arizona State Baseball has a special award for players who have dealt with and conquered tremendous adversity. A recent winner of the Jim Henderson Courage Award was Corey Hahn.

I'm very proud to call Jim Henderson a good personal friend. He has helped me in many ways since our reconnection. He's an inspiration and a constant reminder to keep fighting the good fight even when life is putting me through challenges and adversity.

The Tweaking of Nellie

During the 1990 season I was playing for the Peninsula Pilots in the Carolina League. Around the middle of the season, a pitcher was sent down from AA to join our team.

At the time, he was not doing so well. This stint in A ball might be his last chance if he didn't improve. He threw hard with a really good curve, but threw straight over the top. It was easy for batters to see his release point and his fastball was straight as an arrow.

When he pitched for us, given his stuff, we had high hopes, but he was getting crushed every time out. It was to the point where he started saying things like "I guess I should start looking for another job." Everyone knew he had talent but he just wasn't able to consistently get professional batters out.

After another tough game, this pitcher and I were discussing his pitching mechanics when I said, "Dude, you're 6'4" and throw 90 plus. What if you started stepping directly at right-handed batters and threw side arm? I know that would mess me up as a hitter. What do you got to lose at this point?"

When we arrived at the park the next day, we got dressed and went to the bullpen. His very first sidearm pitch was in the 90s and dropped about 6 inches. It was amazing. Then he did it again, and again. Our pitching coach, Ross Grimsley, came over and started watching. He continued to throw his other pitches side arm, like his curve. Then he threw a slider. I couldn't believe the difference! In baseball terms, "He was WICKED!"

Right away he became our closer—something he had never done before.

His first game was against the Prince Williams Yankees. I knew their shortstop, Dave Silvestri, and warned him as he stepped up to the plate.

"This is not the same guy you faced last week." He said, "Yes it is, I've faced him a bunch of times." I said, "OK, you'll see."

I called for a fastball and it sank 6 inches for a called strike on the outside corner. Silvestri said, "Holy shit Campy, when did he start throwing side arm?" I said, "Today." Then I called a slider and it completely buckled him. Silvestri started laughing because he knew he was overmatched. Another slider and he was out. Silvestri told me after the game it was the most uncomfortable at bat he had had all season!

This pitcher went on to throw something like 16 hitless innings in relief to end the year, then was given an invite to Major League Spring Training, then MADE the Mariners soon after that! All of this within months of being on the bubble of getting released from baseball!

He was later traded from the Mariners to the Yankees to set up Mariano Rivera for many World Championships, before finishing up back with the Mariners. He pitched in nearly 800 games over a 15-year big league career. A great career for a great guy…Jeff Nelson.

Surprise Major Leaguers

There are several players who surprised EVERYONE by even getting drafted let alone having a great major league career. Watching some guys play, like Griffey, it was easy to predict their future Major League stardom. But not these particular guys:

1. In high school, I played American Legion in the summer at CSUF. We were the Fullerton Angels and played against really good teams from the Orange County area. One team was from Edison HS. On that team was a second baseman who was pretty good, but I didn't think he was anything more than an average high school player at the time.

He was one grade behind me, so after I went to USC he was finishing up high school. But my sophomore year, there he was playing for the Cal Bears. I couldn't believe he made the team let alone was starting as a freshman. This guy was never an elite college player statistically speaking. I don't recall him making any All-Pac 10 teams or being invited to play on Team USA which are usually indicators that you are on the rise as a player. He eventually was drafted pretty low, in the 20th round.

Then in my third pro season, there he was AGAIN playing for the Knoxville Blue Jays in Double A. I just kept thinking—this guy is too big and slow for second base—how is he still moving up the ladder? I will give him credit for improving as a hitter—he was clutch when his team needed a big hit. But he just wasn't that impressive to me then.

I lost track of him after '91 until I opened the newspaper and there he was in the Toronto Blue Jays box score. I couldn't believe he was in the Big Leagues at all let alone being only 24 years old. I figured he was called up to fill a roster spot but would be sent back down soon enough.

Well I was wrong. He kept playing and playing and playing…for 17 years. He ended up a 5-time All-Star, National League MVP, and hit more home runs than any other second baseman in baseball HISTORY! That guy was Jeff Kent.

2. Another player who surprised me by not just playing in the Big Leagues but actually becoming a star was a left handed pitcher I caught in the minors. I was sent back to Double A Jacksonville AGAIN in 1993 and he was one of our five starting pitchers. However, he definitely was not our #1 starter at the beginning of that season. I had caught him in the bullpen and his stuff was pretty good, but nowhere near "Randy Johnson" stuff like I had caught earlier at Big League Spring Training.

As the season progressed, I started to notice this guy getting better and more consistent. But what really separated him from the other guys was his competitive drive. When he was on the hill, he was the most intense pitcher I ever caught. His will to win was his secret weapon. I think he believed he could get any batter out at any time. However, sometimes he would get so intense I had to go out and calm him down. I used to try to crack a joke or distract him, but it didn't always work.

That season he finished with a decent ERA throwing about 100 innings but I thought he needed some more years in the minors and would likely end up being a situational pitcher against lefty hitters. But I was sure wrong on this guy.

To my surprise, he was called up the next season at 20 years old and never looked back. He pitched for 16 seasons and became one of the best in the league. He won 22 games with 2.90 ERA in 1999, was an All-Star, and signed a major contract for the Braves in '03. That guy was Mike Hampton.

3. In the fall of my junior year at USC, I started catching a freshman pitcher who was going to be one of our key starters. He threw pretty hard but his curve was WICKED. The problem was, he didn't quite have total control over that pitch so he was working very hard to get better.

One day the pitching coach, Frank Sanchez, asked the pitchers to arrive to practice early for extra conditioning. I was there early also and noticed that the batting cage was set up on the field. Coach Sanchez was going to let the pitchers (who NEVER hit in games) get some swings in, then run all over the field picking up the balls as their workout.

This was comical to me as these guys could throw a ball through a brick wall but couldn't hit the ball out of the infield. Occasionally, one of the pitchers hit a line drive, but just a floater. Until this guy stepped up to the plate.

He had a nice stance but I could tell he was rusty from not hitting since high school. After a while he was in the groove and crushing balls to right center with a nice inside out stroke. He had that natural kind of swing my favorite batters have, like Cabrera, Trout, and Puig.

This pitcher continued to be a starter for us through the '88 season and did pretty well for a freshman. After the season, I was drafted and left to play pro ball while he stayed at USC for another three years. I didn't really follow the team those years so I didn't know how he was doing.

In '91 he was drafted in the 11th round, but NOT as a pitcher, rather as a third baseman. I couldn't believe it! I had never seen him play as a position player; in fact it seemed odd to me that he was a third baseman at all. I just couldn't envision him being anything but a pitcher. But once again I was dead wrong.

He signed with the Brewers at 21 years old and by 24 he made his major league debut at third base. He went on to play in the Big Leagues for 14 years, batting as high as .326 with 115 RBI's! He was a 2-time All Star and was on the Hall of Fame ballot. Did I mention also that he's one of the coolest guys you'll ever meet? That guy is Jeff Cirillo.

I credit these three guys with battling the critics to beat the odds…and proving me wrong!

The "Short Stopper"

From my first high school varsity game until my last pro game was a span of 15 years. I literally grew up playing baseball with the guys on my teams and the guys we played against. I would watch the progress of some of these guys and wonder how in the world they were still playing…like Jeff Kent. So what the hell do I know?

Another guy also really surprised me but in a different way.

This particular guy was my same grade and played shortstop at Savannah HS in the Orange League in Orange County. My school, Valencia HS, was also in the Orange League and I played against him for four years both during the regular season and also summer ball.

Our senior year, I was on second base and asked him during a break in the game if he was being recruited. He told me that he was likely going to go to junior college since we wasn't getting much attention. In summer ball we ran in each other again and he told me he was going to Cypress College that next season.

A couple of years later I ran into him in Tucson where he was playing for the University of Arizona. He was quite good at shortstop and had a cannon. He was also improving as a batter. His older brother was playing shortstop in the big leagues at this point and many thought he had the same tools. He hit .371 in 1988 and was one of the top batters in the conference. He hit better than J.T. Snow that season at U of A!

After the 1989 season I read that he was drafted in the 11th round by the Reds and sent to A Ball. The organization was thinking of converting him to a third baseman or catcher since his arm was so strong, but he wanted to keep playing shortstop like his big brother.

By 1991 our paths crossed once again in Double A. We ran into each other in the outfield in Chattanooga and started catching up. He asked me what I thought about him catching. I said, "Dude, stay away from catcher if at all possible. I'm back there because I HAVE TO or I'd be selling cars by now." He said they were talking about moving him from shortstop since the Reds had some prospects coming up.

The next time we played them we talked some more. He told me that they had decided to make him a pitcher. I couldn't help but laugh out loud and said, "Pitcher? Come on! You didn't even pitch in high school OR college…what are they thinking?" He told me that he could hit the mid 90's with his fastball but was still learning to throw strikes.

I actually felt bad for him at that moment. I thought that he was certainly doomed to fail and all of that work on his offense was for nothing. Another baseball casualty.

To my surprise, he came into the game that night and blew us away. He only had two pitches when he started pitching, a fastball and a slider. But later developed a KILLER changeup.

The next year, luck was on his side. The 1992 expansion draft was coming and teams had the right to protect only 15 players on their roster. I was left off of the Mariners expansion roster and the Reds left this guy off of their roster too. EVERY player who was left off his team's expansion roster prayed to be picked up by either the Rockies or Marlins because he would then have a REAL chance of playing in the big leagues the next year.

This guy was the 8th pick in the first round by the Marlins. I was watching the draft live in Puerto Rico and almost fell out of my chair when his name was called!

He made the Marlins team right out of Spring Training and was in the big leagues...as a PITCHER! He was traded that year when the Padres were willing to trade their superstar, Gary Sheffield, to the Marlins for a number of young players, including my old buddy.

He never looked back. He pitched for 18 major league seasons and went on to become the first pitcher to reach 500 saves, then the first to reach 600, ending his career with 601 and all-time leader, though Mariano Rivera passed him a few years ago. He is one of the most prolific relievers in baseball history with the highest strike out per nine innings ever by a reliever.

I ran into him during Spring Training in '99 after he just signed the biggest contract in Padres history. He was such a great guy that day and treated us like rock stars in the Padres clubhouse. I'll never forget that. It's easy for superstar players to forget guys like me.

From nearly getting released to likely being enshrined in the Baseball Hall of Fame soon. You have to admire the determination and perseverance of the one and only...Trevor Hoffman.

Bo Jackson

Back in the late 80's, the biggest star in the UNIVERSE was Bo Jackson. He had just come off incredible seasons in baseball and football, but as you probably recall, he broke his hip and needed it to be replaced.

By '91 he was signed by the Chicago White Sox and assigned to Birmingham, AL (managed by Terry Francona) to rehab his hip in the AA Southern League. I happened to be in Jacksonville that season and we had a four-game road trip in Birmingham scheduled.

When we checked into the hotel in Birmingham, the newspaper from the day before was in my room. I quickly opened the Sports Page to see a huge photo of Bo Jackson running over the catcher on the Charlotte Cubs, and I mean the catcher was launched into the air and had to leave the game. It was that nasty of an impact! I started thinking, wait a minute, I'm playing against this guy tonight; I better keep this in mind!

At the ballpark, we started our stretching routine in the outfield. Then we heard this massive crash of a baseball against a bat, one that was so loud it was like a firecracker! We all quickly looked up and saw a ball go into the trees about 40 feet behind the fence. The center field wall was already 400 feet so it was bomb!

Of course, the batter was Bo Jackson. He proceeded to belt several more homers and put on a show for the 10,000 fans already at the stadium.

When the game started, he was announced as the right fielder and the crowd went crazy! When he came to bat, he looked at me and said "Hey catch" with a little smile, but he was in the zone.

He hit a routine ground ball to our shortstop who had to hurry to make a bang-bang play at first. His time to first with a replaced hip was faster than any player on our team—and he weighed 240 lbs!

His next at bat, he battled our pitcher, fouling off several pitches. As he ran down the baseline on one of them, I picked up his bat to see how big it was. It was a LOG with a thicker handle than most guys swing. The next pitch we got him, striking him out with a nasty curve. But Bo knows strikeouts and right in front of me he broke his bat over his knee. It must have been incredible to see from the stands, but from 2 feet away it was the most amazing thing I had ever seen on a baseball field.

He got a hit his next at bat and ended up at second base after a ground out. It was then that the photo of the Charlotte Cubs catcher getting crushed by Bo came back into my mind. I quickly thought of an idea to limit that possibility.

Bo was taking a huge lead at second base in order to get a good jump and score on a base hit, but he was getting off a little TOO much. So I gave Bret Boone (our second baseman) the sign to pick him off after the next pitch.

As the pitch was delivered, I could see him taking that big lead again. The batter swung and missed. Bo was left high and dry if I could just get the ball to Boonie. I came up throwing and Bret broke to the base. Bo turned to get back but instead of sliding head first, he went in standing up and just crushed Bret, like the Charlotte Cubs catcher! But Bret hung onto the ball. I had just picked off Bo Jackson!!!

The next game, the EXACT same situation. Bo at second base taking a giant lead after the pitch. This time I faked like I was going to pick him off and he started running full speed to third base. I threw a strike to Frank Bolick and got him again!

When he came up to bat the next time he said, "Hey catch, I'm trying to make a comeback here and you keep throwing me out." I laughed and told him no pick-offs if you promise not to plow me like you did Boonie. He said, "Catch, you know I can't promise that."

It was the first and only time on a baseball field when I felt star struck.

Remembering Tony Gwynn

When I was drafted by the Seattle Mariners, my grandpa was my agent and he negotiated my first contract. The Mariners wouldn't budge on my bonus so my grandpa kept grinding for another way for me to earn a few bucks. We ended up settling on Major League Spring Training. I was going as a non-roster invited player for the 1989 camp.

When I arrived, I quickly realized my place on the team—I was first-string bullpen catcher.

I must have caught 3 hours a day…but it was great catching all of these great pitchers I had only seen on TV. Here are a few of the guys I caught that Spring as a 21 year old—Randy Johnson, Mark Langston, Billy Swift, Tom Neidenfuer, Erik Hansen, Steve Trout, and many more. I had only been catching for about 3 years and these were the best pitchers I had ever caught up to this point.

As the Spring Training games started, I remained the #1 bullpen catcher but didn't complain one bit. It was so cool and I knew this is where I wanted to play some day. Plus, I was making $100 a day in meal money!

Then out of the blue, about 10 games into Spring, the manager threw me into a tie game in the 7th inning against the San Diego Padres at Tempe Diablo Stadium. I was nervous as hell as I ran out onto the field for the first time.

I don't remember who was pitching but I do remember the rest. The first batter that inning was future Hall of Famer, Tony Gwynn. A guy who I always idolized as one of the best hitters in the game. PLUS, he used my dad's C243 bat model.

As he stepped up to hit, he gave me a quick greeting as many hitters do. It was a surreal moment for me. I was catching and Tony Gwynn was hitting!!!

I gave the sign for an outside fastball since the pitcher was a sinker-baller. I set up outside and was preparing to catch my first ever pitch in an MLB game (sure it was Spring Training but all the same players were there).

But Gwynn, who is known for taking pitches and making the pitchers work, hit the very first pitch off the left center field fence for a stand up triple. The manager called for the infield to come in so Gwynn couldn't just stroll home on an easy infield ground ball.

The next batter was John Kruk, and he was CRAZY! As he walked up, he not only greeted me, but started talking to me WHILE the pitch was coming! He was talking smack, saying things like, "What are going to call Catch? You know I'm gonna drive in this run Catch." Then he fouled off the first pitch and was mad at himself for missing it.

He continued talking. "This guy doesn't have shit, I don't care what you call Catch, I'm driving in this runner." The ump was cracking up listening to the ramblings of a mad man. The next pitch, Kruk hit this little fly ball out to left field and Gwynn was tagging up. That's when reality set in.

I thought to myself that I hadn't even caught a pitch yet since Gwynn hit the first pitch and Kruk fouled his first pitch off and hit the second pitch, and now there was going to be a play at the plate with TONY GWYNN!

I got myself into position as the third baseman lined up as the cut off man. The left fielder caught the ball, TG tagged up and was sprinting home for the go ahead run.

As the throw was coming in I was preparing to do what is now illegal—block the plate BEFORE I had the ball. I was in perfect position and I knew if the ball was on line Gwynn was going to have to either slide around me or plow me over. But the throw was just about 6 feet up the first base line and he scored standing up, meaning he was going to plow me if the ball was on line.

I must have played against Gwynn another 20 times over the years as the Mariners and Padres shared the same complex in Peoria, AZ. He was always so professional and was also a real fan of the game. He always maintained the enthusiasm of a little kid playing the game he loved so much.

The day he passed was a very sad day indeed. Baseball not only lost one of its greatest hitters, but it lost an even better man. RIP Tony Gwynn.

Randy Johnson – "The Big Unit"

One of the most successful pitchers in my generation was fellow USC Trojan, Randy Johnson. When I went on my recruiting trip to USC, I met RJ for the first time. We were in the dugout and he had to bend over just to fit in it! I thought, "Are all the college pitchers this tall? How am I going to be able to play against these giants?" Then I watched him pitch and felt bad for the opposing batters because he had NO idea where the ball was going.

I watched RJ pitch a few more times at USC and each time he showed signs of brilliance but then he'd hit a guy, then walk a guy, then a guy would hit a double and two runs would score. Then he'd strike the next two guys out and look untouchable. That was the same thing the scouts saw, and it hurt his draft status.

Scouts all thought he had the potential to make it and maybe even be a star in the big leagues, but his control problems, his inconsistent velocity, and lack of a changeup made it tough for the scouts to tout him as a high first round pick. In fact, many were surprised that he went in the 2nd round of the 1985 draft with the Montreal Expos.

Those first minor league seasons were rough for RJ. He was 0-3 his first season with an ERA close to 6.00 and a WHIP near 2.0. That means ON

AVERAGE he allowed 2 batters to reach base per inning either by a base hit, a walk, or hit batter.

Then he was able to string together three solid years in the minors as he climbed the Expo ladder. Finally, at age 25, he was called up in September after pitching 400 innings in the minors. However, he was still struggling with walks.

In 1988, I was drafted by the Mariners and started my pro career. The next year the Mariners traded Mark Langston to the Expos for a few players, including Randy Johnson. To start the 1990 season, we were together in Spring Training. RJ and I always have had the USC camaraderie connection, although we never played at USC together, and we started catching up about all things Trojan.

This was my second Spring Training so I knew the routine, especially for my role. That role was 50% bullpen catching! I freakin' lived in the bullpen, catching up to 15 guys a day! It wore me out but it also was really helping me improve my catching skills that were ROUGH back then. Then it came time to catch RJ for the first time.

I had a glove contract with Rawlings and they even asked me to be on the Pro Player Advisory Committee so I could inform them about the performance of their gloves. When I arrived to Spring Training, the Rawlings rep met me and we went to the Rawlings truck so I could pick out my gloves. I chose three "Campanis Target Mitt" models that were all slightly different from each other so I could figure out which one performed best. The gloves were still in a box, stiff as a board and not even close to being broken in.

I had a glove breaking system that really works. I strategically put two baseballs inside the pocket of the glove and folded the glove so the thumb side slightly overlapped the finger side. Then I tied a long sanitary sock around the glove, securing the baseballs in the pocket. Then I took the glove to the sink and filled up the pocket with water, soaking the baseballs and the leather in the pocket. Then I unwound a wire hanger, threaded one end through the web of the glove and hung them overnight in my locker, making sure the web was pointed up. In the dry Arizona climate, the gloves would dry overnight and I had at least the formation of a usable glove.

When RJ started playing catch with me to warm up for his bullpen I was using my broken in game glove from the year before. As he started to loosen up, he was bringing serious heat, and we were just playing catch on flat ground! That's when I decided I should switch gloves so he wouldn't tear up my only game-ready glove.

When he was ready for me to catch, I switched to one of the brand new gloves I had just unwrapped from the day before. It was so stiff I couldn't squeeze it, but it had a nicely formed pocket.

As RJ started uncorking that fastball, my new glove started making the LOUDEST popping sound from the stiff, new leather. The POP was so loud my ears would ring temporarily as the sound echoed throughout the stadium. By the end of his 50 pitches or so, that glove was completely broken in and game-ready.

He walked up to me and said, "Damn Campy, that glove pops like a cannon going off! Can you catch me again next time?" Of course I said YES! The next bullpen I used another one of the new Rawlings gloves with the same results...POW!!!

Toward the end of spring that year, RJ was scheduled to pitch on Opening Day, but the Mariners were traveling to play the last few Spring games. The decision was made to have RJ stay back at camp to throw a "B" game against the Padres who we shared the complex with us in Peoria, and I was going to catch him!!!

He was only scheduled to throw a certain amount of pitches but I was fired up. However, the excitement wore out quickly and turned to panic. When he dialed up against a batter, it wasn't anything like the bullpen where I had caught him dozens of times before. He was going 100% and I'm pretty sure he still didn't know where it was going.

This was the first MLB pitcher I had caught where I realized giving location after the fastball sign was ridiculous. So I just put down a "One" and he fired it. Some fastballs cut at the last second, handcuffing me; others sank a few inches and jammed the hell out of my thumb. Then I'd call his other pitch, the slider that snapped much harder than it did in the bullpen. I had never caught a lefty with this kind of stuff before (or since)!

I had hit off of RJ in simulated games in the past. These games were basically "Live" batting practice, but when I faced him, I hit him pretty well although I knew he wasn't going at me with his full arsenal. After catching him in the "B" game, I decided it was actually easier to HIT off of him than CATCH him. RJ threw another couple of scoreless innings and went into the clubhouse to ice down. Just a warm up for RJ but for me, it was an amazing experience catching him!

Later that night, I called my dad to tell him and he remembered that's how he felt the first time he caught Koufax!

My playing days ended in 1995 but RJ was just getting into his groove. We all remember him launching a fastball over John Kruk's head in the All Star game freaking Kruk out so much he turned his helmet around and wore it backwards. And who could forget when he threw a 98 MPH fastball off of a flying bird killing it instantly!

He continued to pitch until 2009 and retired at 46 years old!

He threw 4,000+ innings over 22 major league seasons amassing the second most strikeouts in history, and the third most hit batsmen! He threw two no-hitters, including a PERFECT game—only the 17th in MLB history!

He is the first Hall of Famer I ever played with.

I've stayed in touch with RJ over the years and follow his antics on social media and his killer photography website. He is such a talented photographer and because of his stature as a famous athlete, he gets invited to shoot photos of Rock' n Roll's biggest acts like Metallica, Rush, KISS, U2, and Soundgarden. Plus he has a number of brilliant wildlife, NASCAR, and surfing shots also.

Check it out...*rj51photos.com*. And of course his logo is a dead bird!

8
Shots from the Hip and the Heart

When I look back at my playing days, I'm filled with mixed feelings. What if this didn't happen or what if that DID happen? These questions haunted me.

The mental game helped me reach heights much greater than my talent should have allowed.

Writing this chapter was like a therapy session each time I typed something out. It was a way to remember the valuable lessons I learned but most importantly, to let go of all the baggage and come to grips with the reality of my situation.

Visualizing Success!

When I was a junior at USC I took a class that changed my baseball ca-reer...Sports Psychology. One thing that I had learned by this time in life even though I was only in college, was how important the mental aspect of sports (and life) was to success, mediocrity, or failure. But this class took my knowledge to another level.

Sports Psychology delved deeply into concepts and practices I had never heard of. Preparation, Visualization, Super Focus & Self-Actualization

Preparation: To practice like you want to play. Sounds easy enough but this was to be applied to the mental side of the game. To prepare properly meant that you had taken care of all of the little things and now are ready to perform when called upon. It was more than extra batting practice, it was also staying in good physical shape, getting enough sleep, eating properly and keeping your mind on your goals. You can't succeed without the ba-sics...and preparation was #1.

Visualization & Super Focus: This was the game changer for me! The professor had us go through an exercise in class that really works. He had us put our heads down on our desks and begin to think about our next athletic event. For me it was a baseball game the next day. He continued to say, "Now picture in your mind who you will be competing against. Put a uniform on him and put yourselves in a game situation. Now slow everything down and super focus on your task." For me it was batting against a pitcher from a local college. I remembered how that pitcher started his wind up, where he released the ball and what it looked like from my point of view when was I batting. Basically, I mentally rehearsed that at bat over and over and over in my head before the real thing. I did this again in bed prior to going to sleep and focused on visualizing the ball being released from his hand. This is the same thing Olympic skiers and bobsledders do prior to a run. They visualize their turns.

Right away, the benefits of visualization started to show. I wasn't nervous or anxious like I often felt when batting. In fact, I was quite calm and confident. It was like I had already been there, which I had been in my visualization exercises.

I continued to visualize for the rest of my baseball career. As I laid down every night I would mentally put myself on whatever field against whatever pitcher and visualize the pitch coming in slow motion. I then would prepare to hit the pitch with perfect mechanics and would watch the ball hit my bat. Some nights I would twitch violently when I mentally swung the bat. My wife would say, "Did you hit that one far, Bo?"

This mental exercise totally works and I still do it today preparing for business presentations or music performances.

Finally, the class taught me about a concept called "Self-Actualization." This is defined as the motive to realize one's own potential. This was especially intriguing as a baseball player. How far could I take this limited talent? I learned that no one can become self-actualized unless they first have all of the basics of preparation and visualization down. Without proper preparation we are not even close to our potential. When we are nervous or timid or lack confidence, we are not able to reach our potential.

I coached youth baseball for 13 years and taught every kid I coached the visualization exercise. Some kids would tell me how much it helped them play. My own son swears by it…because it WORKS!

You can benefit from these tactics even if you are not a competitive athlete. Visualize about tasks you will need to perform, meetings you will have, presentations to clients, job interviews, public speaking engagements, asking someone out on a date. WHATEVER it is, visualizing success in advance will take you closer and closer to your full potential.

"When one starts to visualize the impossible, one begins to see it IS possible!"
- Cherie Carter-Scott

Competitive Drive

When I tell people I used to be a pro baseball player, I can tell what they are thinking: You? With that body? The fact is, I was a bit undersized for catcher at 6'0", 195 pounds, but that was not why I made it as far as I did. It was something I still use to this day. It's my competitive drive.

I absolutely THRIVED on the competition. Especially when a pitcher who was supposed to be "All-World" was on the mound; I really loved that battle. I wanted to prove to MYSELF that I could hit the best pitchers and throw out the fastest base stealers. I learned early on that the focus of competitive drive starts from WITHIN with a constant desire to learn and improve.

I remember as a freshman in high school I was called up to varsity baseball. We had a game against Brea who had one of the league's best pitchers. When I stepped up for my first at bat, he started me off with a fastball and I thought, that's not so fast, I can hit this guy! Then he made a mistake and hung a curve and I did what I had done a million times in practice, I waited and hit a shot over the center fielder's head. It's funny that I remember that at bat over 30 years later, but it was the first time I really knew I had a chance to succeed in baseball.

Playing summer ball in high school, I was thrown onto an American Legion team with MEN like Richard Sandoval and Anthony Moreno when I was 15. Guys on this team drove to games, they had beards, and were huge compared to me. Sure, they hazed me a bit when my mom dropped me off at the field, but I hoped my play would win them over after awhile. They just wanted to win and were INTENSE. The older guys on that team taught me to compete at an even higher level.

The competitive drive of pro baseball players is often what get them there, not talent! Most pro level players have a hyper-competitive switch they can turn on, and once in that mode, they are like another person.

This hyper-competitiveness leaks over into card games, darts, girls…you name it. It's part of the beast, the good and the bad of it. I saw this same exact thing when I coached little league for 13 years. The kids that took it personally to compete and succeed, DID!

I put the same focus into other things in my life. My work in advertising/marketing allows me to creatively come up with business solutions. I compete with myself to deliver and execute a successful ad campaign. I play guitar and constantly strive to improve, grow, and create.

There is, however, a dark side to hyper-competitiveness.

Over the years, I have had to pick my competitive battles wisely. For example, my first year coaching little league baseball I was stuck in hyper-compete mode like when I played. It was about winning at any cost. But it was not the right time or place for that. This was for the kids to learn and love playing baseball. For the next 12 years the hyper-competitive guy only came out when I felt the focus shifted to parents/league officials/umpires and not the kids playing the game. And I would go absolutely nuts and get thrown out of games. But I sent the message loud and clear. "HEY DUMBASS ADULT, IT'S ABOUT THE KIDS, NOT YOU!"

"If you want it…go get it." In my experience, when I have been super focused and willing to go that extra mile, I have succeeded. When I was nonchalant and under-motivated about achieving a goal, it always slipped away.

Are you pushing yourself toward your goals every day? What are trying to accomplish? Are you focused? Are you motivated? Do you dream about it? Are you willing to suffer setbacks while accomplishing it?

"If you want to find the real competition, just look in the mirror. After awhile you'll see your rivals scrambling for second place." —Criss Jami

My Roid Rant

One of the things I get asked quite often is what I think about Steroids/ PED's. First of all, I never took any sort of performance enhancement substance. Just drank some protein powder shakes in the off-season when I was lifting and working out.

That was a personal decision I made. The main reason for me was that no one really knew what the side effects were. Then in '92, Lyle Alzado died of brain cancer and it was discussed that his unbridled use of roids was the cause. That was a big deterrent for me when I considered experimenting with roids.

One other thing: I knew many roid users back in the day but I will never "Out" them. I feel particularly strong about this as it was THEIR personal decision based on their own situation.

I will say, I never felt taking steroids was a moral dilemma for me. My choice for not taking steroids was the same reason I never did cocaine: Everyone reacts differently and I didn't see the risk as being worth the reward. I also feared the known side effects like the Neanderthal forehead, the vulnerable ligaments and tendons, but the main side effect was "Roid Rage."

I'd like to do a bit of enlightening. People don't know the basic facts about baseball's banned substance policy, the 1980's & '90's baseball culture or the reality of what roids actually do for players...so let me tell you.

The fact is, when I signed my first pro baseball contract, it was NOT illegal to take steroids in the major leagues—not officially until 1991. In fact, major league players did not get tested for ANY drugs until 2003. If a player was arrested for cocaine possession, then that player was relegated to random drug testing by the league; the same thing with steroids. But if a player could hide it well enough, the league had no right to test him as it was written into the collective bargaining agreement between the players union and the owners.

The culture in baseball in the late 80's was TAKE STEROIDS! That's right. Even our managers, coaches, team executives, and agents encouraged players to take them. why? The Oakland A's had the Bash Brothers (McGwire & Canseco) who we now all know took steroids. But back then, insiders already knew and used those guys as an example of two skinny guys who roided and then crushed balls out of stadiums.

The reality of steroid use is a double-edged sword. By simply injecting yourself with steroids does not make you stronger; you still have to work your ass off in the weight room. The main benefit of steroids is quicker recovery time. Most people I talk to think roids instantly create super human strength but they do NOT.

When players are cycling roids, they work out 6 or 7 days a week and can work out on back-to-back days on the same body part. So roid users can do heavy squat lifting one day and come back the next day and do them again. Normally, there would be too much lactic acid built up to do squats two days in a row, and there would be no real benefit since our bodies require rest to build muscle and strength.

On the other edge of the sword, to me this is why so many steroid users had freak injuries. I know a player who was a big roid user and broke his hand when he tried to check his swing. I know another guy who tore his quad muscle in half fielding a ball. The doctors said repairing that tear was like sewing two paint brushes together. If you look up the injury records for all of the accused roid users, you'll see a consistent pattern of injuries created by too much muscle strength exerted onto the skeletal frame.

I knew of guys who blew out elbows, shoulders, wrists, ankles, and knees from roiding. Those small joints simply couldn't handle the energy generated by the newfound strength.

Let's not forget about the dreaded side effects of steroid use. I'd see guys show up to the stadium looking all bloated. That was water retention from the roids. I'd see that same guy getting massive cystic zits on his back. I'd see guys in their 20's losing hair. I'd see guys eyes turning yellow from liver problems. But the ultimate side effect was what we now call "Roid Rage," and that was REAL.

When alcohol is added to a roid user, you should run for the hills, because there WILL be violence. I saw this way too often but this was pre-internet so the public didn't know how frequently these guys got into fights.

One other factor that I can't medically prove but witnessed was how steroids affect reproduction. Roid users seemed to have more problems with infertility or fathering children with birth defects than the general public. Maybe a coincidence? I don't know for sure, but after all, steroids are hormones so what do you think?

One guy who's been publically blasted for steroid use is Barry Bonds. But let me tell you a little secret. Regardless, he was one of the best hitters in the history of baseball...PERIOD! I caught in Spring Training when he batted and he had no holes in his swing. He stood so close to the plate that his upper body was directly over it. The umpire had to squeeze his head next to mine to see. If the pitcher couldn't hit the spot with the pitch I called, Bonds crushed it. Not the steroids.

This is where critics will say that his steroid use created an unfair advantage of healing quicker than the old school guys, therefore Bonds was stronger day-to-day than players like Willie Mays or Mickey Mantle. I'm on the fence when it comes to the legacy of players like Bonds, Clemens, McGwire, and some of the others. Are they deserving of the Hall of Fame or victims of the "Do Steroids" baseball culture of the late 80's and 90's?

I am anti-steroids & PED's for sure. I just think it is unfair that as a society we've elected to demonize roid users of that era when we cheered for them to hit more home runs. The fact of the matter is, baseball didn't officially recognize steroid use as illegal until in 1991 and didn't even test for them until 2003.

For players getting caught today, I say that player is a complete fool and deserves to be fined and suspended. PED's are clearly illegal and tested by the league, yet guys are still trying to beat the system. There is so much money at stake, I'm sure there are players today looking for the next undetectable PED so they can get that big paycheck.

If I could do it all over again, I would do the same exact thing: I would NOT take steroids.

The Scoop on Umpires

When I was converted to catcher at USC, I was introduced to the Catcher/Umpire dynamic. Rule #1, the ump is always right. Rule #2, if the ump is wrong, see Rule #1. I learned quickly to deal with this dynamic. I figured it was better to be friendly with them, even though that didn't always work. I also learned to use questions instead of statements when I disagreed.

I'd ask, "That didn't hit the corner?" or "Did you get that one low or outside or both?"

The umps would usually tell me why they made the call thus reinforcing their strike zone....which could change game-to-game, inning-to-inning, or pitch-to-pitch. Then later I could say, "Didn't that one look the same as the one you called for strike on the last batter?"

In college we had a very cool and charismatic umpire named Vic, if I recall. Vic kept the game flowing, told me funny stories, and also had an interesting day job. He invented a new protective device he called "The Banana Cup."

In fact, prior to a game he went over to the USC dugout and said, "Campy, get me a bat and I'll show your team the best baseball product on the market today." So we all gathered around Vic as he beat the hell out of his junk with that bat. It was quite a demonstration of his new invention. We all ended up buying one and they worked very well.

When I got to the pros, the umpiring stepped up a bit but so did the egos. They lived a tough life in the minors. They stayed in hotels for the ENTIRE season and drove their own personal vehicles from city to city logging tens of thousands of miles. They worked in crews and they didn't always get along with the guys they spent most of their waking moments with. It was not an easy job, but they signed up for it!

My first year in the minors there was one ump who would put on the best power ump show for the managers but was very insecure…and I knew it. He was great at controlling the game, keeping both managers in check and was very demonstrative when calling a strike.

I remember one game, the pitch was a perfect low and away fastball but it could have been called either way. This ump threw his right arm up and belted out a loud "STEEEEEERIKE." Then he whispered in my ear, "Hey Campy…was that a strike?"

I assured him it was, and occasionally to maintain my unbiased opinion status, I would say a strike he called was actually a ball and he would thank me for my honesty. When I batted, he NEVER screwed me. In fact, he was extra gracious to me, I believe because he appreciated my feedback on his umpiring.

Another thing about pro umpires. They get their head WAAAY in there to see the pitch. The college umps would be a foot or two behind the catcher but pro umps were draped on me so close I could tell what they ate for lunch.

I didn't mind the pro umps being so close to the action until one interfered with my attempt to pick a guy off of first base. The left-handed batter swung and missed. The runner at first base was leaning heavily toward second base. So I dropped to a knee, turned to first, and went to throw a bullet. That's when my right ring finger got stuck in the umpire's mask and ripped off my fingernail. Blood was squirting everywhere. That was some serious pain, and to this day it hurts to cut that nail.

One game in AA, the umpire was not buying my honey nor was he in the mood for any jokes. He was calling a terrible game and I got frustrated so I went to the mound. I told the pitcher that I was going to call a curve so the other ump in the field could see the #2 sign but he was to throw a fastball.

As he delivered the ball I yelled, "Oh Shit!" and ducked, and the ump took a 90 MPH fastball off his left shoulder. I turned around and asked if he was OK as he was laying on the ground. I told him the pitcher crossed me up and I thought a curve was coming. Then I turned back around and gave a little grin to the pitcher thanking him for delivering the message.

Another time, the umpire was being his typical dick self but I was still trying to butter him up. This time the pitcher was giving the ump all kinds of body language when he missed a call. Then the ump told me to go have a talk with him and tell him to stop it…so I did.

Then, a few pitches later, the pitcher gave a big eye roll after a bad call and the ump started yelling at MY pitcher. That's when I went crazy on him.

I don't know why but I got super protective of my pitcher like a mama bear. I laid into the ump with a verbal barrage about his crappy strike zone, his piss poor attitude, his lame power trip, and told him to never speak to my pitchers again. So he tossed me and I was fined $50. But I sure did get my money's worth!

I was forced to umpire Little League games years later for my kid's league. It is not easy nor fun. It did instill a level of respect for doing a job where no one likes you, you have to stand the entire game, and one blown call can change the outcome of the game. I've been out of baseball for many years and there are still guys that were with me in the minors umpiring in the majors today. At least now the instant replay PROVES they are not always right!

Our Wedding

When I signed my pro contract in 1988, the Mariners sent me to Tempe, AZ to begin a 50 game season called "Instructional League."

It was an exciting time. I had a few bucks in my pocket so I bought a "Bonus Mobile," a slightly used 1988 Ford Thunderbird with tinted windows, Centerline rims, and a Blaupunkt stereo. It matched my stone washed jeans, bright neon t-shirts and my epic mullet perfectly.

I checked into the Comfort Inn off of Baseline Road and a bit later decided to go check out the town. I drove down Baseline for several miles into Mesa and decided to hang a U-Turn to go back. As I pulled up to a light, I noticed this hottie driving behind me. At the time, I was the most single guy in America so I had to meet this girl. I was eyeballing her in the rear view and maybe I was hallucinating but I swear she smiled at me.

When the light turned green she was tailgating me BIG TIME. So I sped up, and so did she; I changed lanes, and so would she.

Finally after miles of this, I turned into the left hand turn lane to go back to my hotel, and SHE WAS STILL BEHIND ME! I pulled into the hotel…she followed….I parked…then she parked right next to me!

I ran my hands through the mullet to fluff up the party side and opened the door expecting the hot chick to be there with that cute little smile—but something was wrong. She was in her uniform and late for work—AT MY HOTEL!!!

When I went inside, she was getting ready for her shift as front desk manager. I said, "Didn't you see me driving down Baseline? I was checking

June 30th, 1991.

you out." She said, "Oh, were you the guy in the Thunderbird who I couldn't get around for miles to pass? I was almost late to work because of you!" I couldn't believe it! DOGGED!

I kept flirting with her for weeks but she insisted that she had a boyfriend and would never date a player. My dad came to town and I told him about her. He decided to help me close the deal. So he went to front desk and was hard selling her on just a cup of coffee with me. She politely turned down the offer, but her boss was standing right there. He told her the Mariners account was critical to the hotel and it was her DUTY as an employee to go on a date with me.

Within two weeks we were in love and together every day. Within two years, I asked her to marry me.

In 1991, she quit her job and joined me for the season for the first time in Jacksonville, Florida. Right away, she was working in the stadium box office selling tickets to my games. It was a perfect job because we could go to the field together and she was off by the third inning so she could watch the game.

We intended to get married in Orange County after the season but the GM threw us a curve. Pedro Bragan, GM of the team and son of the team owner, suggested we get married before a game on the field! He even said he would PAY us! He knew it would be a huge attraction that he could even promote on the local TV stations.

Our funds were low at the time so we decided to do it. The date was set for June 30th. Both of our families came out to Jacksonville for the big day.

The wedding was scheduled for Sunday but we had the reception the night before since the team was set to travel to Charlotte after the Sunday day game.

We had a blast at the reception; it was right on the ocean.

The next day it was pouring rain, hard for even Florida, so we were concerned this was going to be postponed. But the weather started clearing up for our 1 PM wedding and 1:30 PM game.

About 5,000 people attended that wedding or game or both. The whole team was in my wedding wearing the Jacksonville Suns uniform. My best man was my old college roommate, the LEGENDARY Dave "Lats" Latter, who was a pitcher for the other team and in uniform also. Bret Boone, who was also an old USC teammate and even older friend, was my other groomsman. We were married by one of the team owners on the field.

As I went to kiss the bride, I had to turn my hat around so I wouldn't poke her in the face with the bill of my cap. After the kiss, we walked through two lines of my teammates holding bats like an arch. She looked beautiful in that dress. I gave her another quick kiss and then headed over to the bullpen to warm up the starting pitcher.

In my first at bat as a married man, I roped a single up the middle; my new in-laws were impressed. My second at bat as a married man...I hit a home run! I could hear my mother-in-law scream, "You really know how to do it Campanis!" Obviously she was not up on baseball lingo but I felt the sentiment loud and clear.

Later that game Lats was called into pitch in a tight game. They were leading by one run. His first batter...ME! As I was announced, the crowd went crazy as they knew it was groom against best man in a tight game. I battled him hard that at bat and finally he walked me to start the rally.

I eventually got to third base. That's when Lats threw a ball in the dirt that got away from the catcher and I bolted home to try to score. The catcher flipped Lats the ball right when I slid into his skinny, little ankle tearing his sock and flipping him onto his back. Now the score was tied.

Lats got out of the inning and went back out in the bottom of the 9th inning. He allowed a base runner and was pulled by his manager. Then my OTHER groomsman, Bret Boone, smoked a double to right field scoring Lats' runner for a WALK OFF WIN! And a loss for my best man.

Decades later, it seems like just yesterday Lisa and I had that first cup of coffee. Only now I love you more than ever.

The Jacksonville 3

I have never taken for granted the physical gifts God gave me to play the wonderful game of baseball. Every prayer I gave thanks. As a kid, I didn't consider the simple joy of playing catch or crushing a home run as a privilege until I met some special people in Jacksonville FL in 1991.

At the beginning of that season, the GM of the team picked me as the main player to attend sponsor meetings, fan autograph sessions, and he even promoted my hair cut on the field prior to a game for Supercuts. I ordered the stylish 1991 mushroom cut that day! The GM liked how I interacted with people and felt I represented his team well. I enjoyed it too.

There was an event earlier that season that changed my life. It was a simple meet and greet with select season ticket holders at a luncheon. As each table was being served, I would walk around and introduce myself and thank them for being so supportive of the team.

At this luncheon there was a table of teens and young adults in wheelchairs. Some of them had paralyzed limbs and others had cerebral palsy or other physically challenging conditions.

As I went to their table, they started asking me questions the other tables had not, questions like, "What does it feel like to hit a home run?" "Does it hurt your hand to catch a 95 MPH fastball?" "How can you even see the ball going that fast?" "Is sliding fun? It sure looks like it is." I was starting to realize what was happening. They had always wondered what it would be like to be on the field, running around in a healthy body, playing a game they loved to watch but could not play. I started to get emotional inside but I had to keep it together.

I ended up sitting down with them for the rest of the luncheon to answer their many questions and to get to know more about them. I learned that they went to EVERY game and sat behind home plate. They had been studying me and had some advice. One teen told me he liked when I threw from my knees and that I should do more of that. So later in the season when I would throw from my knees I'd look up into the stands and try to make eye contact with him. Another suggested that I should remember what I did at USC since my current stats were not even close to those high numbers. I laughed and told him that I wasn't allowed to use aluminum bats like in college but I promised I'd really try my best.

One guy knew EVERYTHING about me, like my mom and dad's names, where I grew up, what high school, college and pro teams I played for. He knew my current batting average and reminded me that if I were to get two hits in my next four at bats I would be back to hitting .275. He also said he didn't expect me to hit .300 but I needed to hit at least .275 if I wanted to get to the show. (He was right!)

I would see these young people nearly every game and would always make sure to visit with them whenever I could. It was funny, they were critical of the manager, some of the other players and even me, but I loved the dialogue. They REALLY knew the game.

One day, one of the guys said this straight up to me. "You are so lucky to be playing pro baseball, but I'd give anything to just be able to play catch." Right there on the field I completely lost it and had to regroup in the clubhouse. I knew how blessed and how lucky I was to be where I was.

So, whenever I scored or something good happened that season I used to look up to them and throw a fist pump in the air. These young people rocked my world. They had really inspired me with their courage and optimism to continue working hard despite the every day trials and tribulations of being a baseball player. All I could think of was…would these kids give up or let a few bad games deter them if they could be in my shoes? NO DAMN WAY!

My Toughest Break

Prior to the 1992 season, the Seattle Mariners added me to their 40-man roster. The reason they did this was to insure that other teams could not steal me in the Rule 5 draft. I was excited for a chance to make the team at Big League Spring Training.

As the Spring progressed, I noticed that the Mariners kept signing other catchers who were a bit older with MLB experience, creating a log jam in the position at Triple A and the big league team.

This log jam meant that even though I was a Double A All-Star the year before, they were going to send me back so I could play every day. I was very disappointed but had no choice...so off to Jacksonville, Florida I went.

I started off the season struggling to find my rhythm. I think the added pressure of being on the 40-man roster was getting to me. I also think that for the first time in my career, I was a lousy teammate, only thinking about myself, my stats, and what the manager, Bob Hartsfield, was writing in his daily reports.

A month into the season, I was really struggling at the plate when we rolled into Birmingham for a three-game home stand. The first game of the series I found myself not playing and relegated to the bullpen. That's when a nice guy who I had met the year before came to say hello. He asked how I was doing and I told him how poorly I was hitting. Out of nowhere he said, "I know just the guy who can turn you around, former All-Star and batting champion, Harry "The Hat" Walker. He has a cage at his house. I'll call him right now and let you know."

Sure enough, Harry knew my grandpa and agreed to work with me the next day!

Striding into the ball at Mariners' Spring Training.

I went to his house in the woods where he had a batting cage set up in the yard with a pitching machine.

"The Hat" showed me things I had never heard of, especially ways to improve my timing, which was way out of sync. Within an hour, I had adopted a new way of thinking about approaching the pitch and got an RBI single in my first at bat using Harry's timing technique that night.

During the course of that season, I grew as a hitter, and when I smoked a nasty slider to right center off one of the best closers in the league, I knew I had turned a corner.

My catching was also improving and I learned to call better and better games. My manager had been tough on me earlier during the season but eventually I think my play finally had impressed him.

With less than a week to go in the season, Bob called me into his office before a game to have a little talk. He said with his slow and deliberate drawl, "Campy, you've improved so much this season. It's a credit to your determination and I commend you for that. I've been on the phone with the big club and told them that I am recommending that you be called up when they expand their roster next week. Congratulations, you've earned this."

I was so happy…it was like I walking on air. But I didn't tell anyone because we had a game to play within an hour. That night I was in the line-up against the Chattanooga Lookouts, Double A team for the Cincinnati Reds.

Future major leaguer Willie Greene led off for Chattanooga and on the third pitch of the game, he fouled a 90+ MPH fastball off my wrist and I heard a POP! Immediately the trainer was on the field with cold spray. It didn't help and I asked him to tape it up.

I played the rest of that game and even got a hit, but when I took off the tape, the wrist blew up like a balloon; I knew it was broken. X-rays revealed a broken pisiform bone in my left wrist. They casted it up but I told the doctors and trainer that I'd be fine within a week. I begged them to just cut off the cast and send me to Seattle! But they said no it was not healed yet, and I was placed on the DL and sent home.

A month later, the Mariners sent me to Puerto Rico when the cast came off and then promptly took me off the 40-man roster. I never made it back to the big league roster and watched my one window of opportunity to become a big league player slam shut in a split second.

To this day, to be so close and have my ultimate dream taken away like that is still the toughest thing for me to accept both mentally and emotionally. More than 20 years of hard work and dedication unfulfilled due to a freak accident, a circumstance totally outside of my control.

The Luckiest Trip

That week after the broken wrist, I had a couple of doctor appointments then waited a day or two until we got paid. We then rented a U-Haul trailer, packed up our junk, and headed back to Arizona.

My wife and I rotated driving and sleeping while my son, Alex, was in his car seat. We decided to try to drive straight to Arizona without staying at a hotel to save money, and that's what we did. We drove 43 hours STRAIGHT and made it to our house in Tempe, AZ early one morning.

When we arrived home, I flipped on the TV to discover something amazing had just happened on our drive. When we left Jacksonville. I didn't even think to check the weather. We just hopped in the car, bumping the cassette tapes, and started rolling west.

Little did we know, as we were driving, one of the most devastating hurricanes in American history, Hurricane Andrew, was heading north through the Gulf of Mexico and right for us with winds over 100 MPH. We were totally oblivious to the impending danger, since we were not listening to the radio. Thanks to dumb luck, we just kept driving west, completely unaware of the devastation that would hit the area in a few short hours. We didn't even get a sprinkle of rain on the windshield…nothing.

I think about this from time to time—had we stopped that first night, we would have likely stayed between Baton Rouge and Lafayette, Louisiana, right where hurricane Andrew hit land, with all of our belongings and a six-month old baby. I was so thankful we made it home safely!!!!

God works in mysterious ways. I was dealt a terrible blow breaking my wrist at such a critical time of my career, but even that seemed so trivial compared to what could have happened if we had been caught in that 100 MPH hurricane.

This is an example of why I try—even when it's VERY difficult—to keep an optimistic attitude and belief that no matter how dark things seem, just like Bob Marley sang on our cassette tape driving home…"Everything little thing is gonna be alright."

Making the "Real Life" Big Leagues

When I look in the rear view mirror at some of the best and most difficult times in my life, I'm starting to realize that things DO happen for a reason, to help us grow even if the lesson is challenging. Let me explain.

Since my earliest memories I defined myself as a baseball player…period. When my first grade teacher asked us to tell the class what we were going to be when we grew up, I said a baseball player. When my high school counselor asked me my senior year what I was going to college to become, I said a baseball player. When USC career counselors asked, BASEBALL!

I had no interest in any other occupation except maybe being a baseball manager or executive after I retired from playing. That was it. I know that in order to excel at something you need to completely dedicate yourself to the belief that you WILL succeed. You must focus with a complete commitment to your goal. And that's what I did; that's what all of my baseball buddies did.

Then on the last day of Spring Training in 1995, after 2+ more seasons of hard work after my fateful broken wrist, they called me into the manager's office to let me know that they appreciated me catching a million bullpens, helping the young catchers develop and mentoring the young pitchers, but they were moving in a "different direction" and released me from my contract.

So there I sat, a baseball player without a team. Harsh reality had collided with my dream.

I started to drive home to tell my wife, but I first needed some time to think things through first. I pulled off the freeway in Phoenix and drove straight to South Mountain where there is a hiking trail to the top with a gorgeous view of the Valley of the Sun.

As I sat on a rock and contemplated my future I kept thinking maybe I could call the Angels or the Mariners? Maybe I could call the Cubs since I had played well against them for years...maybe Independent Ball or Australia? What would my wife say? Maybe I had wasted all of these years and put us in financial hardship to chase a silly dream? What would my dad say? Maybe, to get on the phone and call every team letting them know I was available? So many thoughts were racing through my head as I was staring straight into a major crossroads in life.

Suddenly I was overcome with emotions...so confused, so scared, so worried I had failed so many people. But most importantly, I was afraid of the future. Which translates to being afraid of what "Real Life" was going to be like. Again, my baseball player friends can relate to this one.

When I got home and talked to my wife, she surprised me. She said she was relieved I was done playing. She made sure I knew she married me for me and not my job. Why was I defining my self-worth by my occupation? Her comment really had a big impact on me and I became determined to metaphorically "Make it to the Big Leagues" some other way. She really gave me the courage and support I needed to try something new.

My family was also very supportive when I told them I wanted to move on and try something different. Without the emotional support of my family, this time would have been even tougher and I don't think the outcome would have been the same.

When I decided to move on, I was so happy my grandpa had insisted on including school as part of my contract with the Mariners. They owed me 3 semesters of school, but I had to use them or lose them so I enrolled at ASU in Broadcast Management for the summer session.

When classes started, at nearly 28, I was the old man. But I was motivated to learn new things and find a new career doing something that interested me maybe even as much playing baseball did.

I had a fantastic professor at ASU, Norm Ginsberg, who convinced me to consider advertising. Initially I met with him and told him about my baseball past and thought I would be a good baseball radio or TV announcer.

He simply said, "Why would you want to go back to the minors making almost no money while chasing another dream? You should sell advertising."

I thought, "People actually do that job?"

Before I knew it I had an internship with Kamel Kountry 108 in Phoenix. They would allow me to sit in on their meetings, go on sales calls, write commercials, come up with original ideas and of course do all of the menial tasks interns do. But I did them with enthusiasm and a positive attitude.

My view on life completely changed one day when a special meeting was set up to discuss ideas for a big client and they invited me to sit in. The meeting was being run by the station managers so I just sat and listened. Then to my surprise the General Manager said, "Hey Jim, you are obviously a super creative guy. What do you think we should do?"

I thought, "Did he just call me creative in front of everyone? Have I always had this creative thinking process and just didn't know it? Did my pre-determined mindset of playing baseball cloud this transition period and my potential?"

As I started sharing my idea for this client, I noticed everyone started to take notes. They were genuinely interested in my direction for this campaign. They ultimately used my idea and it was successful. That was a turning point in my new life outside of baseball.

Prior to finishing this internship, they did something unprecedented; they offered me a job as an Account Executive making more money than I made in the past three years playing minor league baseball combined! The money was nice, but the real thrill was the rebirth of my enthusiasm…the feeling of having a "Purpose" again.

I've discussed this with several of my old baseball buddies. We have all had to go through this transition period to some extent. Change is never easy, but going from such a high profile job where they literally announce your name to thousands of fans prior to you going to work is a bigger shift than most people experience.

Over the years, I've gone through many peaks and valleys but I hold tight to the notion of having faith that I will be fine. If you feel lost right now just remind yourself of your best qualities and take comfort in knowing that your passions/interests/talents are like a compass. Follow them to your next destination with open eyes and an open heart.

What I've learned over the years is, when you see that next opportunity presenting itself, keep your eyes focused and take a mighty swing—just in case you connect!!!

Hey, I'm STILL trying to make it to the "Big Leagues!"

The Bitter Years

My friends think of me as a "Mr. Baseball" kind of guy completely consumed with the game. I've told my friends countless stories from those years playing a game that I loved. But what I don't usually share is that after it was over, I went through a long period where I couldn't watch baseball at all.

It started about 1995 when I was released…again. I was offered a couple of contracts to play independent ball but instead chose to just retire and move on. It felt like the right thing to do since the chances of my getting back to where I was just a few years earlier were slim at my ripe old age of nearly 28. But that ultra-competitive drive was still burning and whispering in my ear that I should still be playing.

The decision to find a new career was financial…the best baseball contract I was offered after being released was about $1,000 a month with no paid expenses. That's like paying to play! This was the beginning of what I now call my "Bitter Years." When I say "Bitter" it refers to the gamut of feelings I had not making it to the big leagues; jealousy, sour grapes, disillusionment, and anger.

When I tried watching games on TV back in the mid 90's I simply couldn't watch more than a few minutes before I would get a sick feeling in my stomach. This feeling was from watching countless players that I had played with and against living out their dreams right in front of me. Some guys deserved to be there but others must have been wearing a horseshoe up their ass. They were not that good, but they were the right guy on the right team at the right time…something that never happened for me and it left a bitter taste in my mouth.

It was about this time that my oldest son Alex was getting into playing baseball. We would go out front and play catch just like my dad and I used to. I loved those moments and they reminded me that I still loved baseball. But every time I turned on a game or *Baseball Tonight*, that sick feeling would come back.

I was invited by one of my top clients to play on his Adult league team and felt obligated to play since he was so important to my income in my new advertising career.

In my first game in three years, I hit a home run (with an aluminum bat). I thoroughly enjoyed playing again and my client was even happier about my performance. I eventually became their closer and didn't blow any saves!

But then I'd go home, flip on *Sports Center* and get ill watching some guy I played against break his bat and bleed a double into right field, scoring two to put his team ahead…cue the damn *Sports Center* music; "DEH NA NEH - DEH NA NEH."

At this point you might be thinking, "What a bitter prick this guy is," and I was. I completely admit it.

Then in 1998 my grandpa Al became very ill. My dad called me one night in June and handed the phone over to my grandpa. My grandpa used to ask me how I was playing every time we spoke. It was his was way of starting the conversation. Even though he had had a tough last decade since his infamous *Nightline* appearance, he was upbeat and praised me for finding a new career where I could better support my family. He was slurring pretty badly from recent strokes, but he kept saying over and over how proud he was of me for what I accomplished as a former baseball player and now as a man growing up and moving onto a new chapter in life.

Ironically, the praise I received from my grandpa that night had already influenced me many years earlier. He was a graduate of New York University and his college education had opened many doors for him, including becoming the GM of the Dodgers. He stressed education and when I was offered $50K out of high school to sign, he simply wouldn't allow it.

His stern insistence on having me go to college was the best thing he ever did for me. Not just the knowledge, but the confidence it gave me to realize there really was life outside of baseball. A life that could be amazing doing new things and meeting new people. I thanked him for the kind words and told him I loved him.

The next day, he passed away. There were several mentions of his passing in the paper and on TV. All spoke of the *Nightline* show but only a few mentioned even one of the million GREAT things he had done for the Dodgers and the game. This only fueled my bitterness toward baseball and the sports media, it was growing out of control.

Coincidentally, that same year, in 1998, there was an unprecedented home run race going on between Mark McGwire and Sammy Sosa that had taken America by storm. I would read about the race in the paper with predictions that both players were on pace to break Maris' record. But I hadn't watched an MLB game on TV in over 3 years.

When I saw on the news that McGwire had hit his 61th that season, I told myself it was time to put the bitterness away and watch history in the making.

I think the shift in my attitude was based on the fact that someone from MY generation of baseball players was setting a record set before my dad was even a player. This event made me feel proud inside since I had played against McGwire and had always felt a certain comradery toward him as a fellow USC Trojan. I was really excited and rooting for him to break the record. Or was this a little mind trick I was playing on myself to blind the bitter part of me so I could get back to enjoying the game l love?

Either way, when McGwire hit that 62nd home run, it was like a weight had been lifted off my shoulders. I started to reflect positively on my past career and started to learn to come to grips with the reality of not making it.

The next year my son started Little League and I was asked to coach. The love of the game came flooding back and I did my best to share this love with the kids on the team. I coached my two boys' teams (Alex and then Tommy) for 13 years in total. Those years, and the experiences I had coaching, were some of the best of my life.

Now that I've had many years to consider what was happening during my bitter period I think it was a necessary part of the healing process. I guess these feelings were similar to the way people mourn the loss of a loved one. You dearly miss them, and there is deep void in your heart as you can't bring them back into your life no matter how hard you may try. I suppose I was mourning the loss of the only thing I was really good at and knew I could never go back to that time or those places every again. My dream had died and I simply wasn't prepared for it to end.

Getting through my bitter years was a quiet struggle that I never spoke to ANYONE about. Over time, I learned to cope with the reality that my identity as human being was no longer defined as a "Baseball Player." This process was slow, painful, and quite humbling but it helped me to transition into a new phase of life with new goals and aspirations with a positive attitude and outlook.

Today I can say with certainty that I am once again a full-blown baseball fan. It doesn't matter if it's the MLB, Minors, college or little league, I absolutely love the game. My favorite thing now is to see how many of my old teammates and guys I played against are still in the game as managers, coaches, scouts and executives. I have a new level of respect for guys like Bryan Price, managing the Reds, and Brad Ausmus, managing the Tigers. They have put in the time along with blood, sweat and tears to get where they are today, and I'm a BIG fan.

"*Baseball was, is and always be to me the best game in the world*" – Babe Ruth

The LEGENDARY Dave "Lats" Latter

My old USC roommate/teammate, the best man in my wedding and best man I've ever known, passed away unexpectedly due to complications from heart surgery in October, 2014. He was just 48 years old. That man was the LEGENDARY Dave "Lats' Latter.

But I'd like to reminisce for a minute…back to the late 80's when he met my family for the first time.

My BFF.

As soon as I introduced Lats, he instantly became an adopted Campanis; we all loved Lats. My dad and Lats would often go into another room at family parties and talk baseball for hours. Lats loved it when my dad would get all excited telling one of his million baseball stories. My mom loved him also. He always made her laugh plus he would clear off the table and wash the dishes just to make me look like a crappy son!

Since Lats can't tell this story anymore, I thought I'd write one of his favorites the same way he would tell it. And yes…I'm the victim.

He always started and ended this story the same way:

"OK, here's one of my, oh, top three stories…maybe top two. Me and Camp were sophomores at USC and partying near his parents' house in Yorba Linda so we decided to crash there that night. We were pretty wasted as we walked into the kitchen at about 2 AM.

Right then Camp starts rummaging through the pantry and pulls out a box of Cap'n Crunch, then goes into the cupboard and pulls out a gigantic mixing bowl. He pours half the box of Cap'n Crunch into the bowl and fills it with milk, then gets the biggest spoon he can fit in his mouth and plops down on a barstool at the counter and starts killing it.

At that moment, Camp's dad bolts around the corner wearing nothing but a robe with a hood on it and yells, "Where the hell is your sister?" He's obviously pissed that it's 2 AM and his high school daughter is not home yet. But out of nowhere Campy says, "Did you check her room, I saw her in there." I don't know why he said that because he went right to the cereal and his sister was nowhere to be seen.

As Campy is grinding, his dad comes back into the kitchen and yells, "She's not in there!" And Campy says, "I saw her in there. Maybe she went back out?"

At this point Campy's dad, Big Jim, who I would NEVER mess with, is steaming mad and says, "Wait a minute…you two f**kers are drunk aren't you? You have no idea where your sister is, do you?"

So then Campy looks up from his gigantic cereal bowl and slurs the classic line, "First of all, nobody has a "f**king hood on their robe, and second of all, we don't know where the hell she is!"

In a flash, Big Jim yells, "Then why did you say she's in her room?" and simultaneously throws a left forearm off Campy's chest that sends him flying backward off of the barstool onto the floor. Then Big Jim starts coming after ME! So I ran run around to the other side of the dinner table while he was

chasing me back and forth wearing NOTHING but a wide-open bathrobe...
with a hood!

That's one of my top three...maybe top two stories."

Lats always laughed at this story. It was part of his initiation into the
Campanis family.

For some reason, I still can't come to grips with Lats' passing. Maybe it is
because, I knew the Legendary Dave "Lats" Latter longer than I didn't...We
met in 1985 at the beginning of our freshman year at USC and immediately
became the best of friends.

It's hard to pin down the qualities in Lats that drew me to becoming
friends with him in the first place. Maybe it was his great sense of humor
or his quick-witted sarcasm. Maybe it was this life of the party, good-
looking guy who let me fly "Wingman." Maybe it was because he was a
"Man's man" who the ladies LOVED also. But for whatever reason, we
became friends and stayed best of friends right up until he passed in October of 2014.

Funny thing. My phone has an app that details call usage by user. I decided to see what the usage was with Lats. As it turns out, the app can only
go back 90 days, and it said that we corresponded by text or phone call 89
times with the average phone call lasting one hour. I still really miss our
phone conversations especially when we would tell the old stories that all
seem to start "Remember that chick in San Luis Obispo?" or something like
that.

Lats wasn't just my old USC roommate, college and pro teammate, and
best man in my wedding. He was like a brother to me.

A few years earlier, Dave lost his only brother, Jim Latter, to cancer at
just 46 years old. It was very tough on all of us as we loved Jim also, but it
was extra hard on Dave even though he had to be strong for his mother
LouAnn.

For the last several years, Lats and I would speak on the phone late into
the night about all kinds of things, and all of a sudden he started calling me
"Brother." He said to me, "Now that my brother has passed away, you are

my brother; you are my family." And he meant it with all of his heart…and I knew it.

I felt very special being called "Brother" by Lats and knew it was because we truly loved each other's company. Plus, we had spent so much of our lives together doing things we loved.

Then when Lats was admitted to the hospital, I raced to visit him with a bunch of our old friends, I learned what made Lats so special. I realized I wasn't his only "Brother"…in fact he had deemed like 10 of his closest friends as "Brothers." Then I learned that I wasn't his only daily caller; he had many friends who he kept in contact with on nearly a daily basis. His unique quality was making each one us feel loved and part of his extended family, and that goes back to his friends from Lynbrook High School, USC, pro ball, his work friends and his neighbors.

Lats is survived by his two wonderful children, Brianna and Christian. These kids may have just lost their dad, but now they have 10 "Uncles" who will spoil them silly!

In Lats' honor, his children established The Lats Legacy Foundation, partnering with Dave's beloved alma-mater, the University of Southern California, to establish the USC Lats Legacy Baseball Scholarship. It is awarded annually to a Trojan baseball player who exemplifies leadership on the field and academic excellence off the field.

I could go on for hours about the fun times we had and the crazy things we did. But later in life we also supported each other as we each went through challenges and changes in our lives. Dave was a super smart guy who you could rely on to be there when you needed him.

Lats had "routine heart surgery," and immediately after surgery he got pneumonia…and it wouldn't go away. It zapped his energy and his appetite. He had moments where he felt great, then he would call and tell me how lousy he felt.

On October 16th he was admitted for emergency brain surgery. It turns out his aortic valve became infected and was pumping infectious cells to his brain. The collection of infectious cells in his brain started a chain reaction of massive strokes…over a dozen of them. His first CAT scan showed nearly

100% of his left lobe as stroked out along with stroke spots on his right lobe as well. At that point, there was no chance of regaining cognitive brain function.

Dave had the foresight to establish a living will in which he requested to not be kept alive under these circumstances. Internally I battled with this but didn't vocalize my selfish desire to keep him alive. My naïve optimism was still thinking there must be a miracle drug or procedure. But unfortunately there is nothing that could have brought Lats back and it was decided to grant his request and take him off of life support.

It was a very sad day indeed.

I'll never meet another person who impacted me as much as Lats did.

Afterword: It's Not Over... Til It's Over!

What are we other than our collective memories? These memories permeate our souls with the sights, the sounds, and the feelings from our recent and even distant pasts. These memories and experiences shape our current and future selves. In my case, baseball was at the heart of my collective memory until I was almost 28 years old.

The beautifully manicured field...the pop of the catcher's glove...the crack of the bat...even the smell of Dodger Dogs. How powerful are these memories? The first time I went back to Dodgers Stadium after my grandpa passed away in 2000, I had to leave in the third inning. The memories were just too strong and I was losing it every few minutes. To this day, sometimes nostalgia and lost dreams dominate my memories, and it's still tough for me to walk into Dodgers stadium.

Where does one go and what does one do when that big league dream is gone? What becomes of that brotherhood of hundreds of great people I used to call my teammates? These questions haunted me for years.

Losing Lats right when I was finishing up writing these stories was extra tough. His sudden passing put this thing called life in a broader perspective, and helped me, through the joy and the pain, to understand that the bonds of friendship and love are eternal, and can live on in these stories and in my heart. Lats's passing provided massive motivation to finish the stories and share them with family and friends and the rest of the world to keep his memory flowing.

Dave's passing also allowed me to reconnect with dozens and dozens of former players we both knew, many of whom I am still in touch with to this day. It's almost like Lats planned it that way.

The wonderful game of baseball lifted me to heights many only dream of...and then kicked the ladder out from under me right when I was most ready to shine. The fact that I didn't "make it" didn't mean my competitive streak died, just the ability to play baseball at an elite level. So after taking my "Ambition Disorder" to the real world, I have somehow learned to fit in. After a deal has been made in my business life, sometimes I drop the line, "So...you a baseball fan?" because the game is never far from me nor I from it.

Baseball enriched my life before I even knew what had hit me, and despite the bitter years I went through after I was done playing, writing down the feelings of pain and failure helped me evolve, as did so very much the encouragement I received from so many.

One person from Baltimore whom I never met is a Facebook friend I correspond with often. She is a very wise lady, like a Guru. Her name is Peggy Ruley and she told me that my grief was a longing to return to a place I thought would last forever. That place was being in my 20-something-year-old body, waking up feeling awesome, heading to the park rockin' a stylistic mullet, taking batting practice from a "Dick" and then going "Big Fly" a few hours later, with thousands cheering my name.

I have accepted that those days are over; it's not going to happen again. Well, except in my head, my heart, and in my stories. So if some day you are within earshot of me, watching a game at a local watering hole, I just may drop a few tales on you recalling my life being "Born Into Baseball."

My Gratitude Roster

Life is a team sport, and I have been blessed with so many great friends who have made my journey so much more fun and rewarding. I will be forever grateful to my life teammates, and for the good fortune of having them along with me for the ride.

Alan Lovinger	Billy Staples
Ali Glassman	Blake Baxted
Allen Lane	Bob Arvizu
Andria Payne	Bob Vergura
Andy Bowman	Bob Williams
Angel Burton	Bobby Castillo
Angie Richardson Andrus	Bobby Gomez
Anthony Moreno	Bobby Holley
Arne Valenti	Brad Ausmus
Aunt Judy	Brad Brink
Barbara Young	Bret Barbarie
Barry Turnbull	Bret Boone
Ben Davis	Brian BcA Cramer
Ben Ford	Brian Haney
Bill Buck	Brian Raub
Bill Hall	Cami Lee Dyer
Bill LeSuer	Carmen Torzon
Bill Naharodny	Cathy/Doug Saunders
Bill Valentine	Cesar y Carmen Celia Ascensio
Billy Highsmith	Charles Boyer

Charles York

Chris "Bilski" Billig

Chris Hale

Chris Lonergan

Chris Rojo

Christian & Briana Latter

Christine Duran

Christine Laehle-Brush

Chuck Leonard

Corey Seward

Craig Paquette

Damon Buford

Dan Epstein

Dan Henley

Dan Hubbs

Dane Ilertsen

Danny Hernandez

Darin Krats

Dave Brennan

Dave Chavez

Dave O'Brien

Dave Richards

David & Deborah Wilcox

David Rawls

David Rutherford

Dawn Imig

Debbie Rio

Debbie Standridge

DeDe Shamel

Denise Latter

Derrick May

Desi Relaford

Donny Seals

Doug Robbins

Dusty Raring

Ed Campbell

Eric Cox

Eric Lenaburg

Eric Sheppard

Floyd Kaylor

Frank Bolick

Frank Cruz

Frank David

Frank Gee

Frank Moy

Fred Claire

Fred Valko

Gabe Marquez

Gary Wheelock

Gina Jackson

Greg & Teresa Meeder

Greg Yarber

Héctor Ramirez

Henry Armenta

Irene Terrones

Jack Van Horn

Jackie Nickell

Jake Alba

James Hernandez

Jamie & Jon Davenport

Jason Himelstein

Jay Bagozzi

Jay Rojo

Jeff Cirillo/Sara Landon

Jeff Darwin

Jeff Gay

Jeff Kelso

Jeff Lidskin

Jeff Nelson

Jen Savoie

Jennifer Alyse-Buck

Jennifer McCart

Jerry Plowman

Jill Manville

Jill Neubauer

Jim & Jodi Pritikin

Jim Bowie

Jim Gutierrez

Jim Henderson

Jim Latter

Jim Newlin

Jim Sanford Jr.

Jim/Heather Blueberg

Jimmy Von Eps

Jodie/Jill Latter

Joe Seitz

Joe Slusarsky

Joeseph Acevedo

John "Riles" Reilley

John Daugherty

John Jackson

John Snyder

Jon Leonoudakis

Judah Alan

KC Carson

Kelvin & Delvin Thomas

Ken Fancher

Kevin Farlow

Kevin Lamp

Kim Steagall

Kimberly King

Kraig Washington

Kristin Elfring

Kristy Vaught

Larry LaRue

Laurie Sanchez

Lem Pilkington

Lisa Clark

Lisa Schwebe

Lori Van Gorden

Louann Latter

Luis Loucks

Lynee McIntyre Janes

Lynn Nicholson

Mark & Connie Heavener

Mark & Kelly Tolbert

Mark Cresse

Mark Merchant

Marlon Asher

Martha Billig

Martha/Erika

Marty Winchester

Mary Davies

Matt Andre

Matt Blansett

Matt Walbeck

MC Brown

Melissa Dumoski

Michael & Lori Olivieri

Michael Austin

Michael Fults

Michael Kies

Michelle Balling Smith

Mike "Junior" McDonald

Mike Carter

Mike Diaz

Mike Hampton

Mike Hays

Mike Hedlund

Mike Lynch

Mike McGuire

Mike Pitz

Mike Reinberger

Monica Campanis

Morgan & James Talbert

Mr. Jim Sanford/Mrs. Linda
    Sanford

Neil Heglund

Nelson Simmons

Norm Ordaz

Oscar Rivas

Otis Seizure

Pat Murphy

Paul Burciaga

Paul Crabb

Peggy Ruley

Pete & Tracy Felix

Phil Rodas

Ralph Dick

Randy Roetter

Raul Rodarte

Ray Pallares

Raydeana Covarrubias

Ric Chope

Rich Lodding

Richard Reyes

Richard Sandoval

Rick Lawrence

Rick/Traci Salazar

Rodney Peete

Ron Martinez

Ron Mullins

Ron Raub

Ron Smith

Ruben Gonzales

Rudy & Rosie Esquivias

Scott & Karla Dailey

Scott Harter

Scott Lewis

Scott Rudisil

Scott Stoerck

Sergio Alexander

Shane Lettario

Shane Willits

Shawn Ray

Shuwen Chang

Steve Chitren

Steve Geiweke

Steve Rojas

Steve Travers

Steve Tsai

Steve/Keri/Maddie/Kennedy
    Clave

Stu Paul

Susan Luther

Terrance Morgan

The LEGENDARY Dave "Lats"
    Latter

Tim Flip

Tim McNeil

Tim Quintanilla

Tina Leonard

Todd Borowski

Todd Luciccero

Tom & Debra Barsanti

Tom Owens

Tony Burciaga

Tony Phillips

Tony/Sheena/Tyler James

Tracy Longstreth

Travis Berg

Trevor Garner

Trevor Hoffman

Troy & Todd Wilson

Troy Barnhart

Ty Gainey

Walter Friedman

Wayne & James Chambers

Zig Tyko